# THE PREMIER

## BIG BUSINESS AND GREAT FOOTBALL

### JIMMY BURNS

First published by Pitch Publishing, 2024

Pitch Publishing
9 Donnington Park,
85 Birdham Road,
Chichester, West Sussex,
PO20 7AJ
www.pitchpublishing.co.uk
info@pitchpublishing.co.uk

A CIP catalogue record is available for this book
from the British Library.

ISBN 978 1 80150 982 4

Printed and bound in the UK on FSC® certified paper in line
with our continuing commitment to ethical business practices,
sustainability and the environment.

Typesetting and origination by Pitch Publishing

Printed and bound by CPI Anthony Rowe, UK

# Contents

# Chapter One

# Brief History

A FREEZING English winter day in early 1993, in the first season of the Premier League that had begun the previous summer and had loyal fans of all generations packing stadiums up and down the country, and a fledgling but growing audience on satellite TV. In north London, thousands converged on Highbury, one of Europe's oldest stadiums, given the affectionate nickname of 'the Home of Football' by Arsenal. A young English journalist, my friend and colleague Simon Kuper, was among those gathered to watch a match between the home team and the visitors from the north of England, Leeds United.

Arsenal are one of the longest-established football clubs in the world. They are popularly known as 'the Gunners', as the club was founded in the glory days of the British Empire in 1886 for the benefit of munitions workers in the Royal Arsenal factory. Their opponents Leeds United, founded 30 years later, had as their anthem the no less imperialistic 'Marching on Together', a defiant cry steeped in nostalgia.

Leeds had followed the English empire into gradual decline since the 1960s and 70s when, under the English international-turned-manager Don Revie, they had earned a reputation for a highly physical brand of football: more brute force than art.

The football world changed after the days of Revie. The emergence of a modern, English club game was signalled in

1969, three years after England won the first FIFA World Cup to be held in the English-speaking world. It was the year that the legendary Sir Matt Busby, the manager of Manchester United for 24 years, announced his retirement and Britain's most successful post-war cultural export, the Beatles, performed together for the final time, on the rooftop of Apple Records in London. In the same year, the Rolling Stones performed a free festival in Hyde Park in front of at least a quarter of a million fans, two days after the death of one of the group's founders Brian Jones; Manchester City won the FA Cup in a 1-0 win over Leicester City at Wembley and Leeds United won the pre-Premier Football League First Division.

1969 was the year when Maurice Edwards, a World War Two veteran who became a player then an influential agent during the post-war decades, wrote that there was a 'super league within Division 1', that was beginning to pull away from the rest. According to football writer Jonathan Wilson, 'There were no hedge-funds, sovereign wealth or public investment, and no oligarchs but there was awareness that as English football's popularity grew – and thanks to the BBC's *Match of the Day* and England's World Cup win, it became mass entertainment – there was a risk that a self-perpetuating elite would emerge.'

And yet English club football's evolution to the best league in the world had a way to go, still. It would take nearly another quarter of a century for English football to start the great enterprise of restoring the pre-eminent global status of the game's 19th century founders. The new pioneers of the late 20th century embraced a model for the national league that in time would impact on the character and business of international football as we know it today, with the foundation of the English Premier League. When it reached its 30th anniversary in August 2022 it boasted that it had become the best league in the world.

In January 1993, for the visit of Leeds United, Arsenal's aged Highbury stadium was only two-thirds full with a crowd of just over 26,000. That venue was dwarfed by comparison with the size and reputation of two great rival cathedrals of sport, home to two giant champions of *La Liga* and European football, FC Barcelona's Camp Nou and Real Madrid's Santiago Bernabeu. The historical cultural and political rivalry between *La Liga's* two great clubs had always fascinated me.

Unlike my friend Kuper, I was not at Highbury that day – but I have no regrets. Kuper had bought himself a cheap £5 ticket which meant that his view of the match was partly blocked by several lines of spectators standing in front of him. He failed to get a sighting of any of the four goals scored at his end of the stadium. But watching the match highlights some years later on YouTube, what struck Kuper was that almost every player was white and British, and that the game lacked any refined movement on or off the ball. It was 'dreadful', he said.

The match was a bruising, physical encounter, very different from the skills on display in Spain's *La Liga*, in those times when it was of more interest to me – Johan Cruyff's 'dream team' at Barca, and the similarly legendary Real Madrid of the *Quinta del Buitre* era, with their talented, intuitive, intelligent players who helped develop Spanish club football as a creative spectacle.

In 1988, Manuel Pellegrini, a retired Chilean centre-back who would in time go on to manage top Spanish and English clubs, attended a coaching course at Lilleshall, the Football Association's school of excellence, with the course including classes taught by Alex Ferguson. 'It was tackles and muddy pitches and heads crashing together,' Pellegrini later recalled.

Fast forward to March 2023, on the eve of a Europa League encounter between the latest club to come under his coaching Real Betis, and Ten Hag's Manchester United, and Pellegrini cheekily told *La Liga's* veteran journalist Sid Lowe,

'England has the best league, but the best football is played in Spain.'

Going back to the 20th century, the gap that had opened between top-flight English and Spanish clubs was underlined in November 1994 by Manchester United's 0-4 Champions League group stage defeat by Barca before a 112,000-capacity crowd at the Camp Nou. 'We were well and truly slaughtered,' commented United's manager Alex Ferguson after one of the most humiliating defeats suffered by the English champions since the Scot had taken over as manager. For weeks afterwards, Manchester United would have fans from other English clubs taunting them by singing 'Barcelona' the theme song of the 1992 Summer Olympics created by Queen's Freddie Mercury and the opera singer Montserrat Caballé.

I remember dining with Real Madrid general manager and Argentina star Jorge Valdano in a Spanish tapas bar near Paddington, London, during the UEFA European Championships in 1996. He told me that when he thought of English football he still imagined flying towards the old Wembley and seeing a ball rise up into the air at one end of the stadium and then land at the other – the long ball of English football, full of passionate intent, but devoid of creativity and technique.

The Premier League would come to change all that, with teams still looking for the fastest route to scoring goals, but with new systems and strategies, and the quality of play all improved by the arrival of hundreds of foreigners, among them players and managers and investors who would transform the English game. *La Liga* continued to present a major challenge, with Real Madrid and Barca widely respected internationally as giants of the game, each destined to be responsible for the most enduring rivalry of superstars in modern football history – that between Cristiano Ronaldo and Lionel Messi.

But as Europe emerged from the pandemic in the 2021/22 season, it was the English Premier League that seemed best-placed to strengthen its claim to being the richest, most competitive and passionate domestic league in the world. During the 2021/22 season, two English clubs (Manchester City and Liverpool) and two Spanish clubs (Villareal and Real Madrid) reached the semi-finals of the Champions League. Liverpool were beaten by Real Madrid in the final. But it was the Premier League title race, so competitively fought over by quality contenders Guardiola's Manchester City and Klopp's Liverpool, that drew an enthusiastic global audience, with matches transmitted around the world. Even while the pandemic had restricted the attendance of fans at stadiums which were used to always being filled, the English Premier League had become the most popular competition in sporting history, watched by more viewers than any other league in the world, and by a universal following that ignored national frontiers and cultural boundaries.

Written to mark the 30th anniversary of the Premier League in 2022, this book is a brief but colourful history of English club football, the curiosities and stand-out moments of its most significant teams and the fascinating stories of its key owners, managers, players, fans, and chroniclers. It does not pretend to be a complete let alone definitive history, but I hope readers will find, beyond the purely anecdotal, a narrative that is incisive, enlightening and entertaining.

While I acknowledge the debt I owe to the observations of others as I have written this book, I take full responsibility for selection of content, drawing on my own roots and experiences as points of references. I write from the perspective of an Anglo-Spaniard who has spent his life immersed in the cultures of two great football nations with a history of mutual respect, as well as occasional hostility and rivalry.

I was born in Madrid and brought up and educated in England, thanks to my Spanish mother and English father. My first memory of a football game was being taken as a child by a friend of my Spanish grandfather, Dr Gregorio

Marañón, to see Real Madrid in the Bernabeu stadium and hearing one player's name mentioned more than any other, Alfredo di Stéfano.

My dreams of becoming a professional footballer ended when I was in primary school in London. A tackle by my Basque classmate, the son of a diplomat from Bilbao, cut me down in full flight and left me with a gashed knee and broken finger. From then on, I stuck to being a fan of more than one club in two countries, and pursued a career as a journalist and author, occasionally writing books and articles about football.

These days, when in London, between visits elsewhere in the UK and to Spain, I spend most mornings exercising in a large oasis of urban green space, Battersea Park, next to where the river Thames marks the natural border between the south and north of a metropolis inhabited by the fans of three great English football clubs, Chelsea, Arsenal and Tottenham. In Battersea Park, I often pause to watch young kids kick a ball around, imitating the gestures of the icons they watch on TV or in their computer games. They play near a plaque commemorating the site where the first official match of football, according to English Football Association rules, was played, on 9 January 1864, seven years after the foundation in 1857 of Sheffield FC, the world's oldest football club.

I thank the English for introducing us to a sport that over more than a century has become much-loved by a global community, because you don't have to be born rich to succeed in it or enjoy it, even if the business of football is today in the hands of rich men, and players earn more in a month than ordinary mortals can dream of.

The English were destined to be pioneers of the sport, and their railway and mining engineers taught it to pupils in the Spanish-speaking world from Rio Tinto near Huelva, to Madrid, Barcelona, Bilbao and Buenos Aires. In time it was the pupils who got one up on their masters, and took the game to another level, one characterised by style, skill and success, which their masters would then learn from.

As a schoolboy in London in the early 1960s, I was a fan of Tottenham Hotspur, the first British team to triumph in Europe, following in the footsteps of Real Madrid. I collected stickers of their star player, one of the greatest strikers of all time, Jimmy Greaves. At the age of 13, in 1966, it was English blood, which I owe to my late father, that ran through my veins, and my excitement was boosted when England beat Argentina, then Portugal and finally West Germany to win the World Cup at Wembley, captained by the ultimate Anglo-Saxon gentleman of the game, Bobby Moore.

I remember watching Moore and his team-mates celebrating their victory, greeting the crowds from the balcony of Kensington's Royal Garden hotel, where they were staying near to a royal palace that many years later would be inhabited by Diana, Princess of Wales.

During the late 1970s and early 1980s, English clubs coached by British managers dominated European competitions. The island race, which Churchill had promoted as destined to resist and conquer, and which had emerged full of self-esteem from World War Two, seemed to find itself on the football pitch, only to disintegrate in tragedy.

In 1985, 39 people, mostly Italians, were crushed to death and hundreds injured at a European Cup Final after confrontation between Liverpool and Juventus supporters, provoked mainly by drunken English fans. Four years later, on 15 April 1989, one of the worst disasters in sporting history occurred at Hillsborough stadium in the northern English city of Sheffield, as 97 Liverpool fans died as a result of a crowd crush during the FA Cup semi-final against Nottingham Forest. Hillsborough would later be blamed on poor policing and an antiquated stadium that treated fans no better than herded cattle. However English football became tainted by a reputation abroad for drunken and often violent hooliganism on and off the pitch: the bad boys of Europe – appalling behaviour, poor sporting spirit and a domestic league seemingly in terminal decline with too many mediocre players who smoked and drank too much.

An official enquiry by a senior judge into the Hillsborough disaster produced the Taylor report, which led to major reforms in the domestic policing of English club football, the conversion of all major stadiums into an all-seater model, and restrictions on the consumption of alcohol inside the main stadiums.

My earlier football books mirrored the shifting landscape of the game in the Spanish-speaking world. My boyhood love of the Tottenham of the 60s endured, but with it came an interest in the fanaticism several of my English friends felt for other English clubs, some of which I enjoyed watching playing against the best of Spain at home and abroad. I wrote a biography of Diego Maradona, a history of Spanish football, books on Real Madrid and FC Barcelona and a double biography about the two players that over a decade dominated the game with the most enduring and brilliant rivalry between superstars in any league in Europe, Messi and Ronaldo.

And yet I was spending as much time in the UK as in Spain and as I watched English matches in stadiums, in pubs and in the comfort of my sitting room, I was conscious that something transformational was under way.

After the disaster of Hillsborough, British clubs were ordered to renovate and expand their stadiums or build new ones so that a majority of fans could sit comfortably rather than stand cramped together like matchsticks in a box. The hooligan element was outnumbered by a more diverse and global audience.

It was in October 1990 that the Premier League was seriously discussed for the first time at a dinner hosted by the media executive Greg Dyke, then head of sport of the commercial channel ITV, with representatives of the five biggest clubs in the English Football League. The delegates around the meeting table were the director of Liverpool FC Noel White, Arsenal's co-owner and vice-chairman David Dein, life president of Everton FC Philip Carter, Manchester United chairman Martin Edwards and chairman of Tottenham Hotspur Irving Scholar.

The idea was that the five would sell their TV rights directly to the commercial terrestrial channel ITV, rather than continuing to participate in a package deal with the other 87 Football League clubs. Dyke believed it would be lucrative for ITV if the country's larger clubs were featured regularly on national television and wanted to discuss whether the clubs would be interested in a deal which would give them a larger share of the TV rights money. TV revenue had grown significantly during the late 1980s: in 1986, a two-year television deal was worth £6.3 million; by 1988, a four-year deal was worth £44 million. The money was divided among all the clubs across all four Football League divisions.

The five clubs decided to go ahead with forming an elite league. Plans were drawn up for the new Premier League, enabling it to be launched for the 1992/93 season.

The new league meant massive amounts of money for the participating clubs, of whom there were 20 at the start, and eventually 22. ITV offered £205 million for the television rights, but they found themselves in competition with the satellite service, Sky Television. ITV increased its bid to £262 million but was still outbid by Sky's owner Rupert Murdoch, who felt it would attract new customers.

The Premier League was founded on 20 February 1992, when it was confirmed that the first season would begin in August that year. The original 20 teams were drawn from the 1991/92 season's First Division. The system of promotion and relegation, involving three teams going up and three going down, continued.

But not even those present at its foundation dinner imagined what a global phenomenon the Premier League would become. As the inspirer of the competition, Greg Dyke recalled decades later: 'Who would have foreseen that we'd end up with English football being largely owned by foreign owners, managed by foreign managers, and disproportionately played by foreign players?'

Two years after the historic Dyke meeting, Manchester United showed how far they had moved on from a past overshadowed by tragedy – the Munich plane crash of 6 February 1958, which claimed the lives of 23 people, including eight members of a golden generation of players, full of promise and potential, the 'Busby Babes', trained by pioneering, hands-on coach Matt Busby, who knew youth held the key to United's success and the future of the game. The tragedy would endure in the club's collective memory, incentivising it to rise again, in tribute to those whose lives had been cut short so suddenly, drawing on two ostensibly contradictory English assets: tradition and youth culture. Ten years on, in May 1968, a veteran survivor of the Munich crash Bobby Charlton lifted the European Cup won by Manchester United, the first time an English side had won the trophy.

Early in the first Premier League season, in September 1992, 17-year-old David Beckham, a player who would become synonymous with the modern celebrity culture, debuted for United, and the following spring, a foreigner, the Frenchman Eric Cantona, led them to the inaugural title. Cantona blazed a trail for other stylish and skilled non-English players, and was followed by many European coaches, who came to England and took a lead part in an evolving success story.

The numbers of foreigners entering the Premier League would accelerate following the 1995 Bosman ruling which lifted restrictions on EU players in national leagues. With the foreign players came innovative managers and foreign owners, with a lot of money to spend, even if the political and business credentials of some of these big investors proved controversial.

Among the managers, the arrival of Arsène Wenger at Arsenal in 1996 was a key moment in the history of the Premier League. He transformed the diet of the English players and showed a good eye for bringing in foreign players with talent that could help transform the way a team played.

In 2003, the Russian oligarch Roman Abramovich bought Chelsea, his investment in the club seen by many of its fans as the main reason for its subsequent success at national and international level.

In the words of the football writer Jim White (a Manchester United fan): 'We can wince at the company Abramovich kept. We can be appalled by the way he pillaged the Russian economy. We can wonder how he was ever allowed to seize control of such an important cultural asset as Chelsea FC. But of this there can be no doubt. Roman Abramovich revolutionised English football ... So successful was his stewardship – the club accumulated 19 major trophies in his time – that an inescapable conclusion is he knew what he was doing.'

For the next 19 years after the Russian's arrival, the Premier League benefitted from the modern English custom of welcoming money from almost anywhere in the world, with wealthy Arabs, along with Asian, American and Russian billionaires buying up clubs, securing a major media presence and branding their merchandise.

Some saw English top-flight football becoming a globalised plutocracy. But if it was, as its critics claimed, an overpriced, foreign-owned bazaar, it was because it was facilitated by a free-market and liberal British economy, and because it was nationally and internationally popular, even if there were traditionalists that feared that football was in danger of losing its soul.

England's failure to qualify for the Euro 2008 championships was blamed by the national captain Steve

Gerrard on the influx of foreign players at club level. A group of Manchester United fans would later protest against the club's American owners, the Glazer family, claiming they did not know anything about English football and were taking more money out of the club than investing in it. English fans were the first, in the spring of 2021, to rebel against the idea of a breakaway European Super League, which had six Premier League clubs among its proposed founding members.

And in March 2022, Abramovich had his assets seized and was effectively exiled from the UK after the outbreak of the war in Ukraine, because his money had benefited from and helped finance the Putin regime – something that Chelsea fans and successive British governments had been happy to ignore for years.

Foreign investment across the English Premier League has resulted in multiple teams playing very high-quality and entertaining football, not least Chelsea, who competed with other big clubs for the English title as well as the European Champions League. The clubs fighting each season for the league crown and a place in Europe, and others competing hard on their coat tails or fighting to avoid relegation in games full of drama, made the Premier League the most competitive sporting show in the world. It contrasted with the German, Italian and French leagues, where one or two clubs had tended to monopolise the championship, and *La Liga*, where the main show for many years has been the *Clásico* battle between two ancient rivals, FC Barcelona and Real Madrid, not least in the Messi/Ronaldo years.

* * *

The emergence of a new generation of star English male players in the Premier League – some of them black and ready to stand up against racism – and the competitiveness and quality of the bigger clubs, along with the success of the English women's national squad which won the European

Championship in the summer of 2022, showed the English capacity for renewal and enterprise, reclaiming ownership of the game they had originally delivered to the world.

And yet for all their native talent and diversity, their skills, tactics and management owed much to the pervasive foreign influence that came to characterise English football at club level in the Premier League. It is worth noting here, perhaps, on a point of etymology, that the word 'premier', far from being Anglo-Saxon, is French or Norman in its origin, denoting quality of the higher order, or as the Romans used to say: *'primarius'*, of the first rank; chief, principal; excellent.

If, today, many foreigners as well as Englishmen follow the English Premier League more than *La Liga*, it is because English football has become an alternative history of modern England: a mid-sized nation that has successfully re-invented itself, with its identity moulded by history but capable of evolution, with its strengths and idiosyncrasies and a peculiar relationship with money and how to make best use of it, producing football of real quality as well as entertainment value, with clubs supported by passionate fans.

## Chapter Two

# Mr Nobody

WHEN ARSÈNE WENGER arrived as the new manager at Arsenal in 1996, 'Mr Nobody' was the headline in the popular tabloid the *Daily Mirror*. You could also read in the British media the prediction that a foreign manager could never win the Premier League. And yet, the Frenchman was destined to prove the sceptics wrong. He became very well known indeed and successful, the first in a line of foreigners that redefined the culture of English football.

Initial reactions suggested a man who had fallen to earth, an alien species. A veteran Arsenal fan who had followed the Gunners since the end of the war was asked on English TV what he thought. He replied: 'I know he is a Frenchman. And I know he eats frogs' legs!'

Ian Wright who had established himself as an English international after signing for Arsenal in September 1991 for £2.5m, at the time a club record fee, initially could not believe what he was seeing. He said, 'Wenger looked like a university lecturer' – which is what he was. Although already planning a life in football, he studied economics at university when the dogma of English football seemed to be that you left school at 16 if you intended to take the game seriously. In fact, Wenger spoke like a university lecturer – 'Life is about millimetres, it's about timing,' he said. Such refined reflection was virtually unheard of among the hardcore English fans and players.

Wenger's stratagem was to take the English mentality out of an English team and make his mark on a country that had fought off every attempt at invasion by the French since the Norman army crossed the channel in 1066.

One of the star English black players he inherited at Arsenal, Ian Wright, struggled at first to make sense of him. 'He wore these massive glasses and massive jackets – my name for him was Clouseau.' The reference was to Inspector Jacques Clouseau, a fictional character famously played by the popular English comic Peter Sellers in Blake Edwards' farcical *Pink Panther* movie series as an inept and incompetent French police detective whose investigations descend into chaos.

And yet Wright went on to play a major part in Arsenal's success during the 1990s which owed much to Wenger. The Frenchman later said, 'I felt like I was opening the door to the rest of the world.'

This Premier League French revolution began not with the ball, but with diet.

The Arsenal team Wenger inherited was exclusively English in its eating habits and dominated by English players, some of whom drank as much as their fans. The day would begin with a massive cooked breakfast of bacon and eggs and sausages and a range of additional plate-fillers, dripping fat, from baked beans to fried potato hash and black pudding, plus Coca Cola prior to the match. 'Some of the players went on to the pitch burping,' recalled the Dutch international Dennis Bergkamp, who played for Arsenal from 1995 to 2006. The match would be followed with several beers.

Heavy traditional English dishes, like fried fish and chips and steak were also dished out pre-match. It was not unknown for players to hold competitions as to who could eat the most prior to and after the match, with the record of nine meals held by centre-back Steve Bould. There was much English beer drinking too, every day of the week – pint after pint was consumed after matches and training. Having struggled with addiction for a decade, Arsenal legend Tony Adams finally admitted to being an alcoholic in 1996.

By then Wenger had introduced a strict, healthy dietary and alcohol-free regime, getting players to eat fish and vegetables and encouraging the use of supplements like creatine.

The documentary *Invincible* (2021) focused on Wenger's confidence-instilling fatherliness and connoisseurly appreciation for a balanced team, and how he achieved such nicknames as 'Wengerball' and 'Wruum Wruum', placing him among the pantheon of the gods in the Premier's history.

He began with an English team with one foreign star – Bergkamp – and soon not only used statistics to analyse a player's performance, but also showed how foreign transfer markets worked, with a good eye for getting good value from the star foreign players he pulled in. There were new signings that were largely as unknown to English fans as he was, such as fellow Frenchmen Patrick Vieira and Thierry Henry, whose brilliance he knew about even if many English fans remained stuck in their insularity. Before the players came from Italy's *Serie A* and triumphed in the Premier League with Wenger's Arsenal, Vieira played as a reserve for AC Milan, and Henry as a reserve for Juventus.

From 'Arsène, who is he?', he brought a whole new lexicon to the English Premier League, as he developed an Arsenal team called 'the Invincibles' because they ended the 2003/04 Premier campaign as champions, without a single defeat. Wenger won seven FA Cups and three Premier League titles during his Arsenal tenure before stepping down in 2018, his 22 years as manager the longest and most successful reign in the club's history.

When he arrived at Arsenal, the London club was in an intensifying rivalry with (Manchester) United, dating back to the formation of the Premier League. By 2003, all but one league title had been won by one or the other (the exception being Blackburn Rovers' success in 1994/95). The most hostile encounter between the two teams took place on 21 September 2003 in what became remembered by fans as 'the Battle of Old Trafford'.

Arsenal's captain Vieira was sent off for two bookings, the second for a challenge on United's Ruud van Nistelrooy which the Dutchman made a meal of. When Van Nistelrooy failed to convert a disputed penalty kick just before the final whistle, all hell broke loose. He was jostled and taunted by several Arsenal players and a fight soon broke out.

Once it was all over, it was the Arsenal players who incurred the heaviest punishments: a three-match ban and £20,000 fine imposed on Martin Keown and further fines, totalling £275,00, and bans totalling nine games imposed on Lauren, Ray Parlour, Vieira and Ashley Cole. Identified as the main United culprits, Cristiano Ronaldo and Ryan Giggs were also found guilty of misconduct by the English Football Association, but received lighter fines of £4,000 and £7,500 respectively, and escaped bans.

Although Wenger protested that his players were the victims of 'trial by Sky (TV)', the press saw it differently. As journalist Henry Winter put it: 'Arsenal may have worn yellow, but they were tainted with red. The face of the beautiful game was ravaged with scars and tears.' It was as if a noble professor had been let down by a group of unruly students.

But Wenger was no thug. In his time, he helped change the way the game is viewed in England, expanding the horizon of a closed-off football culture to help turbo-charge its transformation into the home of the most diverse, globally popular and richest national league on the planet. Across two decades, Wenger's Arsenal broke records and changed a club's image for ever.

The first decade of the English Premier League was to be marked by Wenger's challenge to United's evolving reputation as the masters of English football. At the heart and soul of the rivalry were the contrasting personalities of Wenger and the United manager Alex Ferguson. Ferguson's ruddy chiselled features and burly frame, strong Glaswegian accent and reputation as a hard drinker, was in striking contrast to the lean, philosophical school of foreign managers which Wenger personified at Arsenal, when both managers competed against each other. The Frenchman's quiet mannerisms in interviews brought a new sophisticated style of management to English football, while Ferguson, the patriarch, stamped his authority on a club that embraced the global business potential of the game while drawing on deep roots in a history of tragedy and glory.

The Scottish-born 'boss' Ferguson, brought up in the hard, working-class environment of the Glasgow shipyards, was a tough former player with Rangers who had moved to United at the end of 1986 after a successful period as coach of Aberdeen. He had immediately set about strengthening a club that had not won a league title or the European Cup since the halcyon days of Bobby Charlton, George Best and Denis Law in the 1960s. United boasted bigger crowds than their biggest northern rival Liverpool FC, and more fans around the world. This was not just a sympathy vote for the memory of the Munich air disaster of 1958, when eight of their promising young players were killed in an accident as they headed home from a European game. United's popularity among old and new generations was also linked to their reputation for entertaining, swashbuckling football, a reputation Ferguson was determined to enhance.

A trade unionist whose upbringing had been moulded on a Calvinist work ethic, Ferguson took to arriving at his office at 7.30 each morning and got to work on shaping his team. It took another four years for United's fortunes to begin to turn round. In 1991 the club floated on the London Stock Exchange, so as to raise new capital from the public and institutional investors. While many fans were opposed to the flotation, and Ferguson himself was less than happy about it, it laid the basis for the economic transformation of the club into a multinational business, well prepared to tap the commercial potential of the English Premier League and more than capable of exploiting the glory that now began to be relived on the pitch.

Among those who would watch United evolve into a global brand and marketing machine were Real Madrid, under the presidency of Florentino Pérez, a construction magnate who had become a life-long football fan watching Di Stéfano as a boy. Around the start of the new millennium, surveys compiled by Real Madrid's head of marketing, José Angel Sanchez, confirmed the extent to which his club lagged behind United in terms of its marketing reach among non-Latino North Americans and in Japan, China and south-east Asia. A new fan behaviour had also entered the business of football as – thanks to the instant access provided by satellite TV – some were now following elite players as they moved from club to club.

In the early period of the Premier League, Ferguson encouraged a new generation of home-grown young players. He would later reflect: 'I tell the players that the bus is moving. This club has to progress. And the bus wouldn't wait for them. I tell them to get on board. Or they'll miss out. At this club we won't stop, we don't take rests; the procedure goes on and on.'

Players had to fight their way through to the first team and earn their right to remain there. During's Ferguson long regime at United, the club set high standards in the English Premier League, winning the championship 13 times between 1992 and 2013. A myth was created that after leaving Old Trafford there was only one direction any ex-Manchester United player could go and that was down.

## Chapter Three

# Renewal and Style

*5 August 2022: Crystal Palace vs Arsenal, Selhurst Park, Result: 0-2*

The start of a new Premier League season on the first weekend in August 2022 is played out in sweltering heat, effervescent with huge popular enthusiasm.

A week ahead of the start of *La Liga*, thousands of English fans who have stayed on their island, choose loyalty to club over an escape to the beach, to support their teams. They assemble after sponsorship-driven friendly preludes played out by the main contenders in foreign lands, requiring expensive travel tickets amidst flight cancellations and airport chaos.

It's proving a hot summer in more ways than one. With large swathes of the land parched by global warming, the war in Ukraine, China flexing its military muscle over Taiwan and energy prices and the cost of living generally spiralling upwards, football holds out a lifeline of escape and constancy, however delusional.

The sense of re-engagement between fans and clubs comes amid the expectation that the season will be as unpredictable as any since the inauguration of the English Premier League 30 years earlier.

Quite apart from the impact a looming economic crisis may have on the disposable income of fans, there is the question of how the World Cup will affect players and their performance. The showpiece will interrupt the season from the second week of November until the day after Christmas, as the best players in the Premier League represent the nations that have qualified to compete in Qatar. The prospect is that club managers will struggle to develop team spirit and tactics as their key players are diverted to national duties with an uncertain recovery once the World Cup is over. But such fears evaporate as the first match of the season kicks off, with fans from both teams filling Selhurst Park for the encounter between two London clubs with long histories and proud legacies from the south and north of the metropolis – Crystal Palace vs Arsenal.

Near the site of the Crystal Palace – the huge architectural tribute to imperial creativity and ambition moved from its original location in Hyde Park during the Great Exhibition of 1851 and reconstructed three years later before it was destroyed in a fire in 1936 – Selhurst Park is the historic home of a club that aspires to renewal and modernity. After a chequered history as a founder member of the English Premier League, Crystal Palace were relegated in 1993, 1995 and 1998 and went into administration twice in 1999 and 2010. But they recovered and returned to the Premier League in 2013, where they had survived with the support of American investors.

There is a festive, almost carnival atmosphere in the stadium. The Crystals or Crystal Girls are the official cheerleading squad of Crystal Palace FC which is the only club in English football that has NFL-style cheerleaders. Also parading are heroic clowns dressed up as giant eagles, the club's iconic bird.

'The Eagle only appeared in 1973 when Malcom Allison arrived as manager. He re-branded the club, changing the kit to red and blue and nicknaming the club the Eagles,' says Palace fan, Juan Dickinson, on quora.com. 'The Eagle is meant to symbolise the club rising from the ashes of the Crystal Palace, much like a phoenix.'

'Crystal Palace fans say they are the loudest fans in the Premier League,' comments another fan, Gareth Turner.

'They do benefit from an organised singing section, which is led by a drummer. At most grounds the atmosphere will dip for a period, and it is at these times that the Holmesdale Faithful [the organised group, named after the section of the stadium they are positioned in] come into their own, keeping a wall of noise going. Many teams have a hard core of noisy fans for away games, and again Crystal Palace are amongst the loudest and most passionate.'

Patrick Vieira, a former Arsenal captain, was appointed Crystal Palace manager in July 2021. Despite a less than impressive record in his previous job coaching Ligue 1 team Nice, the presence of Arsenal as the opponents on this August day, serves as a reminder of the Senegalese-born Frenchman's glory days as one of Wenger's star players.

Arsenal have as their coach Mikel Arteta. He seemed destined to become manager of the Gunners one day. Wenger signed him as an Arsenal player in 2011 and the Frenchman considered him his anointed *dauphin*. He was known as 'Wenger's son'. When Arteta retired as a player in 2016, Wenger offered him the role of leading Arsenal's Youth Academy, but instead he went to Manchester City as an assistant to Pep Guardiola, a friend as well as an inspiration. The Basque and the Catalan first met in 1997 when Arteta, aged 15, was at FC Barcelona's youth academy *La Masia*, and Guardiola, then aged 26, was captain of the first team.

When asked in April 2021 by John Cross, chief football reporter of the *Daily Mirror*, what he and Guardiola's common interests were, Arteta said: 'We have that obsession about the game, understanding it, and trying to find other ways and the passion to do it on the pitch. It is what we were taught when we were in Barcelona … that is the way we live and breathe football. That's why we love what we do.'

Arteta's dream of reviving Arsenal's Wenger glory days got off to a good start in his first season with the north London club, after he took charge in December 2019, only to stumble in the following season. On 18 July 2020, Arsenal beat Arteta's former employer Manchester City 2–0 in the FA Cup semi-final, and progressed to their fourth FA Cup Final in seven years, and Arteta's first as manager. They beat Chelsea 2-1 on 1 August [the season had been disrupted by the Covid-19 outbreak, so finished months later than usual] and Arteta became the first manager to win a major trophy in his first season in charge of the club since George Graham in 1986/87. But on 23 January 2021 Arsenal were knocked out in the fourth round of the FA Cup by Southampton, subsequently lost 2-1 on aggregate to Unai Emery's Villareal in the Europa League semi-final and ended up eighth in the Premier League, which ended a 25-year run of participating in European competitions.

As a new season gets under way in the summer of 2021 Arsenal are featuring in Amazon's *All or Nothing* series. The documentary details Arteta's mission to revive Arsenal's reputation for excellence, a class act on the pitch attracting a culturally and sexually diverse fan base, the best possible mirror of London at its multicultural and creative best. Young educated African Caribbean girls mix in with successful youths whose parents had emigrated from the Indian subcontinent, along with high-flying City and media white boys and older fans who spent most of their life supporting the Gunners at the old stadium, Highbury, in the days before Arab money made its mark on the English Premier League and Arsenal moved to a new stadium, the Emirates, with its four-tiered bowl and translucent polycarbonate roofing over the stands.

*All or Nothing: Arsenal* begins with fans descending on the spectacular Emirates stadium, in August 2021, with one question on everyone's minds: whether Arteta, who has assembled the youngest squad in the Premier League, is the man to take the club back to the big time.

Among his players is 19-year-old Bukayo Saka, who faced a psychological mountain to climb after fluffing a crucial penalty kick in England's European Championship final against Italy, the biggest moment in the national team's history in 50 years. In the aftermath of the defeat, Saka suffered a social media wave of racial abuse.

If Saka pulled through, it was thanks to growing support for the Black Lives Matter campaign and also Arteta, a former Arsenal captain, placing his faith in the youngster whose humility and resilience had been shaped by a stable family background and the Arsenal Academy.

As they are captured by the cameras off-pitch, in the club dressing room, the car park and team dining room, the players share often banal conversation, talking about family outings to amusement parks or shopping at Ikea. The prevailing image that comes across is that they are not just icons or symbols of a community's hopes. They are normal boys of whom football fans demand so much.

'My main objective is that fans believe in the team and that's been lost a little in the last few years,' Arteta comments prior to the 2021/22 season. 'Football is about giving positive emotions to people and if I can do that, hopefully beautiful things can happen.'

And yet Arteta's ability as a manager is questioned by a critical English media, when Arsenal begin that Premier League season by being beaten away at newly promoted Brentford's Community Stadium. Further successive defeats follow against Chelsea at the Emirates (0-2) and away to Manchester City at the Etihad (0-5), where Arsenal are outclassed by Guardiola's star-studded slick and superior machine. Arsenal fans describe their team at the time as the worst they have seen in their lives.

But worse is to come, when Arsenal lose at home to their north London rivals Tottenham. Only a subsequent victory against Norwich, a newly promoted club, brings Arteta some respite, to survive and hope. Defeat would have meant Arsenal's worst start in the history of the English Premier

League. As the Arsenal player icon of the Wenger years Thierry Henry comments: 'This is Arsenal. Fans expect you to be in the top four.'

Victory comes after Arteta rallies his troops in the dressing room in an emotional pre-match speech focused on team-building and leadership. He tells his players about his early personal history, being born with a heart disease but surviving thanks to the timely intervention of open-heart surgery. The story then fast-forwards to the crushing defeat by Manchester City, when Arteta hits a psychological low from which he recovers thanks to the 'positives' which give him a sense of purpose: 'family, club, players.

'So, believe in yourself as I do. You are really good. The last thing I want to do is blame you in difficult times. My responsibility is to take the shit.'

To Dan Einav, the TV critic of the *Financial Times*, Arteta's visualisation exercises – at one point the tactics board features an illustration of a heart – and speeches about passion and pride, combine the 'intensity of a Silicon Valley visionary and the emotional earnestness of *Ted Lasso*,' [the American sports comedy-drama television series watched by an audience of millions].

After the game against Norwich, Arteta's Arsenal begin a protracted draw back from disaster in a season that remains underwhelming however much the manager tries to provide a master class in team building, worthy of his old masters Wenger and Guardiola and other philosophical gurus of the modern game, from Cruyff to Valdano and Bielsa. Arsenal fans expect better than ending eighth in the Premier.

And so, Arsenal kick off the new Premier season against one of the more modestly financed clubs in August 2022, Crystal Palace, and win 2-0 with a display of sharp as well as creative football, the joyous cries of 'Arsenal, Arsenal, Arsenal' from the visitors' section heralding the prospects of more and better to come. Arteta is encouraged by his team's resilience against opponents who beat them in same stadium in April 2022, severely denting Arsenal's bid for Champions League qualification.

Among those declaring his absolute delight is Ian Wright, the Arsenal and England international turned popular TV commentator. He sees many positive signs in Arteta's team, among them Oleksandr Zinchenko's well-worked corner leading to Arsenal's first goal by Gabriel Martinelli – a great moment for the 21-year-old Brazilian forward in his first match since a £6 million move from Ituano.

Wright picks out two other debutants for glowing praise – Willam Saliba and Gabriel Jesus. Jesus was full of energy and movement up front, following his £45m move from Manchester City, while the 21-year-old Saliba looked confident in his first Premier League match – three years after he was bought for £27m from Saint-Etienne. The defender has spent the past three seasons out on loan but now looks at ease in Arsenal's back line.

Another former star player and now a more outspoken and controversial TV pundit, ex-Manchester United and English international Gary Neville is also full of praise for Saliba: 'I was massively impressed with Saliba,' he tells Sky Sports. 'He actually reminded me of a young Rio Ferdinand. He's such a young defender at 21. Getting through that second half, when Arsenal weren't at their best, would have been the most pleasing thing for Mikel Arteta. Crystal Palace away, that's a tough challenge and that's a big performance from Saliba.'

As for Crystal Palace, there is little to redeem from the match other than the memory of better days. Some of the club's fans still mourn the pre-season departure of the Belgian Christian Benteke to join the American club team DC United, coached by the former Manchester United player and English international Wayne Rooney. The memory endures of a moment Crystal Palace fans will not forget: Benteke's chipped goal from back in 2017, an occasion in itself as memorable as the strike.

On 1 April 2017, April Fool's Day got a dose of reality. Chelsea lost 1-2 to Crystal Palace at Stamford Bridge giving the Premier League's title race one of its unanticipated twists. Chelsea, untouchable for so long at the top and a side that had won 13 games in a row at home, succumbed to a team who had spent almost the entire campaign choked in the grip of a relegation battle. Benteke, a striker who had shown signs of fading form, dribbled from the halfway line. Chelsea's David Luiz attempted to stifle his progress only for the ball to deflect to Wilfried Zaha, sprinting up in support. The Ivorian's return pass found Benteke alone in front of Thibaut Courtois, with the striker calmly waiting for his compatriot to go to ground before lifting a delightful finish into the gaping net. It was his first league goal since the end of January.

As Joe, a Crystal Palace supporter tweeted in December 2019, it was his favourite Benteke – nicknamed 'Big Ben' – moment. Joe simply loved the audacity of the goal, as the Eagles No.17 sat Courtois on his backside before lofting the ball over him. It is a real shame things have gone as stale as they have done in recent years for Benteke, but one thing is certain – Crystal Palace fans haven't forgotten his excellent goal against the eventual champions from that 2016/17 campaign.

## Chapter Four

# Red Devils

FOR MOST of post-war football history, few English clubs have been able to claim such a large international fan base as Manchester United. In 2021, a study found that with more than 1.1bn fans, they were the most popular football club in the world.

The nickname, the Red Devils, was borrowed from a local rugby team who, back in 1934, had dominated a tournament in France, prompting local journalists to dub them '*Les Diables Rouges*'. In time, the nickname became popular at United, partly since it also represented a homage to the early moniker for the club way back in the late 1800s, when they were originally known as the Heathens.

It was the great Matt Busby who led the club out of the Second World War after Old Trafford survived the bombing of the German air force, the *Luftwaffe*, and the Allies defeated Hitler. Busby moulded a group of young players who dreamed of a bright future so there was a tragic irony that such potential was brutally interrupted on German soil.

The Munich Air Disaster in 1958, killed 23 people including eight players – among them captain Roger Byrne, young superstar Duncan Edwards and England international Tommy Taylor – and inspired huge sympathy for the club, leaving a profound mark on United's history. The victims are forever commemorated in a plaque that has a place of distinction at Old Trafford.

Busby had to rebuild the squad, and with it search for a new identity. The Busby Babes, as the team that existed pre-Munich were nicknamed, had become a painful memory, a reminder of the innocence and potential lost in the air crash disaster.

In 1968, a rebuilt Manchester United became the first English club to win the European Cup, and Busby was cemented as a legend. Busby liked the more intimidating image of the Red Devils over the former, more innocent-sounding Busby Babes and he began to apply it to United. In 1973 the club changed its crest to officially include the image of a Red Devil holding a trident. The Red Devil has become an integral part of the United brand around the world, and today the club's mascot is Fred the Red, a smiling red devil, horns and all.

More than 30 years later, Manchester United found themselves initiating another re-invention as they drew fame and fortune from the new English Premier League under a similarly legendary leader, Alex Ferguson. Proud to proclaim his socialist roots and as a supporter of the British Labour Party, Ferguson was initially critical of the Premier League, describing it as a 'piece of nonsense'. The comments came to be seen as somewhat ironic given that Manchester United under his management went on to become the most commercially successful club in Europe, dominating the first decade of the Premier, winning seven of the first nine titles and becoming extremely rich in the process.

It was a period when the Red Devils fans enjoyed celebrity as well as talent and success, with the young superstar David Beckham and the flamboyant Frenchman Eric Cantona both contributing in different ways to breaking the team's and English football's sense of insularity within the hugely expanded commercial parameters of the Premier.

Cantona, the more veteran of the two, played his first season for United in 1993/4 – the second season of the Premier

League – after falling out with the management at Leeds and, previous to that, drifting in and out of various French clubs. Alfredo Di Stéfano had recommended him to Real Madrid in 1989 but was ignored by the then-club president Ramon Mendoza who thought Cantona represented too much of a reputational risk.

Cantona certainly proved controversial in the Premier League, but the harder edge of English football suited him and the fans loved the way he would always surprise them. Cantona had a huge ego and did not take criticism easily. He scored 82 goals for Ferguson's Manchester United, won four league titles and two Doubles (with the FA Cup) and was a catalyst for the most successful period in the club's history.

He would later claim that one of the many good moments he had during his years in the English Premier League was when he kicked Crystal Palace fan Matthew Simmons – a man he referred to as 'the hooligan' – during an away match at Selhurst Park on 25 January 1995. The picture of Cantona flinging himself feet-first at Simmons, remains one of the most iconic images of the Premier League era. What became notorious as Cantona's 'kung-fu' kick came after the player was shown a red card, his first in six months but fifth since being signed for United. As he walked to the tunnel, Simmons took up a position at pitch level, in the first row of the stands, and shouted at him. In Simmons' own version of events, he had simply called out: 'Off, off, off! It's an early bath for you, Cantona.' Other witnesses claimed he had actually shouted: 'You dirty French bastard. Fuck off back to France.'

Cantona was suspended by United until the end of the season and fined £20,000, with the English Football Association then extending his ban until October and fining him a further £10,000. He was also sentenced to 14 days in prison by a magistrate after pleading guilty to common assault, but that was overturned by a judge who ruled the player should not be jailed simply because he was a public figure. Cantona was given 120 hours' community service instead and Manchester United then staged the famous news conference at which the Frenchman simply read a note that said: 'When seagulls follow the trawler it is because they think sardines will be thrown into the sea.' As he prepared to make his exit, Cantona addressed the journalists he had apparently intended to insult, saying only: 'Thank you very much'.

Simmons was handed a £500 fine for abusive behaviour and also received a year-long stadium ban. Following the verdict, the 21-year-old, still in the magistrate's court, launched himself over the bench at the prosecuting lawyer, kicking and grabbing Jeffrey McCann before being led away in handcuffs. Simmons was jailed for a week for the courtroom assault. The judge also ordered him to pay a £500 fine as well as £200 in legal costs.

Cantona considered quitting English football as a result of his treatment by the football authorities but was persuaded by Ferguson to stay. The French player, who liked to write poetry, went on to help United to success in the Premier League and FA Cup the following season.

'The act Cantona perpetrated at Selhurst Park might have been his most worthwhile of all. It was the most important moment in a relationship between players and fans so enduring and spiritual as to be almost without comparison. He was already a United legend. On 25 January 1995, he became immortal,' wrote *The Guardian* football writer Rob Smyth 25 years after the incident.

One of Cantona's colleagues, Roy Keane, recalled: 'Before Cantona came to Manchester United he'd had numerous clubs but had never settled … he wouldn't conform, did things his own way and appeared as if he didn't give a fuck.' But during United's glory days in the English Premier League, Cantona flourished under Ferguson and earned the respect of colleagues and fans on account of his goal-scoring ability, control of the ball and creative passing which could turn a game round in an instant.

The Frenchman taught David Beckham about the power of the media, the sponsor and how celebrity on and off the pitch was a money machine. Beckham credited Cantona for United's early years of success in the Premier League. Beckham himself made history in the league when he scored one of the greatest goals in English football in a game against Wimbledon at the start of the 1996/97 season. He found the net with a swerving and swooping shot from the halfway line. Those who were there that day would never forget it. As Beckham's colleague Gary Neville described it: 'Most players couldn't kick that far and make it look so sweet.' The goal travelled the world on TV and digitally and gave Beckham international fame. United and the Premier League had discovered the meaning of success.

Fast forward and we are in the early weeks of a new season, in September 2022. Manchester United may not have qualified for the Champions League but under their new Dutch manager Erik ten Hag they are aiming to recover some of their former greatness. It is a measure of the club's potential and ambition that in an impassioned atmosphere at Old Trafford, United fans glimpse the glory days of the past when their team beats Mikel Arteta's resurrected Arsenal.

United's own revival is under way despite a widely publicised summer saga over whether Cristiano Ronaldo would stay or go. The summer transfer window came and went, and Ronaldo stayed, after no other club that might value the Portuguese generously, came forward. Ten Hag insisted that Ronaldo could still form part of his plans to rebuild the team and rediscover games of glory.

But the revival of United's fortunes seems not to depend on Ronaldo any longer. One of the star players whose form has dipped in the past season but is motivated by Ten Hag is the England forward Marcus Rashford and against Arsenal, he is back to his best, scoring two goals and showing his versatility as part of United's pressing game, readily switching from centre forward to the wing. With Ronaldo on the bench until later in the second half, Rashford also successfully partners United's big summer signing, the Brazilian Antony, the other goal scorer.

It is an absorbing contest that brings back memories of the two clubs competing for the Premiership crown in the days of Ferguson and Wenger. Arsenal are the better side in quality of passing and intelligence of movement, but United are lethal on the counter, not least with Antony's pace and directness, played with passion and precision.

It is still early days in what turns out to be another hard-fought battle for supremacy in Europe's most competitive league. But as one headline put it, 'Antony's swagger gives United reason to believe'.

In recent seasons the main focus of English club football had been with Manchester City and Liverpool competing for titles, but the match at Old Trafford on that 4 September 2022 had United and Arsenal, two clubs undergoing a renaissance, returning to centre stage, as serious contenders. United fans still protested about their American owners, the Glazers, but they were loving the football played by their team again, as were Arsenal fans. Quality football, and a great spectacle.

# Chapter Five

# Pre-season

*30 July 2022, Community Shield, Manchester City vs Liverpool, King Power Stadium, Result: 1-3*

The Football Association's annual summer 'friendly' match – the Community Shield – is played days away from a new league season, between two clubs whose ongoing title fights have dominated the Premier in recent times, Liverpool and Manchester City, and what a show it is!

No matter that large swathes of the country have their thoughts and prayers focused on the English national team's hopes of beating Germany in the women's European Championship at Wembley the following day. Liverpool FC and City fans ensure that Leicester City's King Power Stadium, with its capacity of just over 33,000, is a simmering cauldron of rival chants as Jürgen Klopp and Pep Guardiola's teams perform the latest act of an enduring battle of wills and skills: two great managers in charge of some of the best players in the world.

The game provides a great deal more entertainment and excitement than is usually the case in Community Shield matches, the well-manicured and watered turf of the stadium contrasting with the parched land of much of England in a summer of unprecedented high temperatures. Liverpool show from the opening whistle they are a team ready for battle, fighting fit, with the Egyptian star Mohamed Salah driving forward on the left wing with speed and skill, as if recharged by the renewal of his contract. By contrast, City struggle to produce their trademark patient build-up play, with Guardiola's latest big signing, Erling Haaland, near-anonymous for most of the match and doggedly staying in an advanced position, seeming to only contribute to disrupting his team's rhythm.

The Norwegian international's sole moment of inspiration comes when he helps ignite City's equaliser by another recent star Premier signing, Julián Álvarez. Before the game is over, and with Liverpool leading 3-1, the tall, long-haired blond Viking manages a point-blank glaring miss, hitting what should have been an easy goal over the crossbar. Part of the attraction of matches between Premier clubs is their capacity to throw up the unexpected, to surprise.

For Haaland, in the words of *The Observer*'s football commentator Barney Ronay, this was a debut not just to forget, but to shred, incinerate and bury at the bottom of the garden, after spending most of the second half, sulking and mooching in the centre circle. Haaland is upstaged by Liverpool's star signing, Darwin Núñez, who comes off the substitutes' bench with half an hour to go and seems instantly at home. 'He ran hard through the middle. He looked direct and clear in his mind. As a case study in buying a player who suits your pre-existing attacking style, this was compelling stuff,' writes Ronay.

The Liverpool fans are electrified, lighting flares in defiance of official guidelines and chanting the Uruguayan's name. The loudest noise emanates from the red section of the venue, just as much of the action comes from those in the same colours. But with Guardiola in charge, Man City fans can afford to be patient. He is a proven tactical master and believes in the theory of evolution. The fight will continue between two great clubs.

Chapter Six

# Russian Club

THERE CAN be few more atmospheric or iconic encounters between two rivals with some of the best players in the world than a Premier League London derby between Chelsea FC and the visitors Tottenham Hotspur at Stamford Bridge.

While Tottenham fans have always seen Arsenal as their biggest rivals, they now also reciprocate Chelsea's fans in mutual antagonism. Chelsea fans have long hated Spurs fans, in the past letting their hatred spill over into racist abuse and physical violence. In March 2015 Chelsea fans made headlines for racist and antisemitic chants on the London underground after their club beat Tottenham in the Football League Cup Final. It was a result that had Chelsea surpassing Tottenham in the number of trophies won, underlining their supremacy in the Premier League, FA Cup and Europe.

The derby match on the second weekend of the 2022/23 season takes place during the hottest summer in living memory, with the stadium exempt from growing hosepipe bans around the country, to allow its turf to remain soft and green, and fans consuming all the beer they can drink before taking their places in the stadium.

There are a few fans drinking water or cans of Coke, but the atmosphere is defined by the beer drinkers. Along the streets of the neighbourhood some of the louder ones are packed into pubs like The Chelsea Pensioner and Tommy Tucker, rehearsing their more visceral chants, as if preparing for battle against the enemy. The sense of tribe, of belonging as well as exclusiveness is embodied by signs warning that the territory extending along parts of the Fulham and King's Roads is for a few hours for Chelsea fans only.

I remember a senior officer of the London Metropolitan Police telling me some time ago that for games judged of high risk, such exclusivity plays an important role in minimising confrontation, as does ensuring the visiting fans' entrance to and seating in the stadium is also carefully segregated. As for mingling with Chelsea fans and joining their section in the stadium as a mere observer, as in my case, the best advice I got from a friend was not to show neutrality, let alone any sympathy with or admiration for the enemy.

My friend has secured me a spare ticket in the thick of the Chelsea tribe, at the opposite end to the visitors. No charge, only some free advice: 'You will have to cheer any Chelsea goal, nor flinch, God forbid, if Spurs score."

For all the beer drinking, I do not see any evident signs of paralytic inebriation. Access to the stadium is controlled by well-trained stewards, and any drunkards face further obstacles in manoeuvring along the close formation of the seating and narrow corridors between the layered rows. I see no one toppling over or indeed fainting from dehydration, which might suggest that the English fans have a certain resilience when consuming large quantities of beer, which is not to say they become particularly Zen-like.

While the fans bond in their support for the team and collective chants, there are some that excel in their physical and verbal expressions which seem to stem from deep-seated, pent-up emotions that find escape during the match.

A few metres to the left of me, a gaunt, sepulchral bearded 30-year-old Chelsea fan has a fanatic's air about him: his eyes with a dark expression, his mouth expelling a litany of abuse, contained anger breaking out. He is of uncertain origin, and is haunted by unfathomable demons and unpredictable outcomes, but he is a Chelsea fan.

To my right, below, an older Chelsea fan, square and stocky, beer-bellied, greets each Spurs tackle and any decision by the referee that goes against Chelsea by gesturing the act of masturbation with his right arm.

I think of the *Clásicos* I have seen in the Nou Camp and the Bernabeu over the years, and one striking aspect of Stamford Bridge is that it is much more intimidating for any outside observer dropping in to see the show. Its relatively small size – just over 40,000 capacity, the smallest and least renovated among the stadiums of the Premier League's big clubs – seems to belong to a bygone era and another league, seemingly at odds with Chelsea's reputation as one of the most successful and richest clubs of the more recent years of the English Premier League. Plans for a new stadium have been discussed and postponed over the years.

Chelsea were given permission to expand the capacity of Stamford Bridge in January 2017, but the plans were put on hold in May 2018 due to what the club described at the time as the 'unfavourable investment climate'. Two years later Chelsea said they would continue to consider options for a new stadium 'should economic conditions improve' but no major progress has been made since then. By the summer of 2022, the stadium's main claim to modernity is the adjacent Chelsea Village complex. Promoted when it was first opened in 2001 as one of the first developments that integrated retail, commercial, hotel and residential uses around a 'top class' football stadium, its size and design today lag behind the bolder architectural urban designs in London, such as the redevelopment of King's Cross, Battersea Power Station and Nine Elms.

Other football stadiums in the Premier League belonging to big clubs also dwarf Stamford Bridge – United, City, Liverpool and Arsenal all have bigger capacities, as does

Tottenham's new stadium (opened in 2017) on the site of the old White Hart Lane. Designed as a multi-purpose venue with a retractable football pitch, which reveals a synthetic turf field underneath for NFL London games, concerts and other events, Tottenham Hotspur Stadium is London's second-largest stadium after Wembley.

And yet, far from diminishing the passion of the fans at Stamford Bridge – where advertising boards claim that Chelsea FC is the true 'Pride of London' and banners from fan clubs around the world are hung from the upper tiers – the cramped environment of the stadium helps accentuate its heat and volume.

The celebration of the Spurs fans, although in a clear numerical minority, explodes as their captain Harry Kane scores an equaliser, securing a draw in the final minutes of a game full of competitive ferocity and quality play. That for much of the match, it is the Chelsea players and the tactical brilliance of their German coach Thomas Tuchel that have the clear edge over Antonio Conte's Spurs, is reason enough for home fans to vent their anger at the referee with the same dedication as they show in approving their team's best moves.

Like officers leading their men as brothers in arms, Tuchel and Conte clash with each other in two eye-popping touchline rows. Tuchel brings back memories of José Mourinho as the German, like a wild pitch-invader, runs jubilantly past the Chelsea bench and an exasperated Conte, and on towards the corner flag after James has restored the Chelsea lead at 2-1.

Some managers, of a less expressive personality, might have been forgiven for feeling somewhat overawed by sharing a touchline with Conte, once a star Italian international player, who as coach has won several league titles in his eight seasons in European club football. But the German relishes throwing down the gauntlet, on the touchline and on the pitch. Beyond showing himself adept at psychology, Tuchel shows his tactical genius, using a 4-2-2-2 formation to overwhelm Spurs' double pivot of Betancur and Højbjerg and the press to shut down the wider rotations of the visitors.

I am accompanied at the match by a young Chelsea fan, Rory, a 28-year-old, whose boyhood football memories are of Gianfranco Zola, the Italian player who was key to Chelsea's resurgence in the 1996/97 season. Those were the days when the coolest (fashionable and attractive) coach in the English Premier League was the stylish Dutchman Ruud Gullit. In his homeland, some of his own countrymen dismissed Gullit as a cantankerous troublemaker. Londoners treated him like a trend-setting celebrity who drew the emerging Labour Party leader and future Prime Minister Tony Blair, among others, to the Chelsea then chaired by Ken Bates.

Gullit wore blue Cerrito suits and no socks, drank cappuccino and was fluent in seven languages – seven more than most English footballers. He made Chelsea the club of choice for the fashion-conscious.

It was all change from Chelsea's previous reputation as the club better known for its street battles and infiltration by the extreme right-wing British National Party, and Gullit himself was a strikingly contrasting image to the English bull-dog terrier, the shaven-headed Cockney Dennis Wise who captained Chelsea, almost the last Englishman standing as the club embarked on an enduring policy of big spends on world-class foreign players.

Fast forward to the game against Spurs in August 2022: Chelsea fan Rory tells me that he wishes his club would encourage more young players coming up through the academy rather than focus its recruitment on high-grade Premier League and star signings from abroad. And yet part of him is also full of admiration for a new arrival, the Senegalese signing from Napoli, Kalidou Koulibaly who is imperious at centre-back and opens the scoring in his first game for the Blues at Stamford Bridge. An impressive young debutant with the club is the Spaniard Marc Cucurella, the star summer signing from Brighton.

In 2018 Cucurella, who had been at Barcelona since he joined the youth squad in 2012, went to Eibar on loan. After another season at Getafe, he was bought by Brighton for £15.4m. Brighton's 2021/22 season ended in ninth place in the Premier League, the highest the club had finished in English top-flight football. Then in the summer of 2022 Cucurella transferred to Chelsea for £62m, making him the most expensive full-back in Premier League history.

In the new season's match against Tottenham, it is the referee Anthony Taylor's failure to penalise Cristian Romero's evident foul, pulling Cucurella to the ground by his long black locks (Cucurella was encouraged by his mother to grow his hair as a school boy in Spain to distinguish him on the pitch) that fuels the anger of Chelsea fans and coach. On the touchline, a Chelsea club employee is waving a large 'No to Hate' banner throughout the match. The gesture contrasts with some of the gestures and chants of the more militant fans. However, a symbol of how the club has managed to confront and exorcise racist attitudes is the presence among several black players in the team of the English international Raheem Sterling, recently signed from Manchester City.

A Chelsea fan, Colin Wing, received a lifetime ban for racially abusing Sterling when Manchester City played at Stamford Bridge in December 2018. In an interview prior to the game against Spurs in the summer of 2022, Sterling says that the incident did not cross his mind when he was looking for the next challenge after deciding to leave City. Sterling is asked if he would be willing to meet Wing. 'I have no hatred or malice towards the individual,' Sterling tells *The Times*. 'That's something that I could do right here, right now, or tomorrow. That's not an issue.

'I think my main focus is to move away from the racial kind of thing and focus more on nurturing and feeding the youth, like me growing up: giving them a map to what lies ahead and showing them that they can manifest a lot of stuff if they just put the time in and look after themselves.'

The London derby is high octane, bruising, and with great tactical play and goals, and hugely entertaining off as well as on the pitch – almost everything you want from a football match at the top level. It is watched by Chelsea's new owner, US financier Todd Boehly, his tall burly frame in the very executive box that for years was occupied by the Russian oligarch Roman Abramovich, before he fell foul of British sanctions against Russia, following Putin's invasion of Ukraine. Youthful-looking, in an open-necked formal shirt coloured a lighter shade of Chelsea blue, Boehly has a memorable first taste of English Premier League football, and is drawn into the rollercoaster of emotions of a game which sees Chelsea twice go ahead, before being pegged back to 2-2 – a Harry Kane equaliser for Tottenham in the 96th minute, the final hammer blow. The American jumps for joy (as Abramovich used to do) when Koulibaly puts the Blues ahead, but by the end of the match he is seated and has his head in his hands after seeing Kane's leveller.

The draw is the final result, after Chelsea fans had taunted Spurs fans with: 'We won it all, you won fuck all!' to underline the huge divide in trophy achievement separating the two sides during the Abramovich years.

As a result of their unseemly confrontation, the two managers get red cards, with the Chelsea manager Tuchel continuing after the match to stir up the hostility the Chelsea fans feel for the referee by insisting that both Tottenham goals should not have been allowed. Tuchel however is destined to follow a long list of foreign managers whose time at Chelsea is cut short due to underachievement. In early September 2022, Chelsea's new owners take a rare gamble for a leading Premier club, by signing Graham Potter, an English coach who has never managed a major club. The new Chelsea hierarchy nevertheless took their decision on the basis of Potter's relatively short-lived but meteoric managerial career, which he undertook after playing with various clubs in the Football League and with Southampton in the Premier.

Potter's first venture into management took off as he lifted the unfancied Swedish club Östersund into the top flight and a place in the Europa League. He then managed, with mixed success Swansea, before achieving his and Brighton's highest Premier finish, ninth, in the 2021/22 season. It was reported that Chelsea's new owner, Boehly, was attracted by Potter's reputation for being non-controversial and collaborating and communicating well with players – credentials needed following Abramovich's departure and the confrontational scenes which Tuchel seemed to relish, without much of a positive result to show for it, in the game against Spurs.

In terms of bad blood however the game was no repeat of the legendary Battle of Stamford Bridge of May 2016, which also ended in a 2-2 draw with Tottenham and gave Leicester City the Premier League title for the first and only time in their history and frustrated the visitors, who had come closest to winning the league since their last title in 1961.

The 'Battle' involved opposing players attacking each other off the ball on the pitch, resulting in nine yellow cards for Tottenham (a Premier League record for any team), and another three for Chelsea, and Moussa Dembélé the Belgian Tottenham player receiving a six-match suspension for violent conduct after he appeared to claw at the eye of Chelsea's front man Diego Costa.

Both clubs were fined by the Football Association for failing to control their players.

In August 2022, the confrontation between the managers verged on the theatrical, rather than seriously hostile. And yet their conduct, not least Tuchel's criticism of the referee Anthony Taylor, risked igniting players and fans in a Premier

League that prided itself on projecting a good image to the rest of the world.

\* \* \*

Prior to new owner Boehly's arrival, Chelsea's recent history was divided into two very clear phases: the era of English owner Ken Bates, 1982 to 2003, followed by the spectacular and polemic 'glory days' of Chelsea's ownership by Abramovich, 2003 to 2022. Chelsea's previous successful era had been from 1955 to 1971.

In 1982 Ken Bates bought a club wallowing in Division 2, with large debts and a notorious hooligan element, for just £1. As one Chelsea fan Charlie tells me: 'I recall 2nd Division games with very low attendances, terrible games, and a despondent atmosphere at Stamford Bridge. Standing on crumbling concrete on sparsely populated terraces, little atmosphere given it also doubled up as a greyhound-racing track. We all knew the debts meant no good players being bought and the 2nd Division would probably be our home for the future.'

Bates was a controversial self-made man, with extreme right-wing views. However, he knew what he wanted and basically transformed the club. After narrowly escaping dropping to Division 3, Bates eventually bought the freehold of the stadium, as the club was about to be evicted from Stamford Bridge. The first season he made large funds available, good players were bought and Chelsea were then promoted to Division 1.

By the time the Premier looked set to transform English football, Chelsea were a well-established club – all thanks to the controversial Bates who amongst other extreme measures, set up an electric fence around the pitch to contain the Chelsea hooligans! The transformation of Chelsea began with Bates but was then taken to another level by Abramovich taking full advantage of a lax regulatory environment.

Before Abramovich's takeover, Bates had brought in a number of highly colourful and successful foreign players: Zola, Roberto Di Matteo, Marcel Desailly, Jimmy Floyd Hasselbaink, etc. And managers such as Gianluca Vialli and Claudio Ranieri. Maybe Abramovich simply continued the Bates model.

Chelsea fans loved Bates, but they came to love Abramovich even more. Bates was an unpleasant character with *cojones* who saved the club and brought great players and trophies (FA Cup and Cup Winners' Cup). He put Chelsea on the international stage: the club's first venture into the Champions League was in 1999. Chelsea were cruising, playing good football, in the top six consistently. And Zola was just magical.

It was the 1990s: a time when the financial centre of London, the 'City', was awash with Russians. As my former *Financial Times* colleague and Moscow correspondent Catherine Belton notes in her best-selling *Putin's People*: 'Instead of Russia being changed through integration into Western markets, it was Russia that was changing the West. The tycoons coming to London, who the West hoped would become independent forces for change, were instead becoming dependent on the Kremlin. They were instead becoming hostage to Putin's increasingly authoritarian and kleptocratic state. Instead of bringing Russia into line with its rule-based system, slowly the West was being corrupted. It was as if a virus was being injected into it.'

The path, according to Belton, had been smoothed in part, when Roman Abramovich bought Chelsea FC in the summer of 2003 for £150 million and catapulted Chelsea into becoming the richest club in the Premier. Abramovich would come to insist that throughout the years of his ownership of Chelsea he invested in two ambitions: to create world-class teams on the pitch and to ensure the club played a positive role in all its communities. His spokesman also insisted that

Abramovich used his box at Chelsea for family and friends and never invited British politicians.

According to Belton, the fact that Abramovich's business interests in the UK were tolerated for so many years was partly because he appeared to have nothing to do with Putin's KGB spies. And yet, regardless of Abramovich's motivation for the purchase of Chelsea, it became a symbol of the Russian cash that was flooding into the UK, and his ready acceptance helped Russian money become part of the fabric of London life.

In London and elsewhere in the UK, many hated Chelsea and their fans but they didn't care! The football brand was powerful, the club was above anything, and the source of Abramovich's fortune was not an issue – well, not until the war in Ukraine.

As they say, the rest is history: 19 years of Russian ownership and 21 trophies. Abramovich got through more top foreign managers than Florentino Pérez at Real Madrid, among them the *crème de la crème* Gullit, Vialli, Ranieri, Mourinho, Luiz Felipe Scolari, Guus Hiddink, Carlo Ancelotti, Rafa Benítez, Conte, and through it all Chelsea won more silverware than any other English club during Abramovich's reign, and the fans forgave everything – even the fact he was one of Putin's oligarchs. The model worked as long as Abramovich's assets were not seized, and no one imagined that would happen until Russia invaded Ukraine in February 2022. Until then, Chelsea fans considered Abramovich a benevolent oligarch. Even after Russia invaded Ukraine, some of them continued to shout their support for him during matches, much to the horror of opposing fans.

Not that Chelsea fans had ever behaved in a way that made them lovable. I remember attending an FC Barcelona Champions League match at Stamford Bridge. I acted as an interpreter for the Metropolitan Police, who warned that all pubs in the neighbourhood were off limits to visiting fans as their safety could not be guaranteed. The Chelsea fans spent the whole match shouting abuse at the visiting fans. The most popularly used term was '*Spiks*', the derogatory Anglo-Saxon word for Hispanics.

But the *cules* had it easy compared to English fans. Tottenham, a club with a strong following among London's Jewish community, in the bad days had to deal with the most racist Chelsea fans making taunting hissing noises in memory of Nazi gas chambers.

When Abramovich decided to invest as the new owner of Chelsea in 2003, he considered Spain and Italy as alternatives. But he decided that ownership there was too complicated politically compared to the liberal market opportunity offered by the Premier. He sealed the deal to buy Chelsea over a bottle of Evian in London's Dorchester Hotel, thereby starting a new era in the Premier League, which had foreigners buying and funding ancient English clubs and transforming them into cash cows. Some of these fortunes were murkily begotten and yet the Premier produced some of the best football in the world, and fans fell in love with it.

With the fall of Abramovich, there was no shortage of bidders to take over Chelsea and a consortium led by Todd Boehly were the eventual buyers. The only condition set by the fans was that the new owner had to be committed to the club and build a new stadium as part of the deal. But there is a curious thing about Stamford Bridge. It is an old stadium, completely unsuitable for a club like Chelsea – just look at the new stadiums of their north London rivals – but it has atmosphere, it is different. The more fanatical fans, from coke-sniffing young executives to alcoholic, working class, racist Brexiteers, love it!

Mourinho appealed to their nature. As Charlie, a Chelsea fan explained: 'Surely the Chelsea team under Mourinho was the ultimate the club has ever seen: Drogba, Lampard, Terry, Cech; a spinal cord that brought Stamford Bridge so much. From a club bought in 1982 for just £1 and almost relegated to Division 3, to then dominate the Premiership, and probably the most successful Premiership club this century, and then being sold for £3 billion as World Club Champions, says a lot about the two owners: both self-made men, who actually cared for the club (unlike Manchester United's Glazer family), had great business sense, changed managers at a drop ... and on selling made a fortune! Bates: £1-£140 million (of which he pocketed £17 million): Abramovich: £140 million-£3 billion (although he hasn't 'made' this money, as such, because his assets have been frozen by the UK government). Who said a football club owner couldn't make money?!'

And yet on 6 April 2021, Chelsea fans at Stamford Bridge got their first glimpse of a future without unlimited riches. In a Champions League quarter-final tie, Chelsea crashed to a 1-3 defeat to Real Madrid. The match showed the reigning champions of Europe (Chelsea) acting like poor folk in a way that allowed the historic emperors of Europe (Real Madrid) an easy win, thanks to the brilliance of Karim Benzema.

Chelsea manager Thomas Tuchel had hoped that the atmosphere created by Chelsea fans at Stamford Bridge would be enough to lift the spirit of his players, evidently affected by take-over anxiety. The rain was pouring down. The fans refused to fall quiet in the face of the growing dominance of the visitors. They roared their support for their team, with waves of noisy taunts shouted at Real Madrid players, not least the goalkeeper Thibaut Courtois, who they felt had betrayed them with the inelegant way he forced his transfer from Chelsea in 2018. For most of the match, the stadium seemed a reminder of the sheer madness of unquestioning fandom, with thousands of fanatics watching every move that might benefit Chelsea, clapping and swaying in unison, a reminder of the passion of English club football. They included fans who romantically recalled the days before Abramovich bought Chelsea when it didn't matter if the club won or lost – all that mattered was that the players, for all the obscene amount of money spent on them, possessed the right attitude, sweated the colours, fought and fell like heroes. But before the end of the match against Real Madrid, there were Chelsea fans abandoning the stadium, disillusioned, their sense of loyalty betrayed.

Chapter Seven

# Pep

MANCHESTER CITY fans have an enduring memory of 13 August 2016, the first game of the new Premier League season at their futuristic Etihad Stadium, under the management of Pep Guardiola.

English football had been transformed over the previous two decades since the foundation of the Premier, with an influx of star managers – but few came with such a track record of recognised achievement in the top-tier as Guardiola. The quick-passing, pressing game that Guardiola had won many glory days with at Barca and Bayern Munich secured a vital three points in victory against Sunderland, thus beginning a revival that would lead to Manchester City – historically the poor pretender compared to Manchester United – turning into one of the top clubs in Europe.

In his first five seasons, the Catalan presided over the most successful period in the club's history, lifting ten trophies and winning every competition on offer in England. He set record after record in that time to leave an indelible mark on both Manchester City and English football, building a legacy which fans hoped would stand the test of time.

In October 2021, as football fans looked forward to the end of the enforced hibernation of the Covid pandemic, the club published performance statistics underlining the team's resilience and dominance in adversity. They had scored more goals (480), struck more shots (3,452) and had more shots on target (1,259) than any other team in the Premier since the start of the 2016/17 campaign, with Liverpool in second place in each of those categories. They had also edged out Jürgen Klopp's men to lead the way for possession (66.98 per cent) and successful passes (118,457), whilst Chelsea (85.69 per cent) were their closest rivals in terms of passing accuracy, with Guardiola's team recording 88.54 per cent across his five seasons.

'These numbers underline the exciting attacking philosophy the Catalan has implemented at the Etihad, but we have also been the leading Premier League team in several defensive areas,' the club proclaimed.

Fans have lived many glory days with Man City since the club was bought by Sheikh Mansour bin Zayed Al Nayyan through the Abu Dhabi United Group in 2008. Up to that point, the club had suffered a long period of decline following the 1960s and 1970s. They were twice relegated in the 1980s and were relegated from the Premier League in 1996. After two seasons in Division 1, City fell to the lowest point in their history, becoming the second-ever European trophy winners to be relegated to their country's third league tier, after FC Magdeburg of Germany.

And yet there was another side to Manchester City which exemplified the complex reality of the English Premier League. In 2008 players and fans were shocked to hear that the club's owner, former Thai Prime Minister Thaksin Shinawatra had gone into hiding to avoid facing trial. The club was then bought by Sheikh Mansour, whose ownership would, with time, become the subject of controversy.

In November 2018, the human rights organisation, Amnesty International accused Manchester City's Abu Dhabi owners of brazenly trying to 'sportswash' their country's 'deeply tarnished image' by pouring money into the Premier League club. It followed a series of incendiary allegations made by the German media group *Der Spiegel* against the club, including a deal for sports rights involving a shell company controlled by a major donor to the British Conservative party via a series of companies and trusts operating in tax havens.

The defunct website 'Football Leaks' made allegations of financial impropriety. The rules are supposed to help level the playing field and stop clubs buying success. The allegations raised questions about City's conduct, the transparency of its financial relationships, and its choice of business partners. One of its sponsorship deals was struck with Arabtec, the largest construction company in the United Arab Emirates, and a firm that has been repeatedly criticised by Amnesty International and Human Rights Watch for its poor treatment of migrant workers. The Premier League has charged Manchester City with 115 financial breaches. City deny those charges, and a decision is expected in summer 2025.

'As a growing number of Manchester City fans will be aware, the success of the club has involved a close relationship with a country that relies on exploited migrant labour and locks up peaceful critics and human rights defenders,' said Amnesty International's Gulf researcher Devin Kenney.

*Der Spiegel's* report confirmed what English Middle East experts like the academic Dr Christopher Davidson had known for some time, that this was inevitable once British football allowed a foreign government to buy a team. As Davidson said following the report, 'What needs to happen now – before Abu Dhabi's money kills the competition and makes football boring – is a debate about whether we let a state linked with human rights abuses invest in British football.'

Sheikh Mansour was still in control of Man City after Russia invaded Ukraine, when he drew protests from the Foreign Office and English members of parliament for meeting Syrian president and Vladimir Putin ally Bashar al-Assad. In the House of Commons, Chris Bryant, chair of the All-Party Group on Russia, questioned if Mansour was a 'fit and proper person', a reference to the criteria the Football Association and Premier League set for new owners.

'What is it that people don't get? There's been a form of barbarous, sustained murder going on in Syria, run jointly by Assad, and now Putin is doing exactly the same in a barbaric war of aggression against innocent sovereign Ukraine. And some people want to meet up with the bully boys?' said Bryant.

Less than a month later, the focus of football fans seemed less on the money or human rights and more on club loyalty – and at Manchester City the mouth-watering prospect of watching football played not just with great style but also of potentially more titles and new records. Ahead of City's home Champions League quarter-final tie, against Atlético Madrid, TV football pundit and former England and Manchester City star Joleon Lescott commented that while Guardiola had sometimes been criticised for supposedly overthinking important matches, his teams remained the best when it came to a possession-based game. 'To beat City, a team has to be at their absolute best,' commented Lescott.

Moral arguments often did not seem to hold water with English football fans.

## Chapter Eight

# 'You'll Never Walk Alone'

IN A city that gave us the Beatles, football fans perhaps have every right to feel that they are God's anointed when it comes to showing the world they feel passionate about the game in a way that reaches out across regions and national boundaries, with a rising anthem to human solidarity sung before kick-off at every game Liverpool FC play at their Anfield home, and at some away games.

'You'll Never Walk Alone' is perhaps the most famous song in football. Since long before the Premier League was founded, it travelled around the world and continued to do so, as the Reds have toured Europe and even further afield as five-time European champions.

But how did it become such a huge part of the club's identity?

The story of the song and its association with Liverpool the team and the city, as well as many other footballing institutions, dates back to the 1960s. 'You'll Never Walk Alone' was originally written by Oscar Hammerstein II and Richard Rodgers for their musical *Carousel,* which was released in the USA in 1945. But it was the version sung by the pop group Gerry and the Pacemakers in 1963, part of the 'Merseybeat' scene led by the Beatles, that became part of the club's identity. So, the popular narrative goes, the lead singer Gerry Marsden presented a copy of the single to the legendary Reds manager Bill Shankly during a pre-season trip that same year and, according to Tommy Smith, a player at the time, Shankly was 'in awe of what he heard'.

A sense of collectivism and civic pride was cemented as culture blossomed thanks to music and football. Firstly, Liverpool's musical revolution in the 1960s, led by the Beatles and new venues such as the Cavern, prompted the city to be named the 'world capital of pop' by the Guinness Book of World Records, with 54 number one hits, more per capita than any other city. Music was not just a pillar of Liverpool's brand which gave the city acclaim across the world, but an important bridge between football and local identity.

Shankly picked the song 'You'll Never Walk Alone' during an appearance on the BBC's *Desert Island Discs* radio show in 1965 ahead of that year's FA Cup Final and the TV footage of that match provides the first evidence of it being sung in the stands. Since then, it has been picked up by a number of clubs. Borussia Dortmund combined with Liverpool fans for a memorable rendition of the anthem when the two sides met in the Europa League during the 2015/16 season. It was particularly popular in Germany and the Netherlands, where Feyenoord sang it, and has gone around the globe to clubs like FC Tokyo in Japan. When Liverpool played pre-season matches in Australia in 2013, 95,000 fans packed into the Melbourne Cricket Ground and produced an incredible pre-match chorus.

The song developed a new meaning and symbolism after the Hillsborough disaster of 1989 which led to 97 fans losing their lives. A full 25 years after the first coroner's inquest concluded the deaths were accidental, the campaigning efforts of the families of the deceased resulted in a new verdict being delivered, stating that their relatives had been unlawfully killed. Throughout that process, the lyrics and themes of 'You'll Never Walk Alone' touched an ever-greater emotional chord.

Krishan Puvvada, an English academic friend of Indian descent who has studied Liverpool's cultural identity in detail, makes the following observation: 'Liverpool became emblematic of Britain's wider social problems in the 1980s. Liverpool FC during the period was the defining motif for Merseyside because it was a deep connector between people and place and because the Hillsborough disaster became a metaphor for how outsiders saw the city's problems. Liverpool FC's relationship with Liverpool is a strong example of cultural nationalism because the club was a marker of belonging to the city and a symbol of the "Scouse not English" self vs other mindset which dominated Liverpool's relationship with the rest of the UK. Liverpool FC was the emblem of Liverpool's cultural identity because it was a focal point of language and shared traditions, sentiment and heritage.'

Today, the words 'You'll Never Walk Alone' appear on Liverpool's crest, based on the design of the Shankly Gates, which were erected outside Anfield in 1982.

According to Puvvada, the fact that Liverpool FC adopted this Scouse song as their anthem underlines the synergy between music, sport, oral performance and regional identity – singing 'You'll Never Walk Alone' on matchdays is a unique opportunity to vocalise what it means to be Scouse, confirming the role of the club as a means of expressing belonging.

The most visceral of these oral performances come from the Kop at Anfield stadium – a stand named after Spion Kop hill in South Africa, where large numbers of Liverpudlian soldiers died during the Boer War in 1900. The Kop has been described as having all the menace of an hysteric's nightmare, underlining the relationship between language, oratory and identity and also the self vs other tribalism which exists between English football teams and the cities they represent. In the words of author and lifelong football fan Grant Farred,

'Anfield was the very incarnation, not simply the symbol, of the city and Liverpool exceptionality.'

Opposing teams have found the sheer passion of the Kop so intimidating as to make even the best-planned tactics of visitors fall apart. In November 2021, Mikel Arteta the Arsenal coach, prepared his team for a visit to Anfield by playing them a recording of the Liverpool fans at a deafening volume on the training ground. Arsenal lost the match 0-4.

Forever 'walking' with the Liverpool fans is the enduring memory of Shankly, who served in the Royal Air Force during the Second World War and was a fierce socialist. Having brought the club national and European glory, Shankly is immortalised in a statue outside the popular Kop end at Anfield.

He became Liverpool FC manager in 1959, while the club was languishing in the Second Division. In 14 years, Shankly took them up to the First Division and then won the title three times, in addition to securing the club's first European trophy in 1973. Says Puvvada, 'Far more profound than the trophies though was the team and manager's adoption of the city's values – fighting spirit, humour and obsession with football. Shankly's Liverpool is littered with stories of simple but effective socialist football and the importance of courage.'

Shankly the legend has replaced Shankly the man in the eyes of most of the Liverpool fan base due to the passing of time. He is simply the grandfather of the modern Liverpool, his musings trotted out by fans whenever it suits, not least his most often-repeated quote: 'Some people believe football is a matter of life and death, I am disappointed with that attitude. I can assure you it is much more important than that.'

They are words often seen on prints, posters, tea towels, mugs and anything else you can stamp a Liverpool logo on and fans will eagerly buy. During the pandemic, when football stopped being a live event attended by massive crowds and the game was played in empty stadiums with recorded crowd applause and chants, the words took on a hollow meaning, before that ended and normality was restored.

Liverpool FC entered a new golden period under German Jürgen Klopp, who was appointed manager in 2015. He guided the club to successive UEFA Champions League Finals in 2018 and 2019, winning the latter to secure his first, and Liverpool's sixth, title in the competition.

Klopp's Liverpool finished second in the Premier League in 2018/19, registering 97 points, then the third-highest total in the history of the English top flight, and the most by a team without winning the title. The following season, Klopp won the FIFA Club World Cup and UEFA Super Cup before delivering Liverpool's first Premier League in 2020, breaking a club record in points. Klopp won the FIFA coach of the year awards in 2019 and 2020.

For decades, English football fans had seen Germans as the hated rivals, with enduring memories of world wars and World Cup encounters, but Klopp's charisma and emotional connection engaged with Liverpool, as he spoke to the fans in their language and with a passion for the game that had him joining Shankly in the pantheon of gods.

Here is Jürgen Klopp discussing the area in the Main Stand at Anfield that he calls his 'safe place' and 'the best pub in Liverpool' and how he felt when he was first shown around Anfield after arriving in 2015.

'So, the first thing which was completely new to me was when I arrived at Liverpool and went [for the] first time to the stadium and they showed me the dressing room, which was not very impressive in the old stand to be honest. Then we went down a floor and they say: "OK, this is your little Boot Room." I said: "What is that?"

'They explained it to me, and it was really nice. [It's] like a little pub in the stadium, it's only for the manager and stuff like this. I liked it a lot.'

As part of the main stand redevelopment in 2016, the Klopp family put their own stamp on the new design of the Boot Room.

'Ulla, my wife, was responsible for the furniture and how it looks. For me, it's the best pub in Liverpool. After a game, we love going there with all my staff and all my friends.'

As was noted on the popular football website JOE, 'Very few fanbases adore and admire their manager more than Liverpool fans do Jürgen Klopp. His warm, welcoming demeanour, commitment to the cause and heavy metal football have made him a fan favourite and he absolutely loves it.'

On a pre-season tour of the United States in 2018, Klopp put the team through an intense training programme to ensure they were ready for another demanding schedule of matches in the Premier and in Europe. But despite the busy schedule and all the training, Klopp still found time to enjoy a drink with Liverpool fans in a local bar. He entered the bar in which musician and Liverpool fan Jamie Webster was playing a gig, and the reaction was priceless. Webster stopped in his tracks, stunned at who he had just seen walk through the door.

He then proceeded to play the famous chant sung around Anfield, 'Allez, Allez, Allez', which had become a sensation during the previous season. Klopp joined in with the fans in the bar to sing the tune, soaking up the love and optimism that flowed through the room.

It was this relationship between Klopp and the fans that helped foster an electric atmosphere at Anfield in the 2021/22 season. Throughout Liverpool's Champions League run, the atmosphere at their home matches played a big part in intimidating visiting teams and Klopp's visible communion with his players and fans played a part in creating that atmosphere.

If Klopp was the foreign manager that connected with the soul of fans and opened their hearts to a world without frontiers, setting aside historical prejudice, the Muslim Egyptian Mohamed Salah did the same as a player. Since arriving in the Premier, transferred to Liverpool from AS Roma in the summer of 2017, he has become one of the most prolific forwards in European football and is a fan favourite at Anfield.

In March 2023, Salah became Liverpool's all-time top scorer in the Premier League after netting his 129th goal for the club with a double in his team's emphatic, record-breaking 7-0 win over Manchester United, the Merseyside club's biggest win over one of its great rivals since 1895, when the Red Devils were still known as Newton Heath.

Cody Gakpo, Mohamed Salah and Darwin Núñez all scored twice in the game and became the first Premier League trio to manage that feat in the 21st century. The 30-year-old Salah leapfrogged Robbie Fowler's previous record of 128 goals, having already surpassed previous club legends Steven Gerrard (120) and Michael Owen (118).

As the English football writer Barney Ronay wrote in a profile of Salah for *The Guardian* in October 2021: 'Salah is, lest we forget, a phenomenon and an outlier. More than any other on-field part, he is the basic magic dust in those six years of Klopp. This is in many ways a co-era: the age of Salah. It is hard to think of other players who have had such an obviously transformative effect. Alex Ferguson had Eric Cantona. Yaya Touré's arrival shifted City from a hopeful project into a culture of relentless success. Salah's first season was Klopp's third at Anfield. Liverpool had improved from eighth to fourth in that time. At which point: ignition.

'In Salah's first year they scored 135 goals and reached the Champions League Final. In his second Liverpool hoovered up 97 points and were champions of Europe. In his third they won the league. In his fourth they collapsed in mid-season. No matter. Salah still scored 31 goals. They ended up safe in third. There has been an urge in the last few days to suggest

Salah has been underappreciated through all this, to inject a little tribal grievance into his brilliance. There is no need. Those who watch know how good he is.'

Chapter Nine

# Merseyside Derby

THERE IS, of course, another Liverpudlian club, Everton, which claims a longer history and was one of the founder members of the Premier and has remained in the top tier throughout its 30-plus years. But Everton have fallen short of Liverpool FC's achievements in terms of trophies, successful managers and star players, and international projection.

I mention Everton in deference to my friend, the Hispanist historian Sir Paul Preston, who has been among several distinguished supporters for whom football is about more than winning, let alone success: it is about emotional attachment. Preston declared himself long ago an Everton supporter although he prefers spending his time writing about the history of Spain rather than visiting football stadiums.

Preston was born in Liverpool in 1946. He took pride at being born into a fairly left-wing family and in his sympathy for the Republic in the Spanish Civil War. 'You could not really be from working-class Liverpool and not be left-wing. Emotionally, in my feeling for the Republic I think there is an element of indignation about the Republic's defeat, solidarity with the losing side. Maybe that's why I support Everton, although Everton wasn't the losing side in my day.'

Another often-quoted Everton sympathiser who has never been a life-long fanatical fan – he prefers music to football – is one of the two surviving Beatles, Sir Paul McCartney (the other survivor, Ringo Starr, once declared himself an Arsenal sympathiser).

McCartney recalled in an interview with *GQ* magazine in 2020: 'There's a great old piece of film from the 1960s of the Liverpool fans singing "She Loves You", with the Kop all singing, "Ooooooh!" All the kids, everyone; it's quite moving. The camera goes in on the crowd and there are all these young Beatles, all these kids with the hairstyle, and they're all singing "She Loves You". They know all the words. That piece of film was always a high spot for me.

'Years ago, I decided I was going to support Liverpool as well as Everton, even though Everton is the family team. A couple of my grandkids are Liverpool fans, so we are happy to see them win this year's Premier League. When people ask me how I can support them both I say I love both and I have special dispensation from the Pope!'

Everton are due to move to a new stadium in time for the start of the 2025/26 season, on the site of former docks on the banks of the river Mersey, two miles away from Anfield (which was actually Everton's original home before they moved following a disagreement over rent). With a capacity of 54,000 it will be an ambitious leap from the 39,000 of the historic stadium Goodison Park. The new home is a project supported by the club's controversial majority shareholder Farhad Moshiri, the British-Iranian businessman who in March 2022 stepped down from the board of USM, a Russian holding company after suspending the club's multiple sponsorship ties with companies associated with its owner, Uzbekistan-born billionaire, Alisher Usmanov after Putin's invasion of Ukraine.

Liverpool FC's owners are the American Fenway Sports Group, whose interests span Major League Baseball and a sports broadcasting company in the US. According to the annual *Forbes* magazine ranking, in 2022, Liverpool FC were the second-richest club in the Premier League, behind

Manchester United and ahead of Manchester City and Chelsea, based on their net worth.

Everton's most legendary manager is Howard Kendall, who won two Football League titles, an FA Cup, three Charity Shields and the 1985 European Cup Winners' Cup, as well as a league runners-up spot and a place in two further FA Cup Finals and a League Cup Final. This was the best trophy haul in the club's history but Kendall was unable to repeat the success when he returned to Everton in 1990, after a couple of seasons managing Athletic Bilbao from 1987-89 and a brief spell at Manchester City. He was appointed Everton's manager for the third time in 1997/98 but left the club by mutual consent having only managed to avoid relegation on the final day of the season.

And yet, regardless of the two clubs' different league positioning and trophy numbers, the Merseyside derby remains an essential part of the city of Liverpool's social and cultural fabric. The rivalry between Liverpool and Everton has had its special identity since they first played a match against each other in 1894.

As the football writer David Hendrick wrote in the *Bleacher Report* in 2012: 'The main thing that separates the Merseyside derby from all others is the relationship between the fans. It is truly unique, much like the city that stages the event. It is a match, and indeed a rivalry which, despite whatever may happen on or around the football, is built on respect between the fans.

'Go to the Manchester derby, the North London derby, the Glasgow derby or any other you can think of and you won't see scenes like you will at a Merseyside derby. You won't see opposition fans sitting amongst each other, you won't see young fans of one club helping an elderly fan of the other to and from their seat.'

Everton have had to suffer in the shadow of Liverpool FC's recent years of glory and the fan 'love-in' under the

German manager Klopp. They began a new season in the summer of 2022 under a rather less talented let alone charismatic manager, the one-time Chelsea and England star Frank Lampard, Everton's seventh permanent manager since the departure of David Moyes in 2013. Lampard succeeded Rafa Benítez when he was sacked in January 2022 after only seven months in charge, unable to produce the good results that he had achieved while at Liverpool FC.

Benítez said after his dismissal. 'It was a big challenge, both emotionally and in terms of sport. My love for this city, for Merseyside and its people, made me accept this challenge, but it is only when you are inside that you realise the magnitude of the task. From the very first day, my staff and myself worked as we always do, with commitment and full dedication. We didn't only have to get results, but we also had to win over people's hearts. However, the financial situation and then the injuries that followed made things even harder.'

The appointment of Benítez, in succession to Carlo Ancelotti, as Everton manager, was a big gamble for Everton owner Moshiri. It was one of the most controversial managerial appointments in Everton's history and turned out to be one of the shortest. Benítez was remembered as an icon at Liverpool FC after winning the Champions League in Istanbul in 2005, when his side came from 3-0 down against AC Milan at half-time to win on penalties.

Legend has it that the Spaniard later earned the wrath of large numbers of Everton supporters after a remark, which he claimed was lost in translation, describing them as a 'small club' following a goalless Merseyside derby at Anfield in 2007. And yet Moshiri believed Benítez's ruthless streak and tactical acumen would bring stability and success following the dysfunctionality and turbulence wrought by the series of managers who were sacked before Ancelotti's return to Real Madrid.

Benítez's conviction that he could win over fans led him to misjudge them as they quickly lost patience with his lack of results, which he blamed on key injuries and lack of investment in new star signings. The fan discontent boiled over, with protest banners and players being abused at the final whistle. With fans in open mutiny, Benítez lost the support of the board. Given Everton's poor performance over the years in the Premier League and the evident superiority of Liverpool FC, and indeed of the other big clubs in the Premier League, no one underestimated the challenge facing his replacement Frank Lampard, the former English international and Chelsea captain who had been out of work since being sacked as manager by Chelsea in January 2021 after his 18-month spell with the club left them ninth in the Premier League.

Despite counting on the support of impassioned Evertonians, who inspired their team to fight a heroic last-ditch fight-back that averted relegation in the spring of 2022, Lampard still began the new season as one of the managers lucky to survive in the top-tier of football and Everton were without a win in the new season before the Merseyside derby against Liverpool at Goodison Park on 3 September ended in a goalless draw. Despite a hard-fought end-to-end game, and some missed chances on both sides, a below-best Liverpool came closest to scoring but for some brilliant goalkeeping by Everton's English international Jordan Pickford.

An Everton fan threw a plastic bottle at Jürgen Klopp and another ran on to the pitch to confront Anthony Taylor, one of the least popular referees in the Premier League. Both fans received automatic lengthy bans from the club under new measures against pitch invaders announced by the English football authorities for Premier League and the second tier English Football League matches. Concerns had been raised about safety at grounds after a number of pitch invasions at the end of the previous season, including one at Goodison Park during a match against Crystal Palace.

Many of the fans who attended the first derby of the 2022/23 season shared a collective memory, which included the 1980s when Liverpool FC were unquestionably the best team in England and arguably the best team in Europe before the city's and English football's reputation was for a while tarnished in the aftermath of the hooliganism that took place at the Heysel stadium in Brussels on 29 May 1985, when 39 people, mostly Italians, were killed after Liverpool fans confronted them before the European Cup Final.

What makes the Merseyside derby different from so many others is that there are no political, social or religious differences between the two clubs, nor a geographical distance and divide. As David Hendrick wrote: 'These are simply two sets of fans from the same city who support teams from the same city, and who are, by and large, very similar, in their love of the game. Derby day in the city of Liverpool is a special occasion and you will see families travelling to the match together. They will often enter the stadium and sit together. Some in red, some in blue. To witness this serves as a reminder that some things in life are more important than football.'

Madrid-based Liverpool fan Steve Brown told me: 'Although I find myself on the opposite side of the football divide from Everton fan Paul Preston, I have always believed that it is indeed fortunate to have two great teams from our city and the rivalry between their supporters is nearly always friendly and good natured. I was at Wembley in 1986 to watch the first ever FA Cup Final between Liverpool and Everton and one of the best moments in my life was to hear 100,000 Scousers singing "Merseyside, Merseyside" in unison.'

There have been fractious moments on and off the pitch in recent seasons of the Premier League, with indications of more violent behaviour by some fans seemingly undergoing an emotional outburst after the confinement of the pandemic and in the face of unresolved social disparity with the more affluent south of England.

But when it matters, Liverpudlians come together in solidarity.

In the summer of 2022, the city was rocked by the tragic death of a nine-year-old Liverpudlian, Olivia Pratt-Korbel – the innocent victim of gun crime. The senseless loss of young lives in the midst of criminal violence has horrified the entire community, and there was a deep sense that the death of a young girl should mark a watershed moment with people demanding an end to the violence.

At the Merseyside derby, Reds (Liverpool fans) and Blues (Everton fans) united to send a message of solidarity to the families of the victims. In the ninth minute of the Premier League fixture, Pratt-Korbel's picture was displayed on the big screen in the ground. Rival fans stood and applauded, while a joint banner was unfurled with two clubs' colours and club badges, declaring 'Enough is Enough – Our City in Unity.'

Chapter Ten

# The Miracle of the Bees

IN A search for Premier League fairy tales or miracles, few clubs can match the David vs Goliath story involving the heroic underdogs, Brentford FC.

On 2 April 2022, Brentford played away at Stamford Bridge and beat the home team, the European champions Chelsea, by four goals to one. The victory by one of the smaller clubs of a football league better known for the giants that had dominated the top flight of English football for years, had a special resonance. Chelsea remained overshadowed by the exile from the UK of their recent owner Abramovich, after the British government claimed to have identified him as one of the oligarchs financing Putin's invasion of the Ukraine. Few people would have imagined that the match would end with Brentford giving the mighty Chelsea a football lesson, but they did, in a kind of mirror image of the heroism of the Ukrainian resistance.

In terms of romance, it was impossible to top the moment when Brentford's Christian Eriksen found himself alone in the Chelsea area and lifted the ball over the goalkeeper Édouard Mendy to give Brentford the lead nine minutes into the second half. It was one of the most emotional moments of the Premier season, the kind of goal that reminds people why the Premier is such a spectacle, rarely predictable, always compelling.

The story of Eriksen and Brentford is almost biblical; football's Lazarus revived after facing death. Eriksen survived a dramatic cardiac arrest episode during a match at Euro 2021. He wished to make a return to European football but had limited options due to his medical condition and his time off from the game. He opted for Brentford – nicknamed the Bees – to aid his recovery and made a return to the Premier League, signing for them 204 days after his terrifying collapse on the pitch in Copenhagen.

Still, there was no doubting Eriksen's talent, and the six-month trial period with a Premier League club battling to avoid relegation, proved a perfect environment to get back into the sport at a competitive level. He was encouraged by Brentford's manager Thomas Frank, who had coached Eriksen as a teenager with the Danish international youth team.

Eriksen's free-flowing style injected life into the Brentford attack, creating chances and making him the darling of the fans. Although he left to join Erik ten Hag's Manchester United in 2022, at the end of his short-term contract with the smaller club, his short spell at the Bees is recalled with fondness.

Brentford fan Roger told me: 'Brentford – one of the miracle fairy-tale stories of the Premier – a veteran community club makes it into the Premier in the first year of the pandemic with a player back from the dead, after inaugurating a new stadium for the new age.'

The club's previous stadium, Griffin Park in the same London Borough of Hounslow – a multicultural neighbourhood which supplies Heathrow airport with much of its ground staff – was inaugurated in 1904. When Griffin Park closed in August 2020, the stadium had become a museum piece for a football world long displaced by the commercial requirements and modernising imperatives of the Premier. Griffin Park was best known for the legend that it was the only stadium in English club football to have a pub on each corner so fans could spend as much time drinking beer as watching the game. A griffin featured on the logo of a brewery which at one point owned the orchard on which the stadium was built. The opening of the new stadium coincided with Brentford's promotion to the Premier League at the end of the 2020/21 Championship season.

The club was founded in 1889 but it was not until the 1930s that Brentford enjoyed a successful spell in the top flight of English football, reaching a peak of fifth in the First Division before being relegated to the lower divisions, where they remained for most of the rest of the 20th century.

The club had little following beyond the town of Brentford, but their local fan base was proud of their history of resilience and survival in the face of adversity. During the Second World War, Griffin Park was hit by two high-explosive German bombs, in 1940 and 1941.

In wartime and peace, fans remained loyal and passionate, turning up for matches regardless of whether they ended in victory or defeat, while celebrating their promotion to the highest level – the Premier – in 2021, for the first time since the 1946/47 season.

Brentford's nickname, the Bees, was created by a group of fans in the 1890s, when they attended a match and enthusiastically shouted 'buck up Bs' in support of their friend and then Brentford player, Joséph Gettings, who played as centre-forward for the club before it became professional, and later became a decorated hero of the First World War.

If Brentford's spirit endured amidst the millionaires of the Premier League, it was perhaps because their fans personified an enduring characteristic of the 'soul' of the English game.

As Johan Cruyff said when the Premier was entering the 21st century: 'If you look at other countries, they have different values: winning is holy. In England you could say that sport itself is holy.'

# Chapter Eleven

# Lionesses

WELL BEFORE kick-off, a joyous, good-humoured and peaceful multitude made its way along football's most famous avenue, Wembley Way, towards the futuristic arch of the new cathedral of the sport rising into the sky ahead.

Wembley Stadium is located in the Brent district of north-west London. The current structure, opened in 2007, was built to replace an older stadium and one of the most legendary venues of world sport which had the same name, on the same site. Old Wembley and its famed Twin Towers was originally built for the British Empire Exhibition of 1924. It hosted the Olympics in 1948 and the football World Cup Final in 1966, which England won. It became an ageing stadium that needed to be torn down but with memories to hold it up for future generations. The architect Lord Norman Foster took on the challenge of reinventing Wembley for a new century, building on its extraordinary heritage and creating a venue that would be memorable and magical in its own right.

In July 2021 when the new Wembley hosted an international final for an England team in the European Championship against Italy, it ended in a riot. The images marred England's first major final appearance since winning the World Cup in 1966. Italy won after a penalty shoot-out. Even before the match was under way, Wembley was stormed by hundreds of ticketless fans and the approach to the stadium resembled a war zone. 'Walking along Wembley Way was one of the worst experiences of the night,' recalled Francesco, an Italian fan. 'It looked like a battleground: trash everywhere, trees being pulled and England fans forcing their way up stairs to the stadium and causing crushes.'

Jon, an England fan, said it was 'the worst football match I have ever experienced – raw aggression the whole way through. Wembley Way was appalling. There were no Covid checks to gain entry as staff were too busy dragging away a number of people who were forcing the barriers. My 15-year-old son said afterwards: "I don't think I like football."'

But that was men, and those who walked along Wembley Way in the summer of 2022 were mainly women and they were on their way to watch a game played by women. No stand-off between male police and drunken male fans. More a carnival than a battle about to commence, with a din of vuvuzelas, exuberant colourful face-paint and fancy dress.

The prevailing image of England's women's subsequent European Championship victory was of 24-year-old Chloe Kelly ripping her shirt off and running towards her team-mates, her shirt swirling above her head, her sports bra displayed. She was rewarded with history's most joyless award of a yellow card. Then nationwide adoration. Lucy Ward, a writer, went viral on Twitter by commenting: 'This image of a woman shirtless in a sports bra – hugely significant. This is a woman's body – not for sex or show – just for the sheer joy of what she can do and the power and skill she has. Wonderful.'

No matter that the goal Kelly had scored was the result of the scrappiest of toe pokes, the kind one sees any day a group of school kids or overweight amateurs kick a ball around in an English park. The game showed star and entertaining quality from two skilled and highly competitive teams. Kelly's goal proved the defining act of England's defeat of Germany, who had previously won eight of the first nine editions of the Women's European Championships. The result at Wembley marked a high point in the history of English football and a seminal moment in women's claim to being more than an accessory to it.

An all-female Royal Air Force squadron performed a spectacular flypast before kick-off. The atmosphere in the stadium was not only feminine but refreshingly bereft of jingoistic references to the Second World War or the nationalist anti-European Brexit. In the visiting section German flags were waved and happily tolerated.

Kelly's iconic moment was reminiscent of another goal celebration, that of Kelly's heroine and role model Brandi Chastain, who tore off her shirt after scoring the winner for the United States at the 1999 World Cup.

Ten years later, with four Olympic gold medals, more World Cups than anyone else and having spent the decade ranked as the world's number one women's team, the USA had become synonymous with dominance in global women's football. The success came from constructing an identity around sheer willpower, the women involved pushing themselves to the very limit, with what became a signature 'never give up' attitude.

US women's soccer had its own troubled discriminatory history and the eventual success was only made possible by the passing of Title XI in 1972, which outlawed gender-based discrimination for federally-funded education programmes. That spurred on the creation of college soccer teams across the United States at a time when women's soccer was rising in popularity internationally.

The Americans in the early years were often technically outmatched by their European counterparts, such as the Germans, who had longer footballing histories and distinct tactical identities like combination play. But it was the Americans' fighting spirit and fitness levels that made a difference and won them their first-ever Women's World Cup in 1991. Up to that point, women players had no motive to play other than to win for their country. Players were earning

$10 a day and worked part-time to make ends meet, but once America's elite women started winning trophies and football exploded as a participation sport for young women, better financial opportunities came on the horizon with advertising, sponsorship and TV rights.

The women's final at Wembley in 2022 showed how far the game of women's football had come in terms of diversity in over just two decades. In the 2002 film *Bend it Like Beckham*, by British film director of Indian origin Gurinder Chadha, cultures clash humorously as an Indian family in London tries to raise their soccer-playing daughter Jess in a traditional way. Intertwined with her story is the struggle of her best friend and team-mate Jules – a white Anglo-Saxon – who struggles to deepen her friendship and her sporting dream amidst the thinly veiled prejudice of her mother, who suspects her daughter of being in a lesbian relationship, not knowing that in fact both girls fancy their male coach.

Unlike Jess's elder sister Pinky, who is preparing for an Indian wedding and a lifetime of cooking the perfect chapatti and curry, and Jules's mother resigned to a lifetime of suburban domesticity, Jess and Jules's dream is to play soccer professionally like their hero David Beckham, the icon of male celebrity who appeals across the sexual divide.

Confronted by her daughter, Jules's mother protests unconvincingly that she has nothing against lesbians as such, declaring herself 'a huge fan of Martina Navratilova', an openly gay tennis champion. The film ends with both families reconciled to their respective daughters' talent on the sporting field. As Jess and Jules prepare to board a plane at Heathrow for the US and the soccer academy that awaits them, they catch a glimpse of a newly arrived celebrity passenger surrounded by an entourage of assistants and journalists. 'It's Beckham. It's a sign!' exclaims Jess of her epiphany.

Twenty years on from that movie, it was a real-life setting that had Chloe Kelly subconsciously digging deep into English cultural history, reincarnating the image of a British folk heroine, Boadicea, the Queen of the British Iceni tribe, who led an uprising against the conquering forces of the Roman Empire in AD 60 or 61 and destroyed the 11th Legion. Not that the Romans were the enemy this time round. The English in the summer of 2022 rose up, once again, against Germany – an adversary in countless football games, in case anyone could fail to remember in the emotionally charged build-up to the latest encounter on the pitch.

Wembley stadium resonated to the sound of 'Football's coming home', a line from the popular song 'Three Lions' remembering England's World Cup Final victory against West Germany in 1966. Ever since England's male team tumbled out of Euro 96, when the song was first written and sung by the English comedians David Baddiel and Frank Skinner, it has endured as an ironic ode to nostalgia, delusion and the underachievement of native English football talent, not least its most poignant verse:

> *That England's gonna throw it away*
> *Gonna blow it away*
> *But I know they can play*
> *'Cause I remember*
>
> *Three Lions on a shirt*
> *Jules Rimet still gleaming*
> *Thirty years of hurt*
> *Never stopped me dreaming*

England women's 3-1 victory over Germany ended 56 years of football hurt since an English national squad had last won a major trophy. I was 13 years old back in 1966. The memory endures of England's blue-eyed blond gentleman footballer Bobby Moore lifting the cup after his team had pulled off their first historic defeat of Germany since 1945.

The year 1966 proved a milestone beyond the football pitch. The pop world accelerated and broke through the sound barrier and, as Jon Savage has written in his book *The Sixties*, it was the year when history seemed to reach a modernist peak. 'A unique chemistry of ideas, substances, freedom of expression and dialogue across pop cultural continents created a landscape of immense and eventually shattering creativity.'

Fast forward and the England women's captain Leah Williamson told the BBC in the summer of 2022: 'We talk and we talk and we talk, and we talk and we finally did it' – bringing echoes of Boris Johnson's 'we got Brexit done' – only he didn't. He simply signed a divorce from the EU without delivering on promises to 'make Britain Great' again and was forced out of office in September 2022, his leadership toppled under a wave of sleaze allegations and failure to tell the truth that contributed to the resignation of two of his ethics advisers, Sir Alex Allan and Lord Geidt.

Amidst all that, and a war in Europe with no clear outcome, a major cost-of-living crisis and with much of the land a great deal more parched than the manicured well-watered turf of Wembley Stadium, England celebrated a piece of good news, however ephemeral can be the emotional fix of winning any game of football, however grandiose the platform, male or female.

From a positive perspective, the Lionesses' victory marked an inflection in the history of English professional football history, delivering diversity and the potential for equal opportunity on a scale scarcely imagined just a few years ago and overturning more than a century of male monopoly and gender bias.

As the author Suzanne Wrack reminds us in the timely *A Woman's Game*, the barriers set up against English women's football can be precisely dated to 26 December 1920, when

53,000 spectators watched Dick, Kerr Ladies FC – a team of employees at a munitions factory in Preston – beat the all-women St Helens 4-0 at Goodison Park, Liverpool. Dick, Kerr & Co Ltd had been a tramcar and light railway rolling stock manufacturer, based in Preston, and was converted to a munitions factory in 1915 as part of the war effort. It was at this time that the votes-for-women suffragettes movement was taking England by storm and Victorian values were slowly being phased out. Women were employed to do the jobs normally done by men who were now on the front lines in World War One, and the girls working in the factory were encouraged to participate in organised sporting activity to help wartime morale.

Initially, the novelty of women playing football was used to raise money for war charities, with crowds flocking to see the so-called 'munitionettes' take on teams of injured soldiers and women from other towns and villages. After they beat their male factory co-workers in an informal lunch-time match, office worker Alfred Frankland decided to take on the role as manager for this Dick, Kerr's women's team and unleash them on the general public. The result was game-changing and instantaneous.

This first match drew a crowd of 10,000, and by 1920, a Boxing Day match against St Helens Ladies was watched by 53,000 spectators at Goodison Park, with another 14,000 locked outside the ground, trying to get in. This astonishing feat was not to be replicated in women's football until modern times. The alpha males dominating the higher echelons of the Football Association felt so threatened that soon afterwards they declared football 'quite unsuitable for females', and prohibited men's clubs from allowing women to use their pitches. It would take another 50 years for the effective ban on women's football to be lifted.

English women's football fought back and Wrack argues that, 'For women, the mere act of playing football is a feminist one and activism still plays an important part.' The US star Megan Rapinoe – FIFA's top women's player in 2019 – is a self-declared 'walking protest' who refused to go to the White House during Trump's presidency.

The 2022 English Lionesses did not come across as suffragettes, but that is not to underestimate their impact in breaking down what for years has been a deep-rooted and exclusive domain of men, with English women's contribution to the professional game far too long lagging behind other democratic nations that have embraced women's football professionally at club and national level.

England women's crowning football glory was achieved by a yoga-practising heterosexual Dutch female manager, Sarina Wiegman, whose small stature and media-shy and non-controversial public persona belie a character who has made difficult decisions throughout her career with an air of authority that has inspired success.

But the credit is also due to a spirited team of English women who played for major football clubs at home and abroad, the majority of them in the Women's Super League, the highest league of women's football in England. Established in 2010, it is run by the Football Association and features 12 fully professional teams, the majority owned by male-dominated English Premier League Clubs. Of the English women who played in the final, four played at club level for Manchester City, three for Manchester United, two for Chelsea and one for Arsenal, while Luzy Bronze, one of the best right-backs in the world, was with FC Barcelona, and Georgina Stanway, who scored a defining goal against Spain in extra time in the quarter-final and was a huge attacking threat in midfield, played for Bayern Munich.

Chloe Kelly, the player who took off her shirt, recalled that as a teenager she grew up on a council estate in Ealing, west London, taking a ten-minute bus ride to Wembley just to buy a match-day programme and then go back home. As a young girl she played football with her five older brothers in a cage pitch. 'Playing cage football really made me the player I am. It added a bit more creativity to my game and the physicality as well,' she said in the summer of 2022. 'The victory in Wembley is what dreams were made of.'

The multinational sports brand logo on her sports bra beamed to millions live on TV and was a reminder that far from chasing windmills, Kelly and her team-mates could look forward not just to honours from the Queen but to lucrative remuneration from the business of football. Opportunities included documentaries, endorsement deals and TV advertisements, with brands building personalities around the players. But there was still a wide gap between men and women to be filled.

According to BBC analysis published in the summer of 2022, the average Women's Super League player earned £47,000 a year, based on available published data from seven of the 12 teams in the women's league. A comparable figure for an average Premier League male player is not easily calculated, and is skewed by the reported £20m-plus negotiated by Cristiano Ronaldo and Kevin De Bruyne at Manchester United and Manchester City respectively. But according to Deloitte, the wage bills at three mid-table Premier League clubs suggest Leicester pay their squad an average of £6.4m, Wolves an average of £4.7m and West Ham an average of £4.3m. If one accepts the Wolves figure as a typical middle ground one for all 20 Premier League clubs, it suggests men are earning 100 times what the women do.

A reference point among the richest clubs in English club football, Manchester City reported a £571m turnover for the 2020/21 season. The club spent 62 per cent of that revenue on players' wages, according to Deloitte, which works out as £354m. By comparison, Manchester City Women's Super League team's accounts reveal £2.9m in turnover for 2020/21 while their wage bill was reported at £3.3m.

Across all major income streams impacting on the business of English club football – ticket sales, broadcast rights and commercial deals, such as sponsorship – women still lagged well behind the men's game.

The women's Wembley final was a sell-out and attracted millions of TV viewers. Women's football in England was drawing in more media coverage and attracting an increasingly big fan base, perhaps because it provided an alternative, more equitable version of the English nation and the game it exported to the world.

Long-term gains will depend on the ability of English women's football and commercial partners to sustain the interest in the game and push for equal pay with the Premier League men. However, attitudes towards equal opportunity as well as diversity in English football have been evolving.

Soon after the English team's conquest, the stand-out star of the Euro 2022 tournament, Arsenal's Beth Mead, modelled some top fashion brands as part of a cover story in a leading English magazine, her blonde hair, usually tied back in a ponytail when playing, cascading over her shoulders as she stood in a movie-star pose. But, just as striking as the images was the text. For in this interview with the Saturday magazine of *The Times*, published a month after the Wembley final, 27-year-old Mead was open about her sexuality and her ongoing relationship with a Dutch female international. The article also named seven other members of the England team who were in same-sex partnerships, openly dating, engaged, or married to women.

Mead told *The Times*, 'From day one in women's football, we made it normal. We've not made it a big deal. In the women's game, you are just being you.'

By contrast, at the same time, there was only one openly gay male player in the top four English professional divisions – Jake Daniels, who played for Blackpool FC in the second tier.

Daniels, aged 17, posted an open letter on the club website in
May 2022 in which he said:

> Everything has happened at once but it feels right.
> When this season started, I just wanted to prove
> myself as a player. I think I have. So this was the
> one last thing in my head that I knew I needed to
> do. Now it's out, and people know. Now I can just
> live my life how I want to and you know what? It's
> been incredible.
>
> The subject of being gay, or bi or queer in men's
> football is still a taboo. I think it comes down to
> how a lot of footballers want to be known for their
> masculinity. And people see being gay as being
> weak, something you can be picked on for on the
> football field.
>
> I am hoping that by coming out, I can be a role
> model, to help others come out if they want to. I am
> only 17 but I am clear that this is what I want to do
> and if, by me coming out, other people look at me
> and feel maybe they can do it as well, that would
> be brilliant.
>
> If they think this kid is brave enough do this, I
> will be able to do it too.
>
> I hate knowing people are in the same situation
> I was in. I think if a Premier League footballer does
> come out that would just be amazing. I feel like
> I would have done my job and inspired someone
> else to do that.

Euro 2022 marked the first time sponsorship was offered
just for the women's tournament, rather than simply being
bundled with the men's tournament as in the past. But there
was one telling fact from the triumph of the Lionesses: the
87,192 crowd smashed the record for attendance at a Euro

match, men's or women's, and the game was watched by millions on TV.

That appeared to tell its own story of how a more sexually as well as socially diverse football game had captured the hearts of fans.

Chapter Twelve

# WAGS

IF THE Lionesses produced a victory for women's self-esteem and equality, the publicity in the same summer of 2022 surrounding the High Court libel case and an estimated £3m in legal fees involving WAGs (an acronym used by populist tabloid newspaper writers to refer to wives and girlfriends of high-profile male footballers) provided an alternative narrative of entitlement.

In 2010, the Equalities and Human Rights Commission (EHRC) criticised the term as sexist and stated that it could be offensive, as it was often used to demean women. Rebekah Vardy reportedly stated that 'WAG is a dated term because we're not defined by what our husbands do. We're individuals.'

It was Rebekah, wife of the Leicester City star Jamie, who lost her libel case against Coleen Rooney, wife of Wayne, the former Everton and Manchester United player turned coach. A damning High Court judgement in the notorious 'Wagatha Christie' case described Mrs Vardy as an 'untrustworthy witness' who was likely to have destroyed potentially crucial evidence on purpose. She was effectively branded a liar and a leaker of gossip.

The saga began three years previously when Coleen Rooney conducted a 'sting' operation to find out who was leaking stories from her private Instagram account to journalists at *The Sun* newspaper.

She identified the culprit with the now infamous words posted on Instagram: 'It's ......... Rebekah Vardy's account.' Vardy denied passing information to *The Sun* and sued Rooney for libel in a doomed attempt to restore her reputation. The feud was dubbed the 'Wagatha Christie' case after the 'WAG' moniker and the renowned author of detective novels (Agatha Christie), in honour of Rooney's sleuthing.

Until the high-profile case occupied headlines, it seemed that the days of the publicity-seeking WAGs with nothing better to do than to appear in celebrity pages as famous footballers' partners were a past phenomenon. Just a year prior to the trial, popular culture commentator Nick Ede was quoted by the Femail section of the *Daily Mail* newspaper saying today's elite footballer wives tend to be 'understated, supportive, academic and subtle', preferring to stay out of the spotlight, and forge careers in everything from physiotherapy to property development and law.

'Gone are the days of fake everything when WAGS were splashed across the tabloids with fake tan, high heels and hair extensions,' he wrote.

Katie Kane, the wife of Tottenham and England captain Harry, posted Instagram updates of their children in England shirts with their faces carefully out of view. The Manchester United and English international Harry Maguire's fiancée Fern Hawkins was a physiotherapist while Mia McClenaghan, the girlfriend of Chelsea and English international Reece James, studied law at Royal Holloway University and actively defended him when he was faced with abuse from racists. Raheem Sterling's fiancée, Paige Milian, pursued a career in sports management and, as a property developer, managed the properties she owns.

One of the original WAGs, Victoria Beckham was neither in court nor at Wembley that July in 2022. But two of her celebrity band-mates from the days before she first met her future husband David Beckham, and upgraded her social status as a fashion designer, Mel C and Geri Halliwell-Horner enjoyed a mini-Spice Girls reunion during the UEFA Women's Euro 2022 final. As the *Daily Mail* reported, 'The 48-year-old and 49-year-old 'Wannabe' hitmakers nailed sports chic in football attire as they watched England's Lionesses beat Germany. Commanding attention in a bright orange top, Melanie combined the neon number with blue bottoms while Geri opted for an all-white ensemble.' The 1990s girl group were rumoured to be reuniting for a world tour as well as an animated movie, with Victoria Beckham even thought to be joining them after missing the band's 2019 shows.

After the Lionesses' victory, messages of support flooded in for the team with each of the Spice Girls full of praise. From their main account @spicegirls tweeted: 'Congratulations @ Lionesses. True #GirlPower right there.'

Mel C then took to her personal Instagram to write: '@lionesses Heroes, one and all!! How incredible to watch a group of young women come together, change people's perceptions and touch the hearts of the whole country.'

## Chapter Thirteen

# Resisting Injustice

FOR MUCH of football's modern history, a generation of top-ranking male players in the Premier League has been defined not just by their performances on the pitch but by celebrity status beyond it, their fortunes made along with the goals scored, and their popularity measured by brand 'personality' sponsorship, and a generally adulatory and well-managed social media following.

However, by the end of 2020, in the middle of the Covid pandemic, one of the Premier League's star players, the English international and Manchester United player Marcus Rashford, had become a fully-fledged national hero for very different reasons.

In the spring of that year, just days after the UK was locked down with the pandemic bringing the 2019/20 season to a halt, the 23-year-old centre-forward began using his free time and growing influence to become a formidable voice for social justice. Rashford spent the early part of lockdown helping to deliver food to families who relied on free school meals (but whose children were now at home, not in school, due to the lockdown). When the government announced the free meals programme would not be extended over the summer holidays, Rashford wrote an emotive and persuasive open letter to Members of Parliament, imploring them to reverse that decision and help feed the 1.3 million families whose children risked going hungry as a result of it. 'This is about humanity,' he wrote in a bold statement. 'Looking at ourselves in the mirror and feeling like we did everything we could to protect those who can't, for whatever reason or circumstance, protect themselves.'

So, by the end of the first bleak year of the pandemic, Rashford had not only been honoured by the Queen, but had achieved national and international recognition for his social activism as much as for his footballing talent.

The young player was one of five children who was raised by a single mother in a working-class Manchester suburb. In his open letter he wrote: 'Food banks and soup kitchens were not alien to us; I recall very clearly our visits … to collect our Christmas dinners every year.'

Rashford's mother Melanie Maynard told the BBC she would sometimes go without food to ensure her children could eat. 'Sometimes it was really bad, I'd rather give the food to the kids than give it to myself; sometimes I didn't get anything to eat. Sometimes we didn't even have a loaf of bread in the house, it's embarrassing to say, but we didn't. So Marcus is only telling the story from how he sees it and the words he has been saying come from the bottom of his heart.'

The then-Prime Minister, Boris Johnson, claimed to have been unaware of Rashford's campaign even when, under immense public pressure, his government announced a £120m summer food fund. When the summer was over, Johnson seemed convinced that the storm had passed – or perhaps he thought the public wanting to see hungry children fed was another lockdown oddity, like illegal private parties. Conservative Members of Parliament were urged by Johnson to vote against a motion from the Labour opposition to extend the provision into the October half-term. Rashford's petition to end child food poverty, relaunched that month, quickly gained over a million signatures. It forced a second government U-turn with the announcement of the Covid winter grant.

The social activism of Rashford – who is described by football writer Simon Kuper as part of an 'unprecedentedly educated and powerful generation of (English) footballers' – has been compared to fellow Premier League and international footballer Raheem Sterling's leadership of an anti-racism campaign in support of Black Lives Matter, and Liverpool's Jordan Henderson, who made large donations to Britain's National Health Service during the pandemic. All three used their considerable football talent as both a way out of poverty and a means to raise social issues by exploiting their public platforms. In Rashford's case it was notable that his focus appeared to stretch beyond race and towards addressing more cross-cutting class-based inequalities.

When the first matches in the Premier League resumed following the relaxation of Covid-19 restrictions on 17 June 2020, the games were played in empty stadiums but broadcast on TV and radio. The players, with 'Black Lives Matter' written across their shirts, took the knee in symbolic protest against persisting inequalities and structural racism, and for the whole of the following season continued to do so before kick-off.

Taking the knee had become a symbol of the Black Lives Matter movement, sparked by American footballer Colin Kaepernick, who adopted the position in protest against police brutality and racism. The campaign was launched after a smartphone video showing a white policeman pressing with his knee against the neck of a black man called George Floyd, until he died, went viral.

In the UK the continuing Black Lives Matter campaign provoked a backlash from those sceptical of social justice movements. Players were booed and abused by some fans on social media for taking the knee at the start of matches.

Although the campaign was supported by England coach Gareth Southgate during the Euro 2020 championships in June 2021, the Prime Minister Johnson was criticised for not being more forthright initially in his condemnation of fans who had voiced their opposition to it. He eventually issued an ambiguous statement that 'the prime minister respects the rights of all people to peacefully protest and make their feeling known ... I would like everybody to get behind the team to cheer them on, not boo.'

The following summer, ahead of the start of the 2022/23 season, the Premier League authorities and club captains announced that players would no longer routinely take the knee ahead of games but would do so ahead of 'significant' moments during the season: the opening matches; games in October and March dedicated to the mantra 'No Room for Racism'; matches played by England at the World Cup in Qatar; on Boxing Day, when the Premier League resumed following the conclusion of the tournament; on the final day of the season and at the FA Cup and League Cup finals.

The Premier League captains said: 'We have decided to select significant moments to take the knee during the season to highlight our unity against all forms of racism and in so doing we continue to show solidarity for a common cause. We remain resolutely committed to eradicate racial prejudice, and to bring about an inclusive society with respect and equal opportunities for all.'

*The memorial to the 96 (later to become 97) fans who died at Hillsborough was finally unveiled at Sheffield Wednesday's stadium. After ten years of protests from bereaved families, the plaque and garden area have been dedicated to the victims next to the ground. Photo taken 8 May 1999.*

*Munich air crash memorial at Old Trafford. Dedicated to the 23 people, including eight players, who lost their lives on 6 February 1958.*

*The new Arsenal manager, Arsène Wenger. Photo taken on 22 September 1996.*

*Manchester United manager Sir Alex Ferguson with the Premier League trophy at the club's victory parade on 13 May 2013.*

*Bukayo Saka of Arsenal playing against Watford at the Emirates Stadium on 7 November 2021.*

*Mikel Arteta, Arsenal manager, encourages his players on 19 February 2022.*

*The Manchester derby on Sunday, 6 December 1992. New signing Eric Cantona makes his first appearance at Old Trafford.*

*Chelsea owner Roman Abramovich (R) celebrates with his players Frank Lampard and John Terry (L) after the Barclays Premiership match against Bolton Wanderers. Chelsea claimed the title after their 2-0 win. 30 April 2005.*

*Manchester City manager Pep Guardiola celebrates winning the Premier League title at Brighton & Hove Albion's Amex Stadium. 12 May 2019.*

*Liverpool fans cheer on their side, 19 April 2015.*

*Statue of legendary Liverpool manager Bill Shankly at Anfield.*

*Jürgen Klopp announced in early 2024 he would stand down as Liverpool manager at the end of the season, having taken charge at Anfield in 2015.*

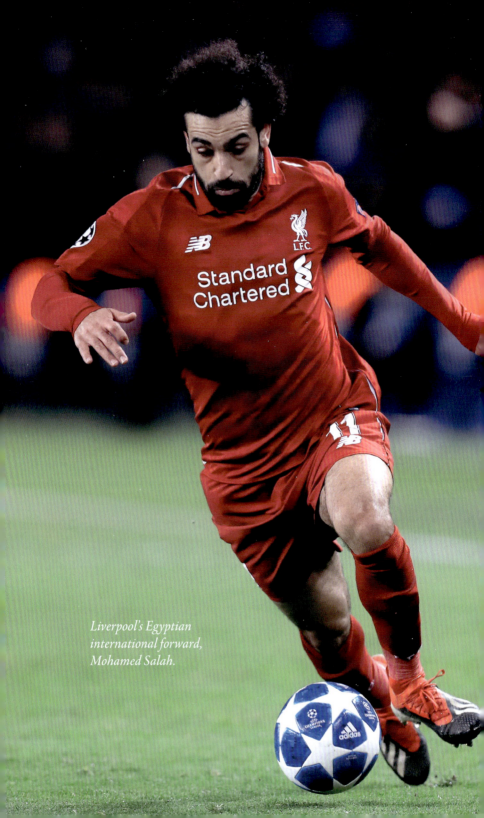

*Liverpool's Egyptian international forward, Mohamed Salah.*

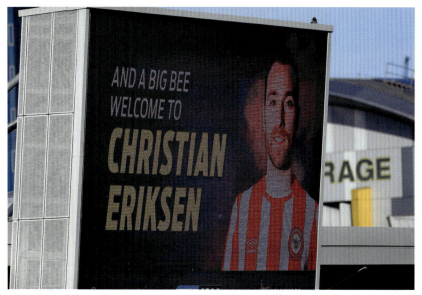

*Brentford celebrate the signing of Danish international Christian Eriksen on a six-month contract on 12 February 2022 prior to their Premier League game against Crystal Palace.*

*England's Chloe Kelly celebrates scoring the Lionesses' second goal in the UEFA Women's Euro 2022 Final against Germany at Wembley.*

*Fans arrive at Wembley Stadium ahead of the Women's Euro 2022 Final.*

*Lucy May Barker as Rebekah Vardy and Laura Dos Santos as Coleen Rooney in the play* Vardy v Rooney: The Wagatha Christie Trial *at The Ambassadors Theatre in London.*

*Section of the Windrush 75 mural in Brixton Village, London, featuring from left to right: Denise Lewis, Sir Trevor McDonald, Naomi Campbell and Marcus Rashford.*

# Chapter Fourteen

# Improbable Foxes

OF ALL the clubs that won the Premier League in the first 30 years of its history, Leicester City's 2015/16 conquest stands out as another rare miracle of David confronting the Goliaths.

On 2 May 2016, Leicester finished top of England's highest league for the first time in the club's history. The feat was widely described at the time as one of the greatest sporting stories of the Premier, which had by then settled into a period of dominance by the much bigger founding clubs, with Manchester United the most successful with 13 Premier titles to date, Chelsea four, Arsenal three, Manchester City two and Blackburn Rovers one.

Leicester had been 5000-1 with bookmakers to win the Premier before that season kicked off. They ended up making history in more ways than one. Jamie Vardy broke Ruud van Nistelrooy's record as he became the first player to score in 11 consecutive Premier League matches and the Algerian winger Riyad Mahrez became the first player from the African continent to be honoured with the Premier's Player of the Year award.

Prior to the 2015/16 season, Leicester City's impossible dream seemed a million miles away. The talismanic manager Nigel Pearson had led Leicester to promotion to the Premier at the end of the 2013/14 season but was sacked on 30 June 2015 with Leicester just avoiding relegation, in 14th place. Pearson's departure came after his son James was one of three Leicester

City players (the others were Tom Hopper and Adam Smith) sacked by the club after an investigation into an allegation that they were filmed making racist remarks while having sex with three Thai women during a post-season tour.

News of Claudio Ranieri's appointment as Pearson's successor did not initially go down well with fans. Yet somehow the 'Tinkerman', as Ranieri was nicknamed, turned his squad of cast-offs and players from lower English divisions and smaller French teams into Premier League champions – just the sixth team to win the biggest prize in English domestic football.

Few people I know have followed Leicester City's fortunes as closely and for so long as Jon Holmes, a former chairman of the club, football media agent and long-standing fan. It was Holmes that recalled Leicester's moment of glory in a piece he wrote for the *New Statesman* in its immediate aftermath, in which he noted that 'it is the gloriously improbable, the sheer unpredictability of sport, but very particularly football, that gives it such opportunity to enrich our lives'.

There had been much talk in the media that the Premier League that had just been won by his club had been the most unpredictable. 'Unpredictable, no; improbable yes,' Holmes insisted.

He wrote about the extraordinary celebration of the title triumph that took hold of Leicester on the Saturday after they secured it. 'The club was based in one of the most unremarkable of English towns. The English author and social commentator J.B. Priestley observed many years ago that nobody appeared to have much fun in it. But that day saw the Italian opera singer Andrea Bocelli, standing alongside Leicester manager Claudio Ranieri [in the centre of the King Power Stadium pitch, then] shed his hood to reveal a blue Leicester City shirt, and the crowd joined in a deafening crescendo to "Nessun Dorma", and the roof appeared to be in danger of coming off the stadium – and the description of this as the greatest story ever was just for a moment not the greatest hyperbole in a world littered with such. And Shakespeare's 500-year-old assertion that Brutus was "'the noblest Roman of them all'" no longer holds. Ranieri is truly the most improbable character in Leicester City's saga...'

When I caught up with Holmes, in the Groucho Club in Soho, London in the summer of 2022, he told me: 'For me personally it was very emotional. I have followed the club for more than 60 years. It constitutes a major part of the fabric of my life and my family history. My father followed the club devotedly for 70 years and never saw them win the league or the cup (but attended four FA Cup finals at Wembley) and sadly died in 2005, before the miracles began. Flukes do not take 38 games although miracles do. What happened was an amazing chemical reaction of footballing elements, and three world class players, Vardy, Kanté and Mahrez coming together.'

A Premier League fairy tale? For Holmes to this day, Leicester City winning the Premier League was probably the best-ever Premier League novel outside of the novella that was Manchester City's 'Agüero moment'.

Rewind to May 2012, and it's the last day of the season. Manchester United have secured a win at Sunderland and look set to lift their 13th Premier League title. With six matches remaining, United had been eight points ahead of Manchester City, but they then faltered with a defeat and a draw in their next three games, while City won all three, to narrow the gap at the top to three points. On the final day, City, coached by Roberto Mancini, and Queens Park Rangers are still playing at the Etihad. A stoppage-time equaliser by Džeko puts City level and United fans get twitchy – but they are still two points clear. And then, with just moments left, Agüero scores a last-gasp winner. The rest is Premier League history. For the first time in 44 years, City claimed the title in what would prove to be the start of a new era for the 'other' Manchester club. Under Mancini's successor, Pep Guardiola, there would be a period of dominance in English football for City, with the club winning five more Premier League titles over the subsequent ten years.

Interestingly, of course it was Leicester City's Premier League win that shook the very foundations of the modern game. It caused the juggernaut clubs the most soul searching. They really did not want gate-crashers at their exclusive parties, and the majority of Leicester's best players were subsequently bought out.

Mahrez remained at Leicester for two more years before transferring to Manchester City, who bought him for £61m. Former Manchester United youth Danny Drinkwater, not considered one of the top players when Leicester won the Premier but still the 'beating heart' of Claudio Ranieri's conquering team, moved to Chelsea in 2017. N'golo Kanté only spent one full season at Leicester City, having joined from Caen in 2015 for £8.1m, before leaving for Chelsea the following summer for almost four times that fee.

Jamie Vardy was one star that remained loyal and glowing in the Leicester firmament. The player had come from non-league side Stocksbridge Park Steels to Leicester City, via spells at Halifax and Fleetwood Town, all within the space of two years, and in one season in the Premier had played a key role in one of the biggest success stories in European club football. Vardy scored 24 goals in the Premier League as Leicester City became champions. After that, the club failed to regain their previous peak, but his goals kept on coming and he won the Premier's 2019/20 Golden Boot with 23 goals.

Leicester might have been destined not to recover their Premier crown again, but their success over the season when they did win brought changes on the social front as they embraced the cultural diversity inherent in the city.

In August 2022 Leicester marked the 50th anniversary of the arrival of Asians of Indian descent expelled by Idi Amin, the dictator of the former British African colony Uganda. Many of the 27,000 with British passports who came to the UK settled in Leicester, making the town home to the UK's largest Asian community. Back in 1972, the Asians from Africa were initially received with mixed feelings by the local majority white population. Some people went out of their way to make sure the refugees didn't feel welcome. Leicester Council took out a full-page advert in a paper in Uganda that most Asians read. It said: 'Don't come to Leicester – there is no housing or schools available.'

But Asians came anyway and were confronted by racist demonstrations organised by the extreme-right National Front, which at the time claimed a strong following in Leicester.

And yet, by 2022, Leicester had become England's most ethnically diverse city, with more than 50 per cent of its population of non-UK origin. Leicester City FC has deeply embedded cultural prejudices which were a challenge to integration: the club's nickname, the Foxes, dates back to much earlier times and came from the predatory animal much in evidence in the local countryside and the hunting on horseback of which was a popular traditional sport among the richer white classes.

And yet in the aftermath of their Premier victory, Leicester City could claim to have developed a more racially diverse fan club. The club, to its credit, under the astute leadership of an Irish female chief executive, Susan Whelan, was diligent in its embrace of a more multi-ethnic population. Holmes recalled how at the start of the new millennium he was taken aback when following a Sikh man in a blue shirt emblazoned Singh 9 to a match. Nowadays there are many Asians among Leicester City followers, even though the Premier League does not attract Asian players as it does black players.

As Vinay, an Asian of Indian descent, who ran a corner store in London and was a Manchester United fan, regularly watching the Premier and the Indian Football League on satellite TV, explained: 'Asian kids get encouraged by their parents to study for a career in non-sporting professions like pharmacy, medicine, accountancy, law ... And when it comes to sport it is cricket not football where a young boy may be pushed, if he has the talent, to become a professional ... India is a cricket loving nation.'

Leicester City struggled, without success, to regain the mountain top of Premier success. While reaching the quarter-finals before exiting from the Champions League in 2016/17, they spent much of the season in the bottom half of the table and on 23 February 2017, Ranieri was dismissed due to the club's continuing poor form, which saw them sitting only one point above the relegation zone. Raineri was replaced by Craig Shakespeare but following a poor start to the next season, he was sacked in October 2017 after four months officially in charge, and with Leicester in 18th place in the table. He was replaced by former Southampton manager Claude Puel on 25 October 2017 and Leicester finished that season in ninth position.

The following season was overshadowed by tragedy. On 27 October 2018, Vichai Srivaddhanaprabha, who fronted the Thai-led consortium Asian Football Investments which had bought the club eight years earlier, died in a helicopter crash outside the King Power Stadium following Leicester City's home match against West Ham United. Vichai was one of five people who died. The others who lost their lives were employees of the club Kaveporn Punpare and Nusara Suknamai, and the pilots Eric Swaffer and Izabela Lechowicz.

The disaster shocked and saddened the club, from staff to players and supporters, who were in much admiration for Vichai for bringing the community together and guiding the club to their surprise Premier League title in 2016. The disappointing results since then were submerged in the outpouring of emotion. The stadium was soon surrounded by bouquets of flowers.

In early November of that year, thousands of Leicester City fans united in Jubilee Square in the city centre before marching to the King Power Stadium ahead of the team's first Premier match at home since the crash, against Burnley, in what was advertised as the 'Walk for Vichai'. Blue and white balloons – the colours of the club – surrounded the square and large banners paraphrased an old Simon and Garfunkel song 'Mrs Robinson'. 'Here's to you Mr Chairman, Leicester loves you more than you could know.' The walk was also named the '5000-1 walk' in remembrance of the bookmakers' odds which the club overcame to win the Premier League.

It was perhaps a symptom of modern Britain, post-Diana. At the time, pre-pandemic and pre-Ukraine, the absence of war and improvements in medicine meant premature death was an out of the ordinary experience, no longer commonplace, emphasised by a sensationalist media. Only a few fans found the hysteria that surrounded Vichai's death profoundly disturbing. Prior to the fatal accident, players were reported to be unhappy with their manager, and the joyous spirit of the league-winning team had gone. There were veteran fans that had become disinterested. Then came the Saturday night, and the accident.

As one long-term fan put it: 'The truth is, there was always a danger in flying the helicopter from the ground like that. It was fortunate not to have come down on a group of people, the nearby main road, a car park or even the ground itself. Then the mass hysteria rivalling almost Diana, for a man who made his money in a far-off land, taking a business decision to shift his wealth into England via ostentatious expenditure. Then he perishes as a result of a hubristic display, the 'shy retiring modest' man in a helicopter with his own name emblazoned on it, crashes in a ball of flame. Only in the week before, he had commissioned a blue carpet for it along the lines of a premier red carpet. What a strange world we live in ...'

The club remained a puzzle to the media and an irritation to the big clubs, under an ownership outside the norm of US, or dodgy middle eastern or Chinese titans. The Thai owners – now Srivaddhanaprabha's son Aiyawatt – remained inscrutable yet tangible.

Free beers and clappers, gifts to the city's institutions and present, if not constantly, at matches, exchanging conversation and handshakes with supporters, uniquely popular amongst fans, who at most clubs viewed owners with suspicion, bordering sometimes on hatred, but were happy to be complicit with them as long as the money kept pouring into the team.

Leicester's story had elements of tragic comedy. The wit and wisdom of Leicester City crowds was a constant source of amusement and the team's surviving star from the glory season, Jamie Vardy, had an interaction which was especially funny. Whenever the opposition mocked his wife, more often than not he scored and gently ridiculed them.

As Holmes spoke of Vardy: 'He is truly an old-fashioned working-class hero, a throwback to the days of the *Hotspur* comic and Alf Tupper, the tough of the track. Just as I recast Leicester's title-winning team with actors from the 60s, Tom Courtenay reprising the Long Distance Runner as Vardy, Omar Sharif as Mahrez, Hardy Kruger as Fuchs, Sven-Bertil Taube as Schmeichel, Albert Finney as Drinkwater, Poitier as Wes Morgan, Bert Kwouk as Okazaki, Bernard Cribbins as Albrighton, Alec Guinness as Ranieri, and so on.'

There are few Leicester City fans around now who can remember the record run of seven top division victories in the 1962/3 season that Leicester broke on 8 December 2019. Jon Holmes is one of them. The 2019/20 season had got off to an incredible start under the latest coach Brendan Rodgers, with the club picking up 38 points from their first 16 matches and going on an eight-match winning streak from 19 October to 8 December.

As Leicester fan Holmes recalled: 'Back then, in the early 1960s, the country was in the shivering grip of the worst winter since 1947, temperatures hardly rose above zero for two months. The Beatles released 'Please Please Me' (in some charts their first number one), Hugh Gaitskell died suddenly and Harold Wilson became the leader of the Labour Party. So long ago, yet the events of that year remain clear in the mind of a few survivors, and the pain of Leicester's collapse at the end of the season, losing the last four league games and the cup final has stayed with them forever, because that side and that run were the kitemark of their highest aspirations for their club. Wilson went on to win four elections, the Beatles became a global phenomenon. In the 1960s there were so many different cup winners, but the Foxes always seemed to be the runner-up. Leicester City have since occasionally threatened but until they won the Premiership, they never consummated the promise of that cold winter.'

The fan who wrote the above in an email to friends was stirred back into writing by the promise of a new beginning: 'something special is happening'. And so, it seemed – and had Liverpool (also on the rise in early 1963) not been quite so imperious in 2019/20, then it surely might have turned out to be 'A Season to Remember', as the players' cup final preview brochure was entitled that year.

Three times during the 1960s, the Leicester City fan who wrote the above travelled with his entire family down the newly built M1 to London, only to return dejected – but in 1963 it really hurt. Manchester United, still recovering from the Munich air disaster, had been poor all season, only escaping the two relegation berths by a fine margin. Yet in the FA Cup Final that late May it was Leicester City that flopped, and the Manchester United team led by their stars Denis Law, Paddy Crerand and Bobby Charlton took home the trophy.

What happened seemed to set the pattern for the ensuing years, hopes continually dashed, until the *annus mirabilis* of 2016, which of course was almost followed by the coming down to earth, in the league at least, in the following couple of years (Leicester City's European adventure being a trip to wonderland).

Then hopes were raised by a virtually new team, just the goalkeeper Kasper Schmeichel and the incredible Jamie Vardy remaining, who broke the record of 1963. Just maybe this time it would be Leicester City who would go on to become a power in the land.

'This is the best squad and probably the best team to wear the royal blue and ply their trade by the canal. Man for man, there has been no parallel in my lifetime. I have seen Arthur Rowley in his swansong, Frank Worthington in his prime, Gary Lineker in his nascency, I have watched Weller and Nish, Banks and Shilton, seen Gibson and McAllister, Mahrez and Kanté, but to watch Vardy plundering new horizons, Riccardo, who would make a Duracell bunny look short-lived, Söyüncü a slab of granite look fragile, Tielemans, Maddison, Praet and Evans stand out like Rolls Royce on Anycar.com, is a revelation beyond any old man's dreams,' recalled Holmes.

But it was tilting at windmills. Despite being in the top four for most of the season, Leicester suffered a drop-off in form, winning only two of their nine games following the resumption of league play after the enforced break due to the Covid-19 pandemic. Three defeats in their last four games saw them slide into fifth – their second-highest Premier League finish in their history, in addition to securing a Europa League place for the following season.

On 15 May 2021, Leicester won their first-ever FA Cup. After finishing fifth in the 2020/21 Premier League, Leicester qualified for the Europa League for the second consecutive year. They played in the newly established

UEFA Conference League before being knocked out by AS Roma in the semi-final, losing 2-1 on aggregate. As a Leicester fan said: 'Given the events that continue to befall England, and the scoundrels who pursued votes, Leicester City fans had to take solace somewhere.'

# Chapter Fifteen

# Stanley Matthews and Gazza

HAD WILLIAM Shakespeare returned and graced our tortured world with his humanistic wisdom and poetry, he would have perhaps penned a moving and incisive tragicomedy led by two contrasting well-known figures of English football.

Here, in deference to the great bard, and with a historical perspective, I select two English candidates: one, a true and noble gentleman, the other a tempestuous and ultimately flawed genius; each, in his own way, possessing a unique talent to play great football.

The footballer who stirred the imagination of my late English father's war generation was the gentleman player Stanley Matthews, or Sir Stanley, as he was ennobled by the Queen – a rare title for a sportsman.

Even as the modern game entered a new millennium, Matthews remained remembered as the best player England ever had. The claim, made by Jimmy Armfield, carries some weight. Armfield was a right-back to Sir Stan's right-winger role for Blackpool, Stoke and then England. It was made among the many tributes that followed the news of the great Matthews's death on 23 February 2000, aged 82. The Premier League by then had been in existence for eight seasons.

In an interview with BBC Sport, Armfield remembered Sir Stan in these words: 'He was impeccable in his behaviour on the pitch. He used to say: "if they kick me, I know I've got them". He was innovative and could do things other people couldn't do and above anything else, he just had fantastic skill.'

Other honoured English football legends – I think of Sir Thomas (Tom) Finney, Sir Robert (Bobby) Charlton – bring magical memories, but with Matthews there was a humility as well as a mystique that made him different. He represented professionalism and clean living and Englishmen, whatever their club, loved him.

The times Matthews lived in were simpler than they are today, no doubt. Satellite TV and the internet, barely imagined, had yet to take a move into the sitting room, players and managers were not pursued by journalists and fans and verbal venting on social media. Simplicity and humility extended to football wages. In the 1950s, Matthews was paid £20 a week by Blackpool, where for 14 years he was just as important as the Tower or the Illuminations.

Matthews's love affair with Blackpool and football developed during World War Two when he was stationed in the northern seaside town with the Royal Air Force (RAF) and played for an amateur team called the Seasiders. After the war, in 1947, Matthews signed for Blackpool for £11,500 and a bottle of whisky, at the start of a dazzling run that lasted to the early 1960s. He had a ruthless streak when it came to playing the ball. He would taunt defenders almost like a matador with a bull. Hs would toe-poke the ball forward a foot or so and invite his marker to come and get it. Few did.

If the physical fitness and mental state of Matthews was superior to other players, that was because of his discipline and dedication, which he owed to his father, a barber and former middleweight boxer. Matthews never smoked or drank and experimented with healthy foods before any other athlete had ever considered them. Matthews would go down to the Blackpool beach, facing the Irish Sea, early every morning where he jogged, stretched and engaged in deep breathing exercises before joining in training with the rest of the team. His fitness level was never in doubt, even when he passed the age of 40. He was the only man to play in the old top-tier First Division as a 50-year-old. Even in the last years of his life, when he was in his late seventies, Matthews would still exercise in the gym. Former England manager Bobby Robson paid tribute to his friend, English football's 'First Knight', on hearing of his death: 'He was one of the greatest players the game has ever seen,' Robson recalled.

English football history would throw up another claim to greatness, but of a more controversial nature. In January 2018, the tabloid *The Sun* ran a story celebrating the resurrection via social media of a footballer whose achievement on the pitch had long been overshadowed by his mental and physical break-down off it. 'Lock your doors and shut your windows, Paul Gascoigne ["Gazza"] is back on Twitter, and he is firing bullets in every direction,' reported the tabloid.

Compared to the stale nature of promotion delivered by media managers running elite player accounts, Gazza's Twitter feed was initially greeted as a breath of fresh air into modern football banter. 'The England legend and all-round lovable rogue has returned to Twitter and is using it to show the full glory of his Geordie wit,' wrote *The Sun*'s Jack Kennedy. The article included a tweet allegedly written by the player:

'I saw Colin Hendry in London once and asked him what he was doing there. He asked me why. [I answered] Because I thought I left you at Wembley.'

Gazza hung up his boots back in 2004, but among the more magical moments he will always be remembered for by English fans, was his goal for England against Scotland at Wembley, during Euro 96, considered one of the best goals ever scored by an English international. He flicked the ball over the Scotland defender Colin Hendry's head with an outrageous moment of skill before burying it into the bottom corner.

In April 2022, a BBC documentary *Gazza*, chronicled the turbulent history of Gascoigne's life from his early days as a gifted teenage midfielder in the 1980s pre-Premier League with Newcastle and Spurs, to his admission for drug addiction rehab to the Priory after he was excluded from the England squad before the 1998 World Cup.

As *The Guardian* critic Barry Glendenning wrote: 'It is a 16-year window in which "Gazzamania" swept a nation that became besotted with the likable, eager-to-please young Geordie, who seemed to have the world at his feet, only to develop a pernicious dependence on alcohol and become one of the most high-profile celebrities to have every indiscretion from a deeply troubled private life trumpeted from the front pages of the tabloid press.'

It was at the World Cup of 1990 in Italy that Gazza became a national celebrity, as much for the skills he showed in England's better games as the tears he shed when he was shown a yellow card for fouling Thomas Berthold having overran the ball. Stretching to retain possession, he slid into a tackle from behind during the semi-final – which meant he would have to miss the final if England got there. In fact, West Germany beat them in a penalty shoot-out at the end of that semi-final.

Until that foul in the 99th minute, Gazza's performance in the match had been brilliant, confirming him as one of the most talented and popular of the English players.

*Guardian* sportswriter Simon Burnton recalled: 'England hearts skipped a beat with every wobble of Gascoigne's bottom lip that night, and player and fans bonded in a display of lachrymose unity.'

A few months later Gascoigne was named Sports Personality of the Year.

The mercurial midfielder had befriended Bobby Robson who, as coach of the English national squad, encouraged a protective father/son relationship. Robson considered him a unique footballer who needed careful personalised management of a kind that verged on indulgence. 'I don't know anybody who dislikes Paul Gascoigne,' Bobby Robson wrote in his autobiography, published in 2005. 'The affection we all felt for him added to the poignancy of his booking [in the World Cup 1990]. My heart sank the moment the referee took out the yellow card. My heart hit my shoes. Because I realised instantly, that was the final for Paul Gascoigne, out. And that's a tragedy – for him, me, the team, the country, the whole of football. Because he was so good, and he was superb in this particular match. The bigger the game, the better he got.'

And yet: 'Had Gascoigne been German he would be *persona non grata* today,' the former Liverpool and Newcastle midfielder Dietmar Hamman, a German, wrote in his book *The Didi Man*. '[After the booking] Gazza went to pieces. The game was still tied, and a job still needed to be done, yet his first thoughts were for himself. When the game went to a penalty shoot-out Gascoigne was earmarked to take [a] penalty for England. He decided that he wasn't in the right frame of mind to take it. For Gascoigne, in that moment, it was all about *him* as an individual, and the way *he* was feeling. It was nothing to do with his duty to the team. If Gascoigne was German his behaviour would have created a national scandal, and the player would be forgotten for ever. If it were possible to erase his name from the team sheet, then it would be done.'

And yet, as later emerged, there was a darker side to Gazza that had been kept from the public eye and would become part of a different narrative: the Gazza monster grafted on to – in the words of football writer Pete Davies – 'the one-in-a-generation model, an immaculate conception born with a ball where the rest of us have a heart'.

According to Davies, the author of *All Played Out*, his eye-witness account of the English World Cup campaign in Italy, there was evidence enough watching Paul Gascoigne that there were devils he carried within him and that he was squandering his talent.

As Davies recalled, Gazza bribed waiters in the team hotel in Sardinia to serve him bottles of fizzy water topped off with a generous amount of wine. After several beers, Gazza would drive off in a golfcart outside the hotel at dangerously lunatic speeds.

Born and raised in Gateshead, Gascoigne signed schoolboy terms with Newcastle United before turning professional with the club in 1984. Three years later, he was sold to Tottenham Hotspur for £2.2 million, where he developed a growing reputation as an emerging young star.

And after the 1990 World Cup, in the words of Pete Davies, Gazza was fed piece by piece to the cheque-book wolves of the tabloids, and 'began literally to be a thing of pieces, a man-boy falling to media bits'. As Gazza's popularity among English fans began to soar in the wake of Italia 90, *The Sun* signed him up on a one-year deal worth £250,000. He won the FA Cup with Spurs in 1991, before being sold to Italian club Lazio for £5.5 million. In Italy, his troubled time off, as well as on, the pitch was once again picked up by English tabloid reporters, with a network of paid informants, including individuals he had trusted as friends.

In July 1995, he was transferred to the Scottish club Rangers for £4.3 million and helped the club to two league titles and two cup trophies. He returned to England in a £3.4 million move to Middlesbrough in March 1998. He made his debut with the club managed by Bryan Robson in the Premier League in the 1998/99 season, before transferring to Everton in July 2000, signed by his old boss from Rangers, Walter Smith, in a move that was questioned at the time. The player still struggled with his demon alcohol and was becoming increasingly injury-prone with a poor fitness record. Several football observers saw a transfer from one Premier League club to another as a mistake that simply delayed the day of reckoning when Gazza would have to face up to the fact that he was way out of step with the fast-developing business of English first-tier football. His star was waning in the new world of a top flight where a lot was demanded from the performance of players, investors, managers and fans in what was fast becoming the richest and most competitive league in the world.

A lapse into alcoholism at the tail end of the 2000/01 season prompted a spell in an Arizona rehabilitation clinic. The following season, 2001/02, saw Gazza featuring more regularly in the Everton first team, but he was rarely able to provide the inspiration needed to take the team to victory. Lack of stamina allowed Gascoigne to play only in bursts before having to sit a game out to recover in time for another 90 minutes.

His departure from Everton in March 2002 ended his days in the Premier League. He completed the season playing at Burnley, in the second tier of English club football known then as the First Division. It was a brief and unhappy time. He was there only three months and made only six appearances. As Gascoigne later wrote in his autobiography *Gazza, My Story* published in 2004: 'I didn't really enjoy my football at Burnley. I found the First Division very tough. The lads were fine and it wasn't them – it was me. Their sort of football wasn't my style. It was all kick and rush. Perhaps I'd lost a bit of the necessary pace for it, but whatever the case I wasn't comfortable with it.'

Unwanted elsewhere in the Premier League and in Europe, Gazza finished his playing days haunted by further bouts of depression and heavy drinking, made no better by his brief experience far from his roots with Chinese League One club Gansu Tianma, and for a few months from July 2004, as a player-coach with the American League Two side Boston United. With his career as a player over, he stated his desire to become a successful coach, a pursuit that failed in a story foretold.

The darker side of his personal life pursued Gazza when, after his spells at Lazio and in Glasgow, he returned to English club football at a time when the Premier League was producing a new generation of players and 'bosses' whose wealth was partly drawn from clean and exemplary personality branding, a role that went against Gascoigne's instinctively rebellious nature and inner demons. The downward spiral of Gascoigne's personal life came to include his abusive treatment of his wife Sheryl, who subsequently divorced him, and his spell at Middlesbrough, where he became so dependent on alcohol that even his team-mates were forced to speak out. In the end, the tabloid media, as much as Gazza's mental and physical vulnerability, ruined the promise of one of England's most feted footballers. He is still described by England's National Football Museum as 'the most naturally talented English footballer of his generation'.

In judging his legacy, one might be tempted to describe him as one of the last of the breed of rock-star-style celebrity footballers – one thinks also of George Best and Maradona – of unrivalled talent brought down by the pressures of fame. In Gazza's case, I cannot improve on the verdict of the author Pete Davies, the football writer who followed his best playing years: 'Promise often goes unfulfilled, but rarely can it have been so very nearly fulfilled before imploding. And seldom has so much money been made out of much hype and hope along the way.'

## Chapter Sixteen

# Germans, Tottenham and Shearer

FOOTBALL WRITING is an acquired and challenging art, and I count myself among the authors who without claiming expertise on the sport itself have delved into a game – its protagonists, stand-out events and passions – because it opens a window into humanity.

Among the books of the genre to have emerged from the Anglo-Saxon world over the last half century, I know I am not alone among colleagues in considering as an exemplary point of reference *The Glory Game* by Hunter Davies. Having written a best-selling authorised biography of the Beatles, Davies turned to writing his seminal book about Tottenham Hotspur's best years. Published in its first edition in 1972, *The Glory Game*, as the title suggests, was a celebration of good football written as a behind-the-scenes portrait of *dramatis personae* during a decade when Tottenham represented English club football at its best, a story throwing up some contrasts with its lesser achievements in what became the Premier League.

*The Glory Game* was penned only ten years after the £20-a-week maximum wage for English professional footballers was abolished. One of the stars Davies writes about is the Tottenham forward Martin Chivers, who during the 1971/72 campaign, hit the best form of his career, scoring 44 times in 64 first-team appearances. Chivers shared a glimpse into his inner soul by confessing that he got scared in bed when his wife was away because he was afraid of the dark.

Few characters can lay a greater claim to being the rock of Tottenham's best years in the 20th century than Chivers's coach Bill Nicholson. Arriving as a teenage member of the ground staff in 1936, Nicholson served as player, coach, assistant manager and manager over the next 38 years, during which time he won nine major honours, one as a player and eight as manager. Chivers was among an array of quality players who were coached by Nicholson. Others included my childhood hero Jimmy Greaves. Greaves was a phenomenal and prolific striker whose name was often followed by 'GOAL!' during the early BBC broadcast commentaries.

Born in Essex in 1940, Jimmy Greaves was scouted by Chelsea and signed for the club in 1955. He played in their famous youth team, scoring 51 goals in his first season, and went on to lift the FA Youth Cup in 1958. At only 17, Greaves made his Chelsea first team league debut against his future club, Tottenham Hotspur, scoring in a 1-1 draw. Greaves was prolific in front of goal, scoring a sensational 124 goals while also being the league's top scorer in 1958/59 (32 goals) and 1960/61 (41).

In the summer of 1961, after an approach from an Italian restaurant owner, Greaves signed for AC Milan after accepting around £7,000 per year – significantly more than his £1,000 yearly salary with Chelsea. However, his time at Milan didn't go to plan, after he fell out with future AC Milan hero Nereo Rocco on numerous occasions.

Greaves moved back to England to Tottenham Hotspur for £99,999, £1 shy of being the first £100,000 player in British history. Greaves hit the ground running at Spurs, scoring 21 goals in 22 games for the Lilywhites. He continued to score goals throughout his Tottenham career, whilst also leading them to FA Cup victory twice, in 1962 and 1967, and European Cup Winners' Cup glory in their 1963 victory over Atlético Madrid – who Spurs destroyed 5-1, as Greaves scored two goals.

The club's glory years under Nicholson's management began with Tottenham winning the FA Cup and Division One, in a 1960/61 double. Tottenham went on to become the first British club to win a European trophy, the Cup Winners' Cup, in 1963. The club won the FA Cup again in 1967, the League Cup in 1971 and 1973 and the UEFA Cup in 1972, all with Nicholson. These feats included many firsts – the first double of the 20th century, followed by the first European trophy win by a British club, the first British team to win two different European competitions and the first to win the League Cup twice.

Nicholson was a complex character. As his wife Darky told Hunter Davies: 'He's very Yorkshire. He never shows what he's thinking. When he comes in from a match, I can't tell from looking at him whether they've won or lost.'

Davies portrayed Nicholson as an obsessive, forlorn, almost tragic figure, who sometimes before a match violently shook from the stress. Nicholson was a stern and uncompromising character. 'I have deep pleasure,' he said, 'in seeing hard work put into effect and being rewarded.' He shaved in ice water, and rarely smiled – a striking contrast to the more charismatic British peers of his time, Bill Shankly and Matt Busby.

As immortalised by the club's official website, Nicholson at Tottenham Hotspur managed the most romantically cherished of English sides during the 1960s and early 1970s, when football was played with bravado, style, skill and grace. His players performed with a flourish, entertaining all along the way. They thrilled supporters crammed into the old White Hart Lane stadium.

But as Brian Scovell wrote in his biography *Football's Perfectionist*, published in 2010, the stoicism Nicholson grew up with in the 1930s in a family of nine children in the Yorkshire town of Scarborough facing the North Sea, suited him well but would continue to make him a football man of the old school. By the mid-1970s, when the idea of a Premier League was still a distant horizon, Nicholson became disillusioned by the modernity of the game. His dislike of the players' growing fashion of long hair dated back to his days as a sergeant physical training instructor during World War Two.

Nicholson resigned as a manager in the autumn of 1974, not at all happy with the rising salaries secured by journeymen players and shocked by the hooliganism that had turned Tottenham's second-leg defeat by Feyenoord in the UEFA Cup Final into the 'Rotterdam Riot' that May.

After leaving the club and then returning as a consultant and ultimately president from 1976 until his death in 2004, Nicholson mellowed and then seemed to blossom in later life. He read the game so well he prophesied the coming of the Premier and UEFA Champions League years before their foundation. Nicholson continued to attend every match that his beloved Tottenham Hotspur played during the first decade of the Premier League at White Hart Lane until shortly before he died on 23 October 2004, aged 85.

Founded in 1882, Tottenham's emblem is a cockerel arrogantly standing on top of a football, with the defiant Latin motto *Audere est Facere* ('to dare is to do'). Under its chairman in the early 1990s, property developer Irving Scholar, it was one of five clubs that most actively lobbied for the foundation of the Premier League, the others being Arsenal, Everton, Liverpool and Manchester United.

For a long period in the first two decades of the Premier, Spurs were outgunned by other big clubs and finished mid-table in most seasons. But even then, they had some star players. One of them was the German international Jürgen Klinsmann, who moved from Arsène Wenger's Monaco to the Premier League for the 1994/95 season and was named English Football Writers' Association Footballer of the Year.

There have been other foreign players who have spent a longer time and been more successful in the Premier, others who left a more lasting mark, or made more of a difference. One of the greatest imports of the Premier League era was Arsenal's Thierry Henry. A member of France's World Cup-winning team, Henry scored 174 league goals in just 254 games and won two league titles for the Gunners in the eight seasons he played in English club football.

'Lightning pace, dribbling ability, rocket shots from range or side-footed finishes from inside the box; Henry had it all,' was the verdict of the *Bleacher Report* in February 2014, making him number one in the 100 ranking of foreign players.

Klinsmann was ranked 53rd, but when he played for Spurs, he had a huge impact. I remember a distinguished female sports journalist friend of mine being obsessed with the player, to the point of having photographs of him decorating her study, and her excitement levels rising whenever she had to cover a game the German played in or a press conference he was at.

Klinsmann was good-looking, athletic, combative, spoke several languages and had a disarming, self-deprecating sense of humour, which helped light up the Premier League in its early days as it reached out to a mass audience. Few Germans had as much positive impact on diminishing the prejudices of an English national football consciousness in such a short period. The fact that Klinsmann came from Germany, the old enemy of two World Wars and the historic rival of the English national team, made his seduction of Spurs's fan base, which had a tradition of followers of Jewish descent, a noble achievement.

Klinsmann had a reputation as a diver, which was, as football writer James Milin-Ashmore put it, in *These Football Times* in 2016, 'blasphemy for an English crowd used to blood and guts'. But Klinsmann responded by diving in celebration after scoring in a 4-3 thriller against Sheffield Wednesday on the opening day of the season. 'The Golden Bomber' used to scare opposing defenders and fans alike, and there was no doubting his importance to the reunified German national team in 1994, when the forward was named as the captain.

Klinsmann had no trouble adapting to English club football and proving his ability and soon became a popular figure. However, the Spurs chairman in those days, businessman Alan Sugar, resisted Klinsmann's lobbying for bigger spending on more exciting players to support him. Klinsmann would later reveal he could tell after a few months that Spurs did not have what it took to challenge for major trophies, and that the best he could hope for was a top-six finish in the Premier. Spurs ended the 1994/95 season in seventh position as they kept to their growing reputation as perennial underachievers.

After ending the season in the Premier, Klinsmann moved to Bayern Munich. A ruthless streak in him had him choosing a German club that had a better chance of winning their domestic league and playing for a European Cup. He was also an important member of the German national team.

Klinsmann was destined to leave broken hearts and fractured teams by the wayside through a nomadic career. Spurs supporters deluded themselves into believing that he would stay for at least another year and lead them to the glory of older days. After Klinsmann had announced his departure from England, Sugar, famed for his bluntness and regular use of swear words, threw the player's shirt on the floor at a press conference, claiming he wouldn't use it to wash his car.

Describing Klinsmann, one English journalist Andrew Antony wrote in *The Guardian*: 'Cunning, cynical, histrionic, the German was the embodiment of all we claimed to despise in British football. Yet just a few weeks later he had the English media, and the nation at large, queuing up to praise his self-deprecating wit, his multilingual sophistication and his sublime talent. He was no longer a mercenary thespian, but a down-to-earth guy who drove a VW Beetle, gave money to charity and was concerned about the environment.

'From the opening day of the 1994/95 season – when he scored on his debut as Tottenham won 4-3 at Sheffield Wednesday and premiered his celebrated celebration dive – to his controversial departure ten months later, Klinsmann bestrode English football like a stallion at a pony club.'

Two *Guardian* articles written by Antony perfectly captured the transformation of Klinsmann in the eyes of the English media. One, written in June 1994, was entitled 'Why I Hate Jürgen Klinsmann'. The other, published a couple of months later, was headed 'Why I Love Jürgen Klinsmann'.

The German returned to Spurs on loan in 1997/98 and played 15 more games before leaving for good. For a long period after Klinsmann's departure, until the late 2000s, Spurs finished mid-table in the Premier League, before managing to break into the top five. With a team that included rising stars Gareth Bale and Luka Modrić in the summer of 2010 (both were destined to move to Real Madrid) Spurs qualified for the Champions League for the first time, nearly half a century after playing in the European Cup in 1961/62, only to lose to Real Madrid in the quarter-finals.

After losing to Juventus in the last sixteen in 2018, the club reached the Champions League Final in 2019, but lost to Jürgen Klopp's Liverpool in Atlético Madrid's Wanda Metropolitano Stadium. Liverpool erased the disappointment of their previous Champions League Final defeat by Real Madrid by claiming the trophy for the sixth time. After the club finished seventh in 2020/21, in 2021/22 Antonio Conte managed Spurs to fourth place in the Premier League, back to a Champions League place for the first time in two seasons.

Among English international and club football's stand-out players in recent years has been Tottenham's Harry Kane.

One of the English journalists who followed his career in the Premier League closely was *The Guardian*'s Barney Ronay. 'It has been fascinating to follow him, from the early days of high-throttle centre-forward play, when he still looked like an ambitious young Edwardian notary clerk who wants to marry your daughter, through to his current incarnation as creator, disrupter, goal-scorer.'

In trying to explain Kane's Premier League goalscoring prowess, Ronay suggested the player became his own attacking innovation, a forward who did not so much play between the lines, as occupy two orthodox positions, the nine and the ten, in rotation. He called him one of 'the last great one-club goal scorers' before Kane left Spurs to join Bayern Munich in 2023, still 47 goals short of Alan Shearer's Premier League record total of 260.

It was Shearer who brought back a sense of national identity and pride when the early days of the Premier League opened its door to foreigners and an increasing volume of international star quality. As a striker with Blackburn Rovers in the early years of the Premier League, Shearer won plaudits for his goal-scoring ability and also as a distinctive homegrown star who showed no inclination to become an expatriate. Whereas Eric Cantona, the Frenchman playing for Manchester United, picked up the Football Writers' Player of the Year Award, Shearer was voted the best player by fellow players the following year.

The contrast in personalities between Shearer and Cantona seemed to open up the cultural divide between England and its continental neighbour. 'For the Blackburn striker, quotations from French philosophers *a la* Eric Cantona are out. Shrieking rows with journalists are out. And two-footed kung-fu kicks at supporters are unimaginable. In fact, a greater contrast between two brilliantly talented footballers would be difficult to find,' wrote Glyn Wilmshurst in *The Game* in May 1995.

Born in Newcastle, into a working-class family – his father was a steel worker – Shearer played his early days in the first-tier division with low-flying Southampton. He began on the substitutes' bench before becoming the most talked-about prospect in English football in April 1988 when he made his First Division debut with the club and scored three goals. That hat-trick scored by the then-17-year-old Shearer meant he had broken Jimmy Greaves's record of becoming the youngest player to score a top-flight treble. It's a record that still stands at the time of writing.

Over five seasons at Southampton, Shearer's scoring record remained modest, but his star potential had him moving to Blackburn Rovers in 1992 for a record-breaking transfer fee of £3.6 million. He missed half of the first season of the Premier League after snapping his right anterior cruciate ligament. But he was soon to rebuild a reputation as a goal-scoring machine, fearlessly physical, combative in the air and a devastating deliverer in front of goal.

Shearer's arrival at Blackburn on 27 July 1992, was a huge factor in the club winning its first top-flight title in 81 years, under the ownership of local businessman and lifelong fan Jack Walker. Returning to fitness for the 1993/94 season, Shearer scored 31 goals from 40 games as Blackburn finished runners-up. In the following season he formed a strong attacking partnership with fellow English international and new arrival from Norwich City, Chris Sutton, with his 34 goals and Sutton's 15 helping Blackburn take the Premier League title from Manchester United. Having finished fourth and then runners-up to United in the first two seasons in the Premier League, Shearer's 34 goals in 42 games helped fire the club to its first league title since 1914, transitioning Blackburn from second-flight strugglers to Premier League supremos.

Blackburn's manager was the Scot Kenny Dalglish who, when talking about his team, had a tendency to allocate praise to the collective rather than the individual. But that was not because he did not appreciate Shearer as a stand-out player but because he had been brought up in the belief, when he was at Liverpool and Celtic, that no individual is bigger than the team.

Shearer was the one player at Blackburn, and possibly in the England team, who had the technical ability that Dalglish had as a young player. Shearer was as different to Cantona as chalk and cheese, but Dalglish's 'all for one and one for all' philosophy echoed *The Three Musketeers* by the French novelist Alexandre Dumas.

For Dalglish, Blackburn and Shearer's achievement helped restore his faith in the value of football after the public success of his reign as manager at Liverpool gave way to public tragedy, that of two stadiums, Heysel and Hillsborough. It was Hillsborough, finally, that led Dalglish to question a sport which had dominated his adult life. 'Nothing is worth one death, let alone 100,' he said before retiring from the game for seven months. It was then that club owner Jack Walker lured him to Blackburn, with the clear assignment of building a winning team.

Blackburn were unable to retain the Premier League title and on 30 July 1996, for another transfer record-breaking £15 million (equivalent to £30 million today) Shearer joined his hometown club and Premier League runners-up Newcastle United, who had been managed by his hero Kevin Keegan before Dalglish took over in January 1997.

In the spring of 2006 Shearer scored a typical powerful penalty for Newcastle against Sunderland, marking the end of an era, as the last of his record 260 Premier League goals.

Here, it is perhaps worth pondering briefly on Newcastle's DNA as a club, to understand the symbolic importance of such a goal. Newcastle United have long been regarded as the 'sleeping giant' of football in England, having last experienced glory days in the 1950s. Newcastle, in the far north-east of

England, is one of the largest cities in the country with only one substantial football team and the club's fans are legendary for their devotion. Even when Newcastle were in the second tier of English football (the Championship) in 2016/17, the home crowd averaged more than 51,000 for each game, 19,000 more than the next club, Aston Villa. And this was despite an ever-deteriorating relationship between the fans and the club's owner, Mike Ashley.

Distinguishing features of fans of the Magpies (the nickname comes from the club's black and white strip) include: an in-bred hatred of Sunderland football club, the nearest sizeable rival; and a propensity to wear as little clothing as possible in the sub-zero temperatures of north-eastern winters.

At Newcastle, Shearer's own stock as a player continued to rise. He hit a new Premier League record of 140 goals and assists in 138 league appearances (112 goals, 28 assists). And yet Blackburn's one and only Premier League title remains also the only major trophy Shearer won in the game, despite going on to become English club football's most potent marksman.

Having made his debut away at Everton on 17 August 1996, Shearer scored 25 goals in his first year at Newcastle, as they tried to win the Premier League title they craved but which would continue to elude the club. The Magpies finished second for the second consecutive season. They never reached these heights again in the first three decades of the Premier League's history.

Shearer retired at the end of the 2005/06 season after his goalscoring ability was slowed by injuries and ageing, to pursue a TV broadcasting career as a respected football pundit.

## Chapter Seventeen

# Icons

DAVID BECKHAM'S rise to fame was not a rags-to-riches tale, it was more like the uncluttered, self-disciplined, sheer aspirational and determined-to-make-it success story that turned Margaret Thatcher, the daughter of a grocer, into an electable prime minister in May 1979, who then ruled the United Kingdom for more than a decade.

Beckham built his own success story out of the one thing that his dad, his mum, his sister, his friends and his teachers thought he would be good at if he only worked at it and could count on good mentors: football.

When Beckham moved from London to Manchester, there was no traumatic displacement. He was simply moving from one family to another, from one protective unit to a much larger basecamp under the control of a paternalistic commander called Alex Ferguson. One can imagine Beckham's life turning out rather differently had he spent his adolescence in Chingford, getting drunk with his friends in the local pub, as the youth of the county of Essex were prone to do at the weekends. Ferguson once remarked that Paul Gascoigne's life would have worked out better if he had become a Manchester United player.

That things turned out rather differently for Beckham was in part due to his father Ted, a Manchester United fan whose loyalty to the club had developed, as it had for so many others of his generation around the world, out of sympathy for the players killed in the Munich air crash in February 1958. Most men in Chingford supported Arsenal or Spurs.

Beckham, as a child, was given his first Manchester United shirt as a Christmas present. He was taken by Ted to see the club whenever they came to London to play in away games. Beckham's early football hero, Bryan Robson, captain of Manchester United and captain of England, dates from these pre-Premier League days. If Robson became an early role model for Beckham it was not because of his hard-drinking habits but his ability to conduct his own life in the way he chose while still playing good football.

Later in his career, as manager of Middlesbrough in the early days of the Premier League, Robson bought Paul Gascoigne from Glasgow Rangers in the belief that the player who preceded Beckham as English football's greatest international star had his talent for football well preserved. But it was a hope which proved forlorn. Gazza's qualities as a footballer – his quirkiness of touch, dribbling skills, strength and balance – combined with his often-outlandish behaviour on and off the field had made him hugely popular among English football fans. But he succumbed to the pressures of fame – alcohol, women, media pressure and his own internal demons which made mincemeat of the talent he had been born with.

By contrast, Beckham may not have possessed such a natural talent as Gazza's, but he managed, more successfully, to save his football from demons. A video of Beckham aged eight, when he was playing for a local amateur team in Chingford called Ridgeway Rovers, captures the image of a young boy – spindly framed and with spikey blond hair sticking out at sharp angles – smiling as he takes a free kick and bends it over the wall and over the goalkeeper into the back of the net.

In 1986, aged 11, Beckham entered Bobby Charlton's Soccer Skills Tournament and was on the winning side at Old Trafford. The prize was a trip to Barcelona and the chance to meet the then-Barca coach Terry Venables and two of the British players he had brought into the post-Maradona squad at the Catalan club: Gary Lineker and Steve Archibald. As I quoted in my book published in 2004, 'I was so impressed with the lad,' Venables recalled, 'that I rang up my dad in London and told him to keep an eye on him.'

Those who already had their eyes on Beckham were scouts working for Manchester United. Beckham joined the club aged 16 as an apprentice. Three years later, in April 1995, Beckham made his debut appearance in the Premier League for United in a match against Leeds. Manchester United at the time were undergoing a revival under Ferguson. The ambition of the Premier League seemed made to measure. The club's finances had been bolstered by new capital coming from public and institutional investors following a flotation on the Stock Exchange. The club was turning into a multinational business more than capable of ruthlessly exploiting glory days on the pitch.

The new chief executive and largest shareholder in the new Manchester United Public Limited Company, Martin Edwards, played a leading role in the foundation of the Premier League, with his club one of those leading the way among the 22 clubs in the old First Division of the Football League. The Premier League held out the promise of an exciting business project that would help the best clubs in the land to negotiate bigger deals with the TV companies, beginning with the £304m contract with BSkyB, the satellite channel that was to have a key role in globalising the business of football and its fan base.

Such deals risked the bigger fish getting the biggest of the income. Ferguson, drawing on his working-class roots from the Glasgow shipyards and his socialist political sympathies, was initially critical. When the Premier League was introduced in 1992, he described it as 'a piece of nonsense' that 'sold supporters right down the river'.

But his remark came to seem somewhat ironic given that Manchester United under Ferguson's management went on to dominate the first decade of the Premier League in a way that no club has done since, winning seven of the first nine titles, with the club reaping the financial benefits of the TV deal Ferguson had initially denounced, along with the additional commercial benefits in sponsorship and shirt sales that came with establishing a global brand.

Beckham spent his formative years at Manchester United with a generation of similar home-grown young bloods – Ryan Giggs, Gary and Phil Neville, Nicky Butt and Paul Scholes – who Ferguson moulded into a winning team; but it was Beckham among his generation, who came to epitomise the huge commercial opportunities of the growing business of football. At the start of the 1996/97 season, Beckham scored one of the great goals in the history of the Premier: a shot from just inside his own half, which swerved and swooped like a missile into the net, beating the Wimbledon goalkeeper Neil Sullivan. English commentators, filled with renewed national pride in the game their nation had invented, pointed out that this was a shot that Pelé had tried and failed.

Beckham himself recalled in his autobiography *My Side* published in 2003: 'I couldn't have known it then, but that moment was the start of it all: the attention, the press coverage, the fame. When my foot struck that ball, it kicked open the door to the rest of my life.'

Beckham's goal achieved international notoriety and made the sophisticates of football in southern Europe and South America take notice of the player's skill and vision. A month later Beckham was promoted to the English national team while Gazza was unceremoniously ditched from it by Glenn Hoddle, the new England manager, who described Beckham as a player 'who sees the furthest pass first'.

But football was destined to be only part of the Beckham story. The encounter that was to spark off the world of football's most enduring celebrity relationship occurred on 15 March 1997 when Victoria Adams, better known as 'Posh', a member of the hugely popular pop group the Spice Girls, exchanged personal telephone numbers with Beckham after watching United play Sheffield Wednesday. As a couple – soon to be married – the Beckhams were followed with increasing obsession by the *paparazzi*, the tabloid press, TV documentary makers and fashion magazines, who saw the combination of a world-class footballer and a world-famous pop star as a media gift made in heaven. Sponsorship and merchandising sales in large quantities poured in.

As Ellis Cashmore wrote in his 2003 book, *Beckham*, the marriage turned the football star into an all-purpose celebrity: 'The synergy produced in the fusion of two performers, each drawn from different spheres of entertainment, created new and perhaps undreamed-of possibilities in marketing, merchandising and promotion in sport, pop, fashion, and eventually patriotism.'

But, at the 1998 World Cup, disaster struck. During the match between England and Argentina, Beckham was lying on the ground after being brought down by Diego Simeone when he suddenly kicked out at the Argentine – a gesture of impetuous folly which earned Beckham a red card. England went on to lose to Argentina in a penalty shoot-out and went out of the tournament. As a result, Beckham became the convenient target to blame for a national football humiliation. In the weeks that followed, effigies of Beckham were burnt by angry zealots. Among those angriest were an endangered tribe, the white working-class male West Ham fans.

West Ham had long enjoyed the reputation of being among the capital's least successful big football clubs with their fans not caring much if they won or lost but being the most grounded in a community. But the working-class East End was a symbol of a culture that had been rapidly vanishing from London's more multi-racial and affluent life. West Ham fans reluctantly ceded to pressure from their club to call off a mass anti-Beckham protest they had planned, showing 10,000 red cards. As the World Cup faded into history, it took about six weeks for the negative reporting on Beckham to fall off the tabloid agenda.

Beckham re-emerged with his image not only intact but seemingly strengthened as a celebrity and player, recognised by Manchester United fans as their Player of the Year. It would prove an on-off love affair between Beckham and the Premier League, ending when the player joined Florentino Pérez's Real Madrid *Galacticos* in the summer of 2003.

The move was a story foretold. Three years earlier, in April 2000, Manchester United lost to Real Madrid in the quarter-finals of the Champions League when *Los Blancos* withstood a late Manchester United recovery at Old Trafford to win 3-2 on aggregate. Beckham shone when his team most needed it, showing creativity and competitiveness and scoring a smartly taken goal. But despite their club's sense of supremacy in the Premier League, United had been outclassed and were unable to defend their Champions League trophy. As the Manchester United captain Roy Keane later wrote in his autobiography published in 2002: 'Real Madrid were technically so adroit we were chasing shadows.'

Three years later, the two clubs met in another Champions League quarter-final. Beckham would later admit to feeling overawed like never before when he arrived to play at the Bernabeu – the stadium's sense of history, grandiose architecture and passionate local fan base conveyed the club's ambition and achievements in European competitions. Beckham's mother, who watched the game that evening, had a premonition there and then that Beckham would end up one day playing in Madrid. And so it came to pass, after Real Madrid won 6-5 on aggregate, with the English champions once again outclassed by the Spanish champions.

Spain had never encountered an English football player with the celebrity status of David Beckham. At Real Madrid, he had to prove he was more than just a brand and was worthy of playing for a club that had gathered leading stars from around the globe.

After winning the Spanish league in 2007, Beckham continued to play for England for another three years and his status as a 'national treasure' was recognised during the London Olympics of 2012, when he carried the flame for one leg of its journey from Athens and was part of the opening ceremony, as he was transported like a Greek god on a speed boat along the Thames – but his involvement in English club football was over and his brand became strongest abroad.

Beckham, during his playing days, grew into the most powerful brand that English football has ever produced, but the Premier League did not make enough of him. Ferguson admired Beckham's professionalism as a player but grew to dislike his celebrity status, believing, like that other Scot Kenny Dalglish, that in football the collective always takes precedence over the individual.

\* \* \*

On 19 October 2002, five days before his 17th birthday, and less than a year away from Beckham's move to Real Madrid, Wayne Rooney scored a last-minute winning goal for David Moyes's Everton which ended Wenger's Arsenal's 30-match unbeaten run. It made him the youngest goal scorer in Premier League history and, within the year, the youngest man ever to play for England.

After Everton, Rooney played at Manchester United from 2004-2017 during which time, playing for club and country, he gained a reputation as the most accomplished English footballer since Bobby Charlton.

Born in Croxteth, a poor neighbourhood of Liverpool, Rooney, the son of a casual labourer, spent his early childhood years in a one-bedroom flat subsidised by the state, and kicking a ball against the wall of his grandmother's house. Aged nine, he joined Everton's academy and soon afterwards, in a boys' match against Manchester United, scored with an overhead kick from 15 metres that had parents from the opposing team breaking into applause.

Rooney was similarly celebrated during an early training session with England when the 16-year-old dribbled past older and much more experienced players and scored.

Rooney's popularity grew partly because, as football writer Simon Kuper wrote in his book *The Football Men*, 'He was treated as the authentic masculine counterweight to Beckham's constructed effeminate beauty.'

But Rooney was also the kind of player that English fans had been waiting for since Paul Gascoigne had pressed the self-destruct button – he not only scored goals, but had that rare thing in English football, an ability to see space.

But like Gazza and unlike Beckham, Rooney was not good at handling the media pressure that goes with celebrity status. When the tabloids reported that he had a taste for prostitutes it put strains on his long-term relationship with his wife Coleen – and he also suffered the abuse of fans when they suspected him of disloyalty by wanting to move clubs. 'The story of Rooney's life became other people wanting a piece of him,' wrote Kuper.

\* \* \*

On 25 February 2017, Harry Kane contributed to Tottenham's 4-0 victory over Stoke City with his third hat-trick in nine games. Kane, then a 23-year-old, was considered by Tottenham fans not just as one of their own but a wonderful goal scorer. Some argued he was not world class, others that he was not even England's best striker, yet the goal numbers spoke for themselves. He had scored over 20 goals in three consecutive seasons and with his first that day against Stoke, reached 100 club goals, across loan spells at Leyton Orient, Millwall and Leicester City and, most emphatically for Tottenham.

'Harry has the profile to be a legend here,' the Spurs manager at the time, Mauricio Pochettino, told Sky Sports, speaking of a player who had already shown the complete ability to wound opposition sides. 'He is one of the best strikers in the world. He is very professional and someone with a strong character.'

The good news for Tottenham was that he also appeared content to stay at the club for some time.

Kane was born in a year that marked the first season of the Premier League on 28 July 1993, in Walthamstow, north-east London, to upwardly-mobile parents Patrick Kane and his wife, Kim.

'He was a lovely boy,' Verna Denny, the welfare assistant at his primary school, Larkswood told *The Guardian*'s James Tapper. 'I remember I lost a ring on my little finger. I was looking everywhere for it and couldn't find it. Harry found it in the playground and brought it to me. I've still got it. When I think now what he's achieved, it's absolutely wonderful. When I think I used to see him kicking a ball around in the playground and he's now playing for England, it's just magical.'

Kane went to a secondary school in Chingford and played for the local youth club Ridgeway Rovers. Beckham, years earlier, had gone to the same school and played for the same youth club. Kane was not cut out to match David Beckham's glamour – celebrity was not part of his DNA. Kane was also a childhood Tottenham fan, while Beckham's early dreams were with Manchester United. Kane got his early football educational upgrade as a boy in the Arsenal academy when he was eight, before returning to Ridgeway Rovers. He eventually landed at Tottenham in 2004, after the Premier League had entered its second decade.

Coming from a family of diehard Spurs fans, and living within sight of Tottenham's White Hart Lane stadium, which was replaced by their new 62,000-capacity stadium on the same site in 2019, it made sense. He made his first-team debut in a UEFA Europa League match in August 2011 but it took a while before he made a distinctive mark. In his early career, Kane was loaned out to several league clubs, including Leicester City, Millwall, Norwich City and Leyton Orient. But it was at Tottenham that Kane was destined to build his career. On 5 February 2023 he became the club's all-time record goal-scorer with the winner against Manchester City at the Tottenham Hotspur Stadium, taking him to 267 goals in all competitions (surpassing Jimmy Greaves's record of 266).

Kane nonetheless at times seems to thrive on low expectations. A video on his social media account showed him practising, overlaid with quotes from his detractors: 'He won't make it', 'Struggled on-loan', 'One-season wonder', 'Not world class'. Determination to prove the doubters wrong seemed essential to his success.

John Viggers was one of the first to see Kane up close, when he was sent on loan from Spurs to Leyton Orient, the other local club, to play League One football.

'A lot of Spurs players came on loan to Leyton Orient: Andros Townsend, Tom Carroll, Harry Kane,' Viggers told the football journalist James Tapper in July 2018. 'Kane was probably the least spectacular, but I remember saying to my mate, "He's the best one of this bunch – he's going to shine in the future."'

The 2014/15 season proved to be pivotal for Kane's career as he became a regular starter in the Tottenham line-up under Pochettino and made his senior international debut as a member of the England squad in a UEFA Euro 2016 qualifying match in March 2015. Kane then finished as the top scorer of the 2015/16 and the 2016/17 seasons of the Premier League.

Kane married a childhood friend and long-term partner Katie Goodland, a university graduate, with whom he has three children. He is understated and lacks charisma. The known Kane family story is unremarkable: his Irish parents relocated to London to have their children and give them a better life. He is different to the stereotype of previous generations of 'celebrity' footballers, with their ostentations and psychological complexities. The fact that he comes across as a normal, humble guy makes him inspiring to many of the more civilised among English fans, but also the target of cruel jokes by hostile tribes of hooligans.

Among the least generous chants emanating from the hard core of home fans at Stamford Bridge in August 2022, in the Premier season's first encounter between Chelsea FC and Tottenham, few were as personal at the one directed at Kane. 'Stop spitting when you talk,' they taunted him. Kane doesn't spit, he speaks with a slight speech impediment from childhood. Chelsea fans mocked that with little regard, let alone respect, for the player's goalscoring record and integrity as captain of the English squad.

He became England's youngest-ever World Cup captain when manager Gareth Southgate chose him to lead his multi-cultural young team at the 2018 tournament in Russia, and he helped reignite the English love affair with the national side. A dream came to a crushing end in a Moscow stadium as England's first World Cup semi-final appearance for 28 years ended in defeat by Croatia, who went on to lose to France in the final. But the English have a history of sometimes making defeats heroic and Kane emerged from the tournament with the reputation of having led from the front with courage and distinction. He was certainly treated better than Beckham had been in 1998. Kane won the Golden Boot for his six goals during the tournament in Russia, equalling Gary Lineker's 1986 Mexico World Cup record for the number of goals scored by an England player.

Kane's numbers when it came to goals during his time in the Premier League were as good as or better than other top players across Europe's major clubs, but internationally he seems to be still a step or more away from being considered a major star worthy of a place at the top table of the world's elite front men. Interestingly, Kane continued to generate a great deal less coverage from the Spanish media than David Beckham had in his days as a player and it is possible that a club like Real Madrid may have been wary of dealing with another Tottenham player, and the club's chairman Daniel Levy, after their not entirely happy experience with Gareth Bale.

Tottenham, with their lack of trophies in the Premier League, lagged well behind the big guns of Manchester City, Manchester United, and Chelsea. A comment one read in the English media was that, for all the headlines and plaudits Kane had received in England, there had not been that standout moment that would catapult him into the global conversation. And yet by 2020, the English forward had become one of the most prolific strikers in the Premier, with proven accuracy in front of goal and ability to link up well with other forwards.

Kane had a difficult summer in 2021. He and his teammate, the Korean Heung-Min Son, had been the only positive note in a wretched 2020/21 season for Tottenham. But Kane was caught up in a running saga over a possible move, which did not materialise, to Manchester City. The saga went on for some time until the English media reported that City were not prepared to meet Tottenham chairman Daniel Levy's £150m valuation of the player. It was only under Antonio Conte, who replaced Nuno Espírito Santo as head coach in November 2021, that the England captain appeared to be happy to be extended a lifeline to stay at Tottenham.

In January 2022 Conte reinforced his belief in Kane as a key member of the team. He told the English football media: 'First of all, we are talking about a really good person and a really good man. And I think this is the most important thing. I am happy to have him in my team because for sure we are talking about the top player, a top striker in the world, and if we want to win or if we want to think to build something to win, Harry must be a point of start. He is a point of reference in the dressing room and an experienced player. I am totally enthusiastic about his involvement in the team and the Tottenham project.'

The extended media speculation as to whether and when Kane might transfer to Manchester City took place on either side of the England captain leading Gareth Southgate's team to the brink of England's first trophy in 55 years, only to fall agonisingly short in a penalty shoot-out defeat by Italy in the Euro Championships Final. The match against the Italians at Wembley in July 2021 was overshadowed by hundreds of drunk hooligans and ticketless fans storming through security cordons before and during the match as police and security lost control. Huge crowds of rowdy troublemakers had thronged the showpiece venue for hours before the 8pm kick-off on 11 July, openly drinking and in some cases snorting cocaine after Covid restrictions had been eased. An official enquiry led by Baroness Casey of Blackstock later described it as a 'source of national shame'.

Kane condemned the behaviour, and also the racist abuse on social media of three young black English players – Bukayo Saka, Jadon Sancho and Marcus Rashford – who missed their penalties in the final shoot-out. He stated the team wanted nothing to do with the sort of fans who aimed their abuse at the young players who missed from the spot.

'They deserve support and backing, not the vile racist abuse they've had since last night,' Kane said. 'If you abuse anyone on social media, you're not an England fan and we don't want you.'

As Kane turned 29 in July 2022, ahead of a new season, transfer speculation receded and he declared himself committed for at least another season to Tottenham, his boyhood club which he had dedicated the entirety of his peak years to. He had yet to win a major team honour with Tottenham, whose last piece of silverware had come in the 2007/08 season when the club won the domestic Carabao Cup. They had come close to winning the Champions League in June 2019, losing to Liverpool in the final in Madrid and that disappointment still weighed on Kane's conscience. Before that match, the then-Tottenham manager Pochettino took the gamble of selecting the England captain despite him not having played since April because of an ankle injury. He replaced semi-final hat-trick hero Lucas Moura, but gave a very lacklustre performance and had no impact against Klopp's team.

But in a frenzied summer transfer market in 2022, Tottenham had strengthened their squad in support of Kane, with some impressive signings and had in their latest manager Antonio Conte, a proven winner who had returned to the Premier League to win more trophies. Kane was taking a career gamble, pursing the noble task of driving Spurs on towards one trophy, any trophy. As *The Guardian*'s football writer Barney Ronay wrote: 'It makes Kane a note of interest, a genuine star outside the elite; and who knows, perhaps the last great one-club goal scorer, out there in pursuit of his own white whale.'

Kane comes from a working-class background and is reasonably good-looking, a mix of Celtic piper and Anglo-Saxon warrior. What he lacks because he has deliberately avoided it, and also because it does not come naturally to him, is the character of a full-blown celebrity. But Kane has avoided becoming a victim of the pressures of fame which have had better players squandering their talent as they dealt with controversy, and in some cases, scandal.

On 12 August 2023, Bayern Munich announced they had signed Kane on a four-year contract, the most expensive signing in Bundesliga history costing €100m plus €10m in bonuses.

## Chapter Eighteen

# TV Pundits

'SITTING ON high stools in a TV studio in front of an invited audience fielding questions from the presenter Dave Jones, the pundits Roy Keane, Micah Richards, Jamie Carragher and Gary Neville do not so much resemble a crack team of in-house analysts assembled to publicise Sky Sports' coverage of the imminent Premier League season as a has-been boy band announcing a comeback tour prompted by multiple mid-life crises or a large bill from HMRC,' wrote Barry Glendenning, in *The Guardian* in August 2022.

Such a scene is also a reminder that there is still life after playing in the Premier League.

The occasion was a preview of the new season's popular weekly slot *Monday Night Football*, on Sky TV, which analyses the weekend games from the richest and most powerful football league championship in the world. Sky Sports was one of four Premier League rights-holders as it entered a new season in 2022/23, the others being BT Sport, Amazon Prime and the BBC.

Those on view that Monday were just a sample of the growing number of pundits that helped bring the Premier League to a massive and diverse audience, in pubs, sports bars and home sitting rooms, among them women and Asian and black members of English society, who feel intimidated by the thuggery and racist abuse that sometimes surfaces at stadiums.

All four pundits mentioned above used to play at the highest level of English and European football. When retirement beckoned, they faced up to the limited choices open to men whose age has put them beyond the fitness required to cope with the intense competition of elite football. Only a select group of players have the psychology or skills to turn into coaches of top teams, but knowledge and experience and some decent coaching in communications skills can prepare a former player for a new phase in life in front of a large TV audience and guarantee a large salary package.

English football punditry and coverage has become a much more technologically sophisticated and highly paid operation than it once was, pre-Premier League, with multi-angled shots, numerous graphics, instant replays and statistics that in the old times would have been buried in a dusty archive. The modern-day pundits belong to a very different world to that inhabited by the legendary BBC football commentator Kenneth Wolstenholme, who died in 2002, aged 81, just as the Premier League was getting into its second decade.

Wolstenholme was one of the pioneers of European post-war sports broadcasting, at a time when the BBC as a public corporation had a virtual monopoly when it came to English football. He became the first commentator on the BBC's *Match of the Day*, which in modern times has faced much tougher competition for viewers.

Wolstenholme's most famous comment was, 'They think it's all over, it is now,' at the end of England's 1966 World Cup Final win over Germany. He was England's voice of football over nearly a quarter of a century with the BBC, hugely respected by players and fans who tuned in to the radio and terrestrial TV coverage.

Today's TV and internet audience embraces greater diversity, reflecting the growing role of women in the sport, and of ethnic minorities otherwise defined by the official UK government website as non-white British.

One of the best-known modern-day pundits is Irishman Roy Keane, who captained Manchester United during the late Ferguson years. Keane can be as combative and outspoken as he was as a player although, mellowed by time, he insists he does not bear grudges and tries to be scrupulously fair in matches, despite an enduring capacity for coming up with a pithy word or phrase.

Towards the end of the 2021/22 season Keane declared without a blink in a live broadcast that there were up to six Manchester United players who should never represent the club again after the Red Devils were outclassed in a Sunday afternoon derby, when two goals each from Kevin De Bruyne and Riyad Mahrez propelled Guardiola's Manchester City to a 4-1 victory.

As Mark White commented in *FourFourTwo* in November 2023: 'The hand grenade in the ball pit. The argument in the empty room. The dark side of the moon. You don't have to have agreed with anything that Roy Keane has ever said; nor do you have to have appreciated anything achieved in his trophy-laden career. But you can't live without him. Keano is the chief firestarter of football punditry.'

Certainly, both Keane and another former United player-turned-pundit Gary Neville do not pull their punches when it comes to criticising poor performances, even of the club they once proudly played for, although Neville often plays the role of checking and countering any hint of bias by Carragher whose *alma mater* was Liverpool, where he dedicated his 17 years as player.

Richards, a former Manchester City star, is English-born of West Indian Caribbean descent, a reminder that those whose ancestors were discriminated against as unwelcome immigrants from the Commonwealth have pursued successful careers in football as players on the pitch and entertainers off it. Other black players who have transitioned to celebrity TV commentators include former internationals like the ex-

Arsenal player Ian Wright and the ex-Manchester United player Rio Ferdinand. Anti-racism group Kick It Out runs sessions for aspiring broadcasters as part of their Raise Your Game programme, an attempt to broaden social access in all areas of the football industry. For Kick It Out chief executive Tony Burnett, lack of diversity does viewers a disservice. 'In a multi-cultural society, it's critically important there is a range of talent working in the industry, both to inspire the next generation and to offer a better understanding of the sport itself,' he said.

For *FourFourTwo*'s Mark White, 'The best pundits don't just explain what's going on, they make you feel a part of the event; they illuminate things you would never have thought to look for and even in a goalless match, they might just have an entertaining moan about a player's potential.'

In the autumn of 2023, *FourFourTwo* ranked Wright, Richards and Ferdinand at five, six and eight in the list of the top ten Premier League TV pundits. A woman of mixed race and a former star football player, Alex Scott, was ranked number four. Scott was born in East London to a British mother with Northern Irish, English and Lithuanian-Jewish heritage and a Jamaican father. Once considered one of the country's greatest and most dangerous female full-backs, Scott was a key fixture on the right of defence for both Arsenal and England for well over a decade.

Despite having to suffer misogynist remarks and racist comments via social media, Scott declared she felt it was her responsibility to change perceptions when she joined a BBC panel for the Women's European Championships in the summer of 2022, which drew record audiences as the English 'Lionesses' progressed to their historic victory.

Alan Shearer led the ranking as the Premier League all-time scorer when he was a player and is now its most respected pundit, having made a seamless transition from goal-getter to analyst on the BBC's *Match of the Day*. The plain-speaking

Shearer is excellent value for any kind of comment on movement or finishing by forwards and keeps a special eye out for any emerging signs that the old-style striker in his mould may be undergoing a revival, which some believed it was, even under Guardiola early in the 2022/23 season, with Manchester City's new signing Erling Haaland playing more as an orthodox striker, rather than as a false 9.

The Premier League *Match of the Day* programme has been anchored by the veteran former England striker Gary Lineker since 1999. The one-time Leicester City and Tottenham player is also fondly remembered by older FC Barcelona fans from the 1980s, as he earned the nickname Matador while playing there, when Terry Venables was his coach. Playing in the world's biggest club football fixture, Lineker scored an *El Clásico* hat-trick, as Barca famously saw off Real Madrid 3-2 at the Camp Nou. Such a memorable performance came in Lineker's first season in *La Liga*, following his transfer from Everton after the 1986 World Cup.

The Leicester-born forward landed the World Cup Golden Boot in Mexico, scoring six goals for England, who were defeated at the quarter-final stage by Diego Maradona's Argentina. He transferred from Barcelona to Spurs in 1989 and left there after three years, before the start of the first Premier League season, and ended his playing days in Japan with Nagoya Grampus.

Lineker's claim to fame as a player is as a rare footballing hero. In a country that until the English women's team won the Euros in the summer of 2022, had under-delivered for over 50 years, he holds the record for the most goals for England at the World Cup finals. As a player Lineker owed his popularity not just to his prowess as a striker but also to his remarkable disciplinary record; he was never cautioned by a referee for foul play. Good-looking, literate and personable, Lineker, thanks to some good advice and coaching, used his knowledge and natural talents to transition to television and became one of the most recognisable faces in global sports broadcasting.

He became British TV's leading sports anchor, watched by millions every Saturday night, and his status as the BBC's highest-paid presenter, earning an estimated £1.35 million a year, has contributed to making him a more controversial figure as England has become a more socially and politically divided nation in a poor economic climate. Lineker came to personify the tensions and divisions of Brexit and concerns over the environment and asylum policy which have left few areas of British society unaffected. BBC guidelines recommend that its employees aim for impartiality. Lineker defended his public comments about current affairs, saying he could air his personal views because his was a sports programme not a political show and he was on a freelance contract so was subject to different rules.

The once 'Mr Nice Guy' of 1990s, 'cool Britannia' English football was reinvented by the hostile right-wing tabloid media as the voice of the loathed liberal elite, envied for his huge salary and vilified by trolls on social media for condemning Britain's vote to leave the European Union, defending the rights of refugees against 'racist' Conservative party policies and accusing Boris Johnson of lacking integrity as a politician. In December 2021 Lineker used his popular Twitter account to describe Johnson's less than truthful accounting for partying at his official residence during the Covid lockdowns as 'unforgivable'.

In August 2022, as the country baked in the hottest summer ever, he criticised Conservative MPs who voted against imposing a legal duty on water companies to reduce sewage discharge into rivers and the sea. Then in March 2023, Lineker was embroiled in a fresh controversy after tweeting that the language in which Rishi Sunak's government had set out its asylum policy was 'not dissimilar to that used by Germany in the 30s'.

The populist and rabidly nationalist tabloids like *The Sun* and the *Daily Mail* showed their hatred for him. *The Sun* splashed its front page with an article claiming Lineker was 'peddling lies' with his comments in defence of child refugees. So how did the ultimate sure-footed smooth operator provoke such a storm? It was a question Lineker was asked by the *Financial Times* journalist David Bond when *The Sun* launched its tirade against him.

Back came Lineker's answer. 'The only reason it ballooned a little bit was because the press picked up on it and decided I wasn't really entitled to any kind of opinion – which obviously is a nonsense because everybody's entitled to opinions. I just felt the European Union, okay, it's got its weaknesses, but the moment it started to get into a little bit of trouble we just ran away. The funny thing is I don't regard myself as particularly liberal. I just think I'm kind of humanitarian. I've always been interested in politics; I've always followed it very closely, but I've never really offered my views. I suppose going on to Twitter gives you a kind of platform to do so if you wish.'

His tweets are sometimes as clinical and brutal in delivery as his goalscoring, but do not always hit the target as intended. In the summer of 2022, he was forced to delete a contentious tweet in the aftermath of the England women's team's Euro 2022 victory. It was Chloe Kelly who sent Wembley Stadium into raptures with the winning goal – just four months after returning to action from injury. The goal triggered a mass outpouring of emotion across the nation, with many taking to social media to hail the Lionesses for their success.

Kelly's celebration – taking off her shirt and wildly spinning it above her head while sporting a Nike sports bra – was an iconic moment, as much of liberation as victory.

Following the final whistle, Lineker wrote on Twitter: 'The @Lionesses have only gone and done it, and Kelly is England's heroine, bra none.'

The tweet ruffled a few feathers, with women in particular taking exception. Journalists and fans continued to react even after the tweet was deleted, with freelance journalist Flo Lloyd-Hughes tweeting: 'From a man that has had so much power and influence and never used it to support women's football. Yikes!' Another person tweeted: 'Seriously Gary ... biggest moment in women's football and you choose to make a joke about her sports bra, give your head a wobble.' Further comments accused him of 'casual sexism'.

Following that backlash, Lineker insisted he would not be bullied into self-censorship even if he did delete the tweet, claiming that his critics had missed the context of his comment. 'It was just a play on words given the celebration. I do rubbish like that constantly on here, including on men's football. I've deleted it as many people didn't see the game so missed the context.'

For some sections of the UK press, which had always enjoyed a love-hate relationship with Lineker the celebrity, his tweet deletion was a moment of humiliation to relish. But within a short time, he was once again on air, leading a discussion on the upcoming Premier League season.

For *Match of the Day* Lineker travelled from the English capital to the BBC studios in Manchester by train and returned often before the night was out by car to his London home. His high-paid celebrity world was very different to his early childhood in Leicester when, as he once told a *Financial Times* journalist, his working-class family 'worked its socks off all the time.'

He was in fact the son of a Tory-voting market-stall owner, and Lineker was given his middle name Winston, in memory of Britain's wartime leader Churchill, with whom he shared the same birthday.

While Lineker was against Brexit, the county of Leicestershire, along with many working-class white English football fans, voted to get out of the European

Union in the referendum. As the *FT*'s journalist David Bond commented, 'As a player and now as a broadcaster, Lineker has witnessed first-hand the transformation of English football from a game best known for its hostile grounds and muddy pitches to a star-studded, global entertainment business where even quite average players can enjoy multi-millionaire lifestyles.'

In an interview with the *FT* published in December 2016, Lineker said he was perfectly comfortable defending the sky-high wages earned in the business of football. 'Football gives so much to so many people, it's so important to people and every fan at every club wants their club to sign a big player. If you're the best at what you do in the entertainment or sporting world you will get well paid – that's how it works. You can argue all day that there are also people doing more important things in the world who don't get paid well at all but there's nothing footballers can do about that.'

On air, he continues to be periodically prompted as a point of reference to recall his times as a former star player, the high points of his playing career – Tottenham games, World Cups, Barca. Yet, for all his glory on the pitch, and the rewards of his life in TV, one event endures in Lineker's memory as perhaps the most joyous, magical experience of his sporting life: the day, 2 May 2016, Leicester City – the club he was born into – won its first Premier League championship.

In March 2023, Leicester City's stadium was where Lineker sought safe haven to watch his club play Chelsea as, notwithstanding the photos taken of him watching the match by the media, he escaped temporarily from the latest and most controversial fall-out of one of his massively followed tweets, in a row over impartiality. Lineker had been suspended by the BBC from fronting *Match of the Day* after tweeting criticism of the government's hard-line asylum policy which set out to ban migrants who arrive on small boats from settling in Britain.

He tweeted: 'This is just an immeasurably cruel policy directed at the most vulnerable people, in language that is not dissimilar to that used by Germany in the 30s, and I'm out of order?'

Lineker is a sports presenter, not a political presenter or news journalist. He is an effective and engaging communicator and knows a great deal about football – with a social media following that had, by then, reached 8.7 million followers on Twitter. But the BBC's Executive Complaints Unit ruled that, although the star was not required to uphold the same impartiality standards as BBC journalists, he had an 'additional responsibility' because of his profile.

'We expect these individuals to avoid taking sides on party political issues or political controversies and to take care when addressing public policy matters,' the ruling said.

By declaring Lineker's 'recent social media activity to be a breach of our guidelines' and deciding to take him temporarily off air, the BBC provoked an outpouring of criticism of its action on the basis that it was an unjustified curbing of free speech on an important issue of public concern and that the broadcaster was bending to political pressure from hard Brexiteers and racists. Among the many celebrities and public figures who took Lineker's side were BBC colleagues, including fellow football pundits Ian Wright, Alan Shearer and Alex Scott who did not appear that Saturday on *Match of the Day* 'in solidarity' – one of a number of boycotts that caused considerable disruption to the corporation's football coverage.

In her book *The Light We Carry*, published in 2022, Michelle Obama argues that as a result of social media, 'We live in a time when reacting has become almost too easy, too convenient.' She goes on: 'Rage spreads easily, along with hurt, disappointment, and panic. Information and misinformation seem to flow at the same rate. Our thumbs get us into trouble, becoming easy vectors for our fury.'

And yet it seems from the comments of people who know Lineker well, that he genuinely feels strongly about the social issues he speaks out about. He has, for example, contributed an article to a charity book about refugees. He also hopes he might influence at least some of the millions that follow him – another example of the activism that had taken hold among some players, as a counter to the hooliganism and prejudice that still persists in English society, not least among some football fans.

And yet with or without 'Gary', the Premier is first and foremost about football, not politics let alone morality – or so it would seem from figures showing that some 2.5 million people tuned in to watch, rather than boycott, the *Match of the Day* show which went ahead without TV pundits on the Saturday of the boycott, up nearly 500,000 from the previous week's 2.09m viewership.

Chapter Nineteen

# Hooligans

WHAT IS it about some English male football fans that has earned them a reputation for being violent drunkards?

I owe to my former *Financial Times* colleague Brian Groom, a historical perspective that takes us back centuries. 'Life on the Anglo-Scottish border was not for the fainthearted. One six-a-side football match in 1599 between men of Bewcastle, in England, and the Armstrongs of Whithaugh, on the Scottish side, was followed by "drinking hard" and a thwarted ambush. The final score was two dead, 30 taken prisoner and many hurt, especially John Whitfield, whose bowels came out, only to be sowed up again.'

As Groom notes in his book *Northerners: A History, from the Ice Age to the Present Day* (2022) the Middle Ages in the British Isles were to bring 600 years of border warfare and English and Scots wrestled over the boundary. For border residents, fighting could be brutal, with homes and towns on both sides sacked and burned. Nonetheless, for all the bitterness between people on either side of the border over calls for independence by Scottish nationalists opposed to Brexit – a majority of Scots voted in the referendum to stay in the EU – the culture of football violence has been provoked more by local club loyalties.

The most bitter rivalry in the Scottish league – that between the region's two biggest clubs, Rangers and Celtic – has its roots in religious sectarianism mirroring Northern Ireland's years of civil unrest and terrorism (Rangers-Protestant, Celtic-Catholic) while the enduring battles off-turf as well as on it of the Premier League south of the border are to do with where you were born or spent most of your life in England.

From the mid-19th century, northern England, with an expanding industrialised working class serving the Empire, led the world in football's development as a game for the masses. The region was noted for its culture of sentimentality and heavy drinking, not least at weekends, largely as an escape from and a reaction to the hard work in the factories, pits and shipyards, giving rivalry between the region's clubs a particular intensity.

Northern England did not invent the rules-based Association Football – London did – but it can claim to have turned it into a professional spectator sport. Major sports gambling companies, including Littlewoods and Vernons, were northern companies. Betting pools based on predicting the outcomes of top-level matches were founded in Liverpool in the 1920s.

Football took hold in the northern region of England, in Yorkshire and Lancashire. Sheffield FC, founded in 1857, is recognised by FIFA as the world's oldest club.

The English Football Association initially tried to outlaw professionalism but accepted it in 1885. The English Football League was created in 1888. All 12 founder members came from the North and the Midlands, and they dominated the League until the 1920/21 season, when the Football League Third Division was introduced – which became, in effect, the Third Division South of the following season, when the Third Division North was also introduced. This expanded the league's operational radius and the total number of clubs increased from 44 to 66. The North provided at least 50 per cent of Football League clubs at all times before 1920, and usually 40-45 per cent until the late 1970s, when the figure fell to about 35 per cent. The proportion remains about the same today in England's top four divisions, including the Premier.

Rivalry between the region's two biggest counties Lancashire (Manchester) and Yorkshire (Leeds) is known as the War of the Roses, a reference to the bloody encounters between royal houses in medieval times which were immortalised in the theatrical saga of nationhood and power as imagined by the great English literary icon William Shakespeare.

Within the northern county of Lancashire, encounters between two big teams, Liverpool and Manchester United, vying to be considered champions, have a history of mutual abuse that pre-dates the Premier. During the 1980s, Manchester United's Old Trafford Stretford End taunted Liverpudlians with 'Sign on, sign on, and you will never get a job'. Later the terraces of Liverpool's Anfield stadium responded with 'There's only one Harold Shipman' referring to a doctor based in Manchester who at the start of a new millennium was found guilty of the murders of 15 women by lethal injections of diamorphine, and was estimated to have drugged to death countless others, from children to pensioners, making him the most prolific English serial killer in modern history.

When in the summer of 2022 I asked the anglophile Spanish author Ignacio Peyro what he remembered about Premier football from his five years as director of the Cervantes Institute in London, he told me about one event which had stuck in his memory. It was when he went to see a match between Newcastle and Chelsea at Stamford Bridge. 'It was mid-morning, and I came across a group of Newcastle fans naked from the waist upwards, already drunk waving their shirts and chanting – and this was mid-winter! What I thought were the rowdiest most violent fans were probably about 15 per cent of the total attendance – so to some extent it was a 'controlled' scene – but I couldn't help wondering what English football must have been like in the days before

Premier League stadiums were reformed and there was limitless access to alcohol.'

Stamford Bridge was one of several Premier League stadiums that had bars serving alcohol in the corridors, where fans could drink as much they liked before they actually moved into the main alcohol-free arena to take their seats. Many of the ticket-holding fans had already imbibed in large quantities in nearby pubs in the hours leading up to the match.

I have come across many civilised teetotal Spanish friends who have emerged shocked by the drunken thuggery after their occasional forays into the heart and soul of English football when visiting the land of 'Perfidious Albion'. Over many years of following football in Spain as well as England, I recall some of the prejudiced attitudes of extremist fans like the *boixos nois* (FC Barcelona), and *ultra surs* (Real Madrid), but the football tribes have always been more numerous and vocal in England, while racism can be found in both countries.

Maybe the difference is that English tribes have deeper roots in local history as do their clubs. There is also the large amount of beer the English fans consume without eating and the relatively flexible regime police and club authorities adopt when it comes to allowing consumption of alcohol.

In the summer of 2022, another Spanish friend of mine, José Luis Hens, who happened to be a Betis fan, went to see a match at one of the relatively new arrivals to the Premier League, Brentford FC. He emailed me afterwards noting the strange rules on drinking he encountered.

He wrote: 'As long as there is a good sports director and good professionals, Brentford FC is an incredible idea, but I don't see a long-term future for it. A lot of respect, a lot of tolerance, but also a lot of nonsense, like for example selling you alcohol inside the stadium but that you have to drink it in one go near the latrines since that same alcohol that you bought is supposed to be the one you won't be able to imbibe watching your team live. Would it not be easier not to sell alcohol, at all? If you drink, don't drive or don't go to football, because if you drink you still won't be able to comply to the letter of club regulations, as it seems that security is supposed to have orders to enforce those six values that Mr Thomas Frank, the admirable Danish coach suggests as an inspiration of the noble project of Brentford FC in the Premier League: 'Togetherness, respect, honesty, trust, professionalism and humility.'

Walter Oppenheimer, who had lived and breathed Anglo-Saxon lands as a writer for the Spanish newspaper *El País* for much of his professional life, provided me with an interesting analysis of the drinking habits of football fans, from the perspective of an outsider looking in, in this case a Spaniard living in England. As Oppenheimer wrote towards the end of the 2021/22 Premier League season:

'In Spain it is taken for granted that the English are class-oriented, but the Spanish, with their Mediterranean climate and natural *bonhomie*, get along with everyone and, when it comes to having a drink, they do not distinguish between rich and poor, upper class or lower, dark or light skin. In reality, at least in terms of alcohol consumption in football stadiums, the English treat the rich exactly the same as the poor, while in Spain the rich or influential with access to an executive box can drink but the ordinary fans attending the match do not have the right to consume alcohol.'

No doubt it is an established truth that football and alcohol go badly together and that violence in the stands disappears if beer also disappears – echoing the Betis fan's report on Brentford FC. In England, with a legendary history of violence in football, alcohol can be drunk inside the outer walls of stadiums while in Spain, where there have only been occasional problems, it has been prohibited since 1990.

In the summer of 2022, as a new Premier season got under way, I could think of mitigating factors. There were more controls than met the eye of the untrained observer, from the use of security cameras in English stadiums to anticipate non-desirables, to the large number of well-trained stewards who could support the police in quelling any minor disturbance before a major battle breaks out. I could find little evidence that having a match start in the morning or afternoon during a weekday or at the weekend made much difference in England, where any fan knows he can get his hands on some beer, at whatever hour, even if he has stashed it under his bed.

The fact remains that English fans have for a long time developed a habit of drinking a great deal as part of their tribal pre-match bonding, and the most extreme elements among them are more hostile, intolerant and unruly at both home and away games, than would be expected from the longest-established liberal democracy in Europe.

English fans also have a proven track record of exporting their worst habits. I remember watching a group of Manchester United fans occupying a popular 'cerveceria' beer bar near Barcelona's central square Plaza de Catalunya on the night before a Champions League game at the Camp Nou. I saw the Englishmen occupy the bar mid-afternoon, setting up their emblems and chanting like an army claiming territory – their sense of entitlement drawing on some subconscious identity of nationhood that admires British troops for their courage and endurance far from home, dating from the legendary marauders that inhabited Saxon lands.

By the time I passed the bar again near midnight, it was trashed, every bottle, glass, chair, and table broken – the English still inside, dancing and chanting in tribal euphoria, the Spanish woman owner out on the pavement, in tears.

In his observations of the mob culture of English football published in 1992 – the foundation year of the Premier League – under the title *Among the Thugs*, the American journalist Bill Buford was amazed by the complicity of tolerance that made it possible. The police were prepared to handle thousands of drunk and loud people, and train station managers erected barricades to facilitate the flow of traffic for the inebriated population. And yet Buford also wrote that working-class Englishmen, very often white young men, expressed their dissatisfaction with their current economic situation by lashing out against their immediate surroundings after a football event. A minority of English fans who regularly behave like hooligans are more likely to feel unstable in the world and unwelcome in corporate environments; they also feel very threatened by globalisation. They prefer to explain any personal setback they experience as being the fault of 'the other guy' (usually someone non-white or 'foreign') or an opposing fan whatever colour, rather than their own failings.

The hooligans Buford encountered were both a look into the past and into the future, and seemed to present a clear and present danger to the more moderate fans who wanted to simply to enjoy a game. Buford wondered why families insisted on paying to attend what was often a miserable event. After attending games around the country, he confessed to have found himself understanding the tribal ritual. It was addictive.

Towards the end of *Among the Thugs*, Buford considered why a certain breed of English men were so prone to be troublesome. He concluded that the effects of rioting produce endorphins in the brain that are similar to ingesting drugs. Simply put, they riot because it's fun. It's also an instant way to feel that they're connected to their community and can act in ways that are larger than themselves. These positive benefits are not, in their social situation, delivered to them, so they act out, as society gives them nothing beyond the stadium.

Throughout the 1960s and 1970s, football violence was largely confined to football stadiums, but the trend to move outside has been increasing since then. A watershed in the history of English football hooliganism was the Heysel disaster of 1985, in which a 'charge' by Liverpool fans at rival Juventus supporters caused a wall to collapse, resulting in 39 deaths. English teams were banned from European club competitions until 1990. In the 1990s, following the introduction of all-seater stadiums, in the wake of the Hillsborough disaster, nearly all football violence occurred outside stadiums, and it was usually brought swiftly under control.

Perhaps one of the most significant factors in reducing the problem of hooliganism has been the widening interest across all levels of society in the sport since the 1990s and the influx of huge sums of money into the Premier League, raising both the quality and comfort of the match experience. At the same time, the influence of improved police technology and methods, along with an unwillingness of a majority of law-abiding fans to tolerate hooliganism, have pushed it away from the mainstream and into its new, less overt forms.

If hooliganism declined in overall scale and scope, it continued to occur. As Paul MacInnes of *The Guardian* noted, during the 2021/22 season, with a lingering threat of resurgent new strains of Covid, if there was one thing everyone in English football could agree on, it was that there were unnerving levels of disorder at matches: rules were being ignored, safety measures overwhelmed, arrests made on a regular basis. The newspaper listed as just a 'sample' of the incidents reported by police over the season as England emerged from lockdown: fights between Tottenham and West Ham fans on two occasions; projectiles thrown from the stands at Everton's Goodison Park and Chelsea's Stamford Bridge; and the use of banned pyrotechnics from the seats of other stadiums. There were pitch invaders at Norwich, Leicester and Arsenal (more than once), trouble on the streets of Nottingham after the local derby match with Leicester and 18 arrests before, during and after a match between Middlesbrough and Derby. There was also the riot that descended on Wembley in the summer of 2021 on the night of England's first championship final since 1966.

Statistics released by the UK Football Policing Unit (UKFPU) in January 2022 showed a 36 per cent rise in disorder at matches and an increase in arrests of 47 per cent in the first half of the 2021/22 season compared to the same period in 2019/20. On-and-off lockdowns had kept people mostly in their homes for 18 months and out of stadiums for almost a season and a half. Upon their return, there appeared to be a release of pent-up energy and a rise in what Geoff Pearson, a senior lecturer in criminal law at Manchester University and leading expert in football hooliganism, called 'carnivalesque' behaviour with transgression at its core.

'I do think there has been a post-pandemic increase in antisocial behaviour and low-level nuisance disorder more broadly,' Pearson told *The Guardian* in February 2022. 'There's a subculture who go to football, mainly lads and anything from teenagers through to 60-odd, who go for a transgressive experience. Watching the football is only one element of what is important to the day. Getting absolutely blottoed in whatever way, having a sing-song, hanging around with your mates, expressing your identity and coming back with a bunch of stories that will get you through the working week is what it's about.'

Dr Martha Newson, a cognitive anthropologist based at the universities of Oxford and Kent who has researched social cohesion and football fans, was quoted in the same article: 'There's a seamless transition between football culture and the rest of society. There's no sort of lag. It's just an instant mirror holding up what's happened to society but amplified because of this ritual, high-affect state you're in [as a fan]. There's a massive amount of tension in the country at the moment so it comes out in football.'

If the Premier League remained admired for the good football games it produced, it was because the English police did not do a bad job for a majority of the season, controlling the potentially more violent elements among the fans. And judging by the experience of the Champions League Final of 2022 between Liverpool and Real Madrid, English fans thought they had reasons to believe that English policing worked better than the French, and the English FA worked more responsibly in protecting the rights of non-violent match-goers than UEFA, European football's governing body.

The Champions League Final, in Paris, featured two heavyweights of European football. It was meant to be a glorious occasion. It wasn't. The match was overshadowed by the descent into chaos of its organisation, with tear gas, riot police and thousands of onrushing teenagers. The breakdown of civilised behaviour among mainly socially alienated young Frenchmen and UEFA's organisational failings created the overriding memory of many Liverpool fans who were there on the night.

Who was to blame for Champions League Final trouble?

According to eye-witness accounts, in all of the chaotic rushes on the streets of Saint-Denis, there were no Liverpool or Real Madrid shirts, nor were there any English or Spanish voices. The travelling support came for that reason only: to support their team. It was local youths from poor neighbourhoods who appeared to jump the gates of the stadium and then flooded into the surrounding area. Mishandling, miscommunication and misrepresentation around security and tickets contributed to a dangerous situation that could have turned into something far worse.

## Chapter Twenty

# Money Machine

AS THE English braced themselves for a deepening cost-of-living crisis in the autumn of 2022, one area of their society, the Premier League, was alive and well and kicking in its 30th anniversary year.

Forget the doomsayers of Brexit, the astronomical energy-price rises, the uncertainties of the war in Ukraine, the most globally overheated and flooding climate in living memory. English stadiums were packed to capacity, millions tuned in on their TV sets, advertising and sponsorship by betting companies, among other businesses, provided a lucrative source of revenue, with mega-clubs engaged in a frenzied buying and selling spree of stars for record transfer fees in pursuit of triumphs in national and international competitions, and ever more lucrative broadcasting and sponsorship deals.

Well before the closure of the summer transfer window, the Premier League had spent over £1.5bn, with foreigners among the big signings – Darwin Núñez to Liverpool (£65m), Casemiro (£60m) and Antony (£85m) to Manchester United, Erling Haaland to Manchester City (£52m), Raheem Sterling (£47m) to Chelsea, and Gabriel Jesus (£45m) to Arsenal.

The Premier League's signing of a £2.7bn, six-year TV deal with Comcast NBC, part of the largest American multinational telecommunications conglomerate, not only pushed the league's turnover above £6bn in 2022 but also marked the moment at which income from foreign media rights exceeded domestic income.

As the author David Goldblatt, reflecting on three decades of hyperglobal rise and rise of the Premier League, noted in *The Guardian* in August 2022: 'First, the Premier League outstripped domestic viewership. Then the entire foreign XI fielded by Chelsea in 1999 announced the globalisation of the league's labour market; foreign players now make up threequarters of the clubs' squads. Foreign managers, once entirely absent, are now in the majority, as are foreign owners, who hold majority stakes in 16 of the 20 clubs.'

Ownership can be a contentious subject for all stakeholders of a football club, but particularly so for football fans. There were fateful days in April 2021 when the owners of 12 of Europe's biggest clubs, including six from the Premier League, unveiled plans for a European Super League (ESL), a breakaway competition to rival UEFA's Champions League. In just three days, the plans were kicked into touch by a rebellion led by English supporters of some of the major Premier League clubs. Leaks of the ESL plan had its powerful club executives describing domestic football supporters as 'legacy fans'. The suggestion was that traditional home-based support was perceived by some club owners as a poor relation to an overseas armchair fan base or 'fans of the future'. What the ESL had in mind was maximising profits through global expansion with like-minded invitation-only clubs. But it encountered a backlash from fans of the clubs involved, as well as politicians, governing bodies like UEFA and clubs that felt side-lined.

The fans' outrage over plans for the ESL was based on fears of a gradual erosion of community-based loyalties and the creation of a new world dominated by a select group of rich clubs and matches that only those who could afford travel and high ticket-pricing could enjoy watching live.

Yet, airbrushed from such a narrative was the extent to which fans, complicit in the evolving business of English football, had colluded with the controversial foreign ownership of some clubs, cheering from the side-lines. At Stamford Bridge in 2022, less than a year after the fans' revolt against the ESL, Newcastle United fans barracked their Chelsea homologues with a banner that read 'We're richer than you'. In October 2021 the British billionaire retail entrepreneur Mike Ashley had sold Newcastle for £305m to Saudi Arabia's hugely rich Public Investment fund, a thinly disguised adjunct of the Saudi regime. To the question as to why the desert-dwellers, whose favourite hobbies included horse-racing and hawkery, had taken an interest in an apparently declining symbol of north-east England's working man's pride, the English football writer Jim White had an answer.

'Because they (the Saudis) know full well that every challenge the new turbocharged club makes for trophies, and every victory they achieve is a giant twin tub to launder the reputation of one of the world's least attractive dictatorships … As they back a bunch of England-based footballers charmingly decked-out in shirts designed to resemble barcodes, it will make them appear benevolent investors, helping to revive a much-loved sleeping giant of a civic institution… In the modern sporting world, money talks. And the least attractive people talk the loudest,' White wrote in his column in *The Oldie* magazine in August 2022.

Justin, a Newcastle fan told me: 'In 2021 an English businessman, the chief of Sports Direct, Mike Ashley sold his 14-year-old ownership of the club to a Saudi-backed consortium for £300m. There may have been some misgivings about the source of the funds that would undoubtedly flow into the club as a result of the takeover. But the fans' greater concern was to get rid of Ashley after 14 years of perceived chronic under-investment and poor management, and to see their club progress to a position where it could challenge for titles rather than having to fight off relegation every season. There was therefore considerable excitement around the fans of Newcastle stadium St James' Park for a new era in the club's rich history.'

Perhaps it was true that English football fans still worshipped at the temples of Newcastle's St James' Park, Manchester City's Etihad or Arsenal's Emirates, as their ancestors did in church. The game was not exactly the opiate of the masses, as Karl Marx said, but it was big business enjoyed by millions. As Gary Lineker commented in BBC Two's *Kicking Off: The Rise and Fall of the Super League*: 'Football is not a religion. But it's not far off for many people. They don't want it messed around with.'

What price your soul? English fans in recent years have welcomed transfusions of large amounts of money, without questioning its provenance, and transfer fees leading to six-figure weekly salaries, and players' shirts sullied not with blood and tears but with sponsorship logos, some of which tempt the financially and psychologically vulnerable to gamble with money they don't have to pay the bills with, let alone support their children's education.

Despite an All-Party Parliamentary Group on gambling-related harm and campaigners calling for tighter regulation to protect children and other vulnerable groups, by the latter stages of the 2022/23 season there was still no government action and football clubs seemed confident they had seen off any threat of banning gambling sponsorship by law. Instead, a plan being discussed by the Premier League would have it agreeing voluntarily to changes to the front of shirts, leaving betting companies to promote themselves in Premier League stadiums and also on other parts of club shirts. The BBC reported in February 2023 that eight of the 20 Premier League clubs displayed gambling company names on the front of their shirts, although they were banned from junior replica kits.

As noted in a report by *Brand Finance* in 2021, the promise of investment into a club in the form of stadium expansion, improved training facilities and increased spending in the transfer market was a lucrative proposition. 'There is no greater proof of the benefits of a large investment from a foreign owner than that of Manchester City, who since being taken over by the Abu Dhabi Investment United Group have gone on to win five Premier League titles, two FA Cups and six League Cups. The benefits of the vast investments that foreign owners have the potential to make, extend beyond the field of play too, with the Greater Manchester community benefitting from the gentrification of the area.'

However, the counter-argument for foreign ownership was that there were some investors who lacked an in-depth understanding and respect for the traditions and history of a football club, and this developed poor relations with fans. In August 2022, thousands of Manchester United fans marched to Old Trafford before the Monday night game against Liverpool in protest at the club's ownership by the US Glazer family who had owned it since 2005. A 'United for sale' banner featuring a photo of British billionaire Sir Jim Ratcliffe, who seemed to have a greater emotional connection with United and had indicated he was interested in buying the club, was on display during the walk.

United's home league game against Liverpool in May 2021 was postponed because of fan protests. The fixture was meant to be played behind closed doors because of the coronavirus pandemic but thousands of United supporters gathered outside the ground in the hours before the scheduled kick-off and around 200 then broke into the stadium.

As Dan Coombs explained on the Red Devils' fans website United in Focus in August 2022: 'The Glazers are the only owners in English football to take out dividends to pay themselves, collecting around £11 million twice a year. The club's debt stands at £500 million, and is no closer to being paid off. United's income simply goes towards paying interest payments on the debt, rather than reducing it.'

The romantic idea around which many fans revolve is that players wearing their club colours have somehow committed themselves to values and identity of enduring vitality. The feeling of communality is a sentiment that requires a significant suspension of disbelief, wrote *The Guardian*'s Jonathan Wilson, further commenting in August 2022, 'Players will move on for better offers. Clubs will jettison players they no longer need just as quickly ... Football is a brutal, mercenary world, the sense that it somehow matters based not quite on a fiction, but on something that is, at best, fleeting and ephemeral.'

Chelsea fans who protested against the ESL, chanted in support of their Russian owner Roman Abramovich, even as Putin's army and air force was pounding Ukrainians, before welcoming the club's new owner, a consortium led by the Los Angeles Dodgers baseball club's part-owner, the US financier Todd Boehly, whose acquisition in a £4.25bn deal, was the biggest of any football club in history. The sum, surpassing the £790m paid by the Glazer family for Manchester United, freed Chelsea from British government restrictions relating to sanctions imposed on Abramovich, who had owned the club for nearly two decades. As part of the UK's sanctions against Russian funds, Chelsea had been unable to acquire or unload players or renegotiate contracts with existing squad members while operating under a special licence. The intervention by the British government in the few weeks it lasted was the closest an English club has come to being nationalised in the 30 years of the Premier League's existence. It revived the frustrated dreams some English fans had of taking greater ownership of their clubs.

The new owner, Boehly, a capitalist not a socialist, wasted little time in pursuing a lavish spending spree, with Wesley Fofana, Raheem Sterling, Kalidou Koulibaly,

Carney Chukwuemeka, Marc Cucurella, and Pierre-Emerick Aubameyang all bought by Chelsea for significant transfer fees as the new season got under way. Chelsea were the biggest spenders in the Premier League in the summer of 2022, with a record total estimated at £261 million (United were the second biggest spenders). The total spend for the whole of England's top division was also record-breaking, topping the £2bn mark by the time the summer window closed at the beginning of September.

Like a lot of businesses, English football clubs' revenue plummeted during the first full year of the pandemic but by the start of the new season in 2022/23 the Premier League was looking richer than ever.

Nor did Brexit seem to impact negatively on the Premier League. Through Brexit, the UK government's declared aim was to take control of its borders, money and laws while protecting its economy, security and Union. In practice, it was sectors like student and lower-paid employee mobility, trade in certain goods and tourism that were negatively affected. But fears that international player recruitment and sales involving the Premier League might be similarly impacted under Brexit, ending the freedom of movement between the UK and the EU, did not materialise. Signings from EU countries were now subject to the same permit guidelines, including a points-based system based on international and club appearances and the reputation of the seller, as those applying previously to transfer of players from outside the EU. But while this arguably opened up the market for senior players and stimulated transfers between Premier League clubs, the jury was out on the impact of Brexit rules that banned the signing of under-18-year-old overseas players. While previously such players may have been brought in by a Premier club as potential future high-value stars, the ban shifted their focus to recruiting standout young talents from clubs within the UK and fulfilling the homegrown quota for squads in the Premier League and Champions League.

Arsène Wenger, the Frenchman who won Arsenal hearts and minds as one of the Premier League's most intelligent, trailblazing managers, warned in June 2020 (the UK had voted to leave the EU in 2016) that Brexit could have a negative impact on English top-flight football, predicting that it could result in the best players going to other countries instead of England. The 2022/23 transfer market proved him wrong.

What certainly is true is that one early ramification of Brexit was that of consolidating the financial muscle of the elite clubs, with less predictable consequences for smaller clubs. Unlike English clubs in the lower divisions, the richer mega-clubs seemed to have little difficulty in being active on the foreign as well as domestic transfer market, while the Premier League's publicity on its 30th anniversary reassured the public that the money being spent would go into improving the UK's grassroots football and young British footballers.

Meanwhile the best foreign managers in the world, mostly Europeans, consolidated an unrivalled position in the Premier League in a Brexit Britain. Of the 20 Premier club managers that began the new season in August 2022, over half were European, with seven British, and one American. The shift to foreign coaches was a trend established pre-Brexit because they achieved the best results and return on investment. This was reflected in the fact that of the 11 managers who lifted the Premier League trophy in the three decades following its foundation, apart from Scots Kenny Dalglish and Alex Ferguson, all came from outside the UK, mostly hailing from Europe. The one exception Chilean Manuel Pellegrini.

From 2007 to 2013, Ferguson won the Premier League title with Manchester United five times, Wenger won three league titles at Arsenal in 1997/98, 2001/02 and 2003/04 and Carlo Ancelotti won Chelsea's third Premier League title in 2009/10.

Claudio Ranieri stands out as the most memorable underdog winner from possibly all 11 managers to have lifted the trophy. His appointment was followed by Leicester City winning the Premier in the 2015/16 season. Antonio Conte was the seventh foreign manager to win the title and he did it the following season with Chelsea. José Mourinho won successive titles in 2004/05 and 2005/06, and in 2014/15 during his second spell at the club.

In 2019/20, Klopp guided Liverpool to their first top-flight title in 30 years. Guardiola won four Premier League titles in his first five seasons at Manchester City. In two of them, Guardiola's side beat Liverpool to the crown by one point.

Carlo Ancelotti claimed one victory for Chelsea and Roberto Mancini one for Manchester City. Since Ferguson's last triumph, six managers have steered four different teams to the pinnacle of English football and none of them have been British.

As Wenger recognised, the Premier League depends on worldwide exposure, with the best players and worldwide ownership, with multi-billionaire owners from around the world. The Frenchman told English journalists in June 2022, 'I believe you're intelligent enough in England and love football enough not to destroy what is basically a diamond.'

Paradoxically, the scale and nature of foreign ownership and the global nature of the Premier's TV rights and players, is a very English story. England has historically been a land that has attracted exiles, elites and immigrants, with its two biggest cities, Manchester and London, maintaining multicultural societies that belie the reputation for exclusion and insularity that the more extreme nationalists among the most virulent Brexiteers campaigned for. English football continues to offer glimpses of another more diverse and caring England – and here I would highlight the victory of the English women in the Euro championships, the anti-racist stance taken by a generation of Premier League players and clubs and United's Marcus Rashford's campaign in support of alleviating poverty.

And yet the astronomical salaries football stars earn compared to ordinary 'non-elite' workers, pensioners and others scraping enough money to pay their energy bills in the winter, seem at best unreasonable, at worst scandalous.

# Chapter Twenty-one

# Snapshots of a New Season

THE START of the 2022/23 season, which marked the 30th anniversary of the founding of the Premier League, saw Chelsea away from home to Everton at Goodison Park. The sheer vocal support of fans – loyal for better or for worse, in baking sun as in chilling pouring rain, as is the nature of so many English club followers – lifts the spirits of Everton, the club seemingly condemned to being considered the 'other' Liverpool club and that much of the world chooses to ignore. Those fans had already played a critical part in the battle to avoid relegation from the Premier League in 2022, under the newly appointed manager, former Chelsea player Frank Lampard.

Goodison Park – one of the oldest stadiums still standing in the Premier League – is a venue where Chelsea had not won a match in six seasons. In August 2022, the visiting club was coming to terms with the meaning of the post-Abramovich era, with new owners and a team trying to forge a strategy in a frenzied transfer climate.

Memories of Chelsea's last win at Goodison Park in April 2007 merely served to underline how far Chelsea has fallen behind what appeared to be the two dominating forces of the Premier League, Manchester City and Liverpool, and their stronger London rival, Tottenham Hotspur. The statistics alone may not tell the full story of the beating heart and less noble financial shenanigans of the Premier League, but they were revealing none-the-less in terms of what made the difference between victory and defeat. In the 2016/17 season, Chelsea finished on the brink of the league title, with Antonio Conte's side scoring 85 times, starring players of the quality of Diego Costa (20 goals) and Eden Hazard (16). In subsequent seasons, Chelsea's score tally dipped – 62, 63, 69, 58, and 76. Compare this over the same period with Manchester City – 99, 83, 102, 95, 106, 80 – and Liverpool – 94, 68, 85, 89, 84 and 78. The overall difference to City was 152 goals and 85 to Liverpool.

Chelsea's manager Thomas Tuchel began a new season, 2022/23, conscious that he might have to quit or wait to be sacked if Chelsea failed to reach the next season's Champions League. (He was sacked the following month.)

Of the opening matches of the season, Everton v Chelsea proved the most lacklustre. Despite the early summer splurge by Chelsea's new co-owner Todd Boehly, on Raheem Sterling and Kalidou Koulibaly, the club seemed to mirror the poorer Everton with their lack of effective play. As Chelsea captain César Azpilicueta said after a game in which his team secured a 1-0 win through a Jorginho penalty: 'It is five seasons since the last time we won the Premier League. We need to score goals if we want to win anything.

'Lately, the last couple of games in the Premier League, we didn't score enough and with a half-chance we concede. So that's our problem, and that's why we finished third, 20 or more points behind Manchester City.'

Chelsea's new signing, Sterling, deployed as a 'false 9' with Kai Havertz and Mason Mount on either side of him, lacked consistency, and the team lacked a natural goal scorer. And yet Chelsea's defence also seemed in need of renovation, with Tuchel appearing to make an argument as to why Chelsea should step up their efforts to sign £85m-rated Wesley Fofana, the Leicester City left-back, which they did before the summer transfer window expired in September. At the age of 21, the long-term future that Fofana might provide contrasted with the reality that three of Chelsea's defence force – Azpilicueta (33 in August 2022), Thiago Silva (38 in September) and Kalidou Koulibaly (31) – had a combined age of more than a century.

As for Everton, spare a thought for the young player of undisputed potential, Antony Gordon who had the luckless task of being asked by Lampard to play as a makeshift number 9 and who found himself the butt of less than generous comments from Everton fans, noting that his newly dyed blond hair simply underlined his poor heading ability.

Hair styles, like clothes have a tendency to come in and out of fashion, in football and in other celebrity circles. In the mid- to late 1990s, it suddenly became popular for everyone to dye their hair peroxide blond, with the likes of Paul 'Gazza' Gascoigne and Robbie Fowler setting the trend among English footballers. The style was everywhere at the start of a new millennium, then disappeared, before coming back again in 2016 and it seemed there were several footballers who were happy to bleach. We saw superstars like Messi and Neymar temporarily discarding their naturally dark crop of hair.

The England squad promised to all dye their hair blond if they won the European Championships in 2021. They didn't. England lost to Italy in the final in a penalty shoot-out. One player, Phil Foden, who had dyed blond, reverted to his natural colour, while he and his team-mates focused on 'taking the knee' in the spirit of anti-racism.

\* \* \*

*7 August 2022: Super Sunday*
Manchester United, once regarded as one of the best-loved and most successful clubs in the world, had yet to recover the glory days they had experienced under the legendary Alex Ferguson, whose achievements no successor had managed to emulate.

The club's latest 'boss', the Dutch former Ajax manager, Erik ten Hag, the fifth man appointed to take the helm since Ferguson, was under huge pressure to resurrect a club that has failed for so long. Not since Johan Cruyff moved from Holland to FC Barcelona in the 1970s, had a move from Holland generated such expectation in a legendary club in desperate need of regeneration.

Part of the initial challenge facing Ten Hag was what to do with Cristiano Ronaldo, the media controversy over whether he should stay or go proving an unresolved distraction in the build-up to the new season. Ronaldo, at the age of 37, was evidently a different proposition to the 18-year-old Ronaldo that Ferguson had signed from Sporting Lisbon back in August 2003, when Beckham left Manchester United for Real Madrid. As David Conn wrote in *The Guardian* in January 2011: 'Manchester United's signing of a callow, improbably talented Cristiano Ronaldo in August 2003 was a defining moment for the Premier League and modern football itself, heralding a dazzling new superstar for a fledgling millennium.'

Ronaldo once called the signing of his first United contract 'a dream' fulfilled. He had been a fervent follower and full of admiration for the Red Devils and their treble-winning team. Few football fans can forget that Manchester United team and their achievement that for two decades would not be equalled: that of winning the Premier League, the FA Cup and the European Cup. 'Remember' – that was the one word that Ferguson wrote down as he emerged from a brain haemorrhage in 2018. He remembered the team of mainly young, gifted players – Beckham, Scholes, Giggs, Sheringham, Gary Neville, Butt, Giggs, Keane – all were under Ferguson's patriarchal influence, the supreme commander. Ferguson was more master motivator than master tactician, of the old school, before women laid their claim to top-flight football: 'Tactics don't win football matches. Men win football matches,' Ferguson would say.

His dressing room talks were not master classes on whiteboards but rousing tribal rallying cries on the eve of battle. Young men, some of whom he had known since they were children, were told to remember the sacrifices of their parents and grandparents.

When the BBC journalist Nick Robinson interviewed Ronaldo for a documentary on Ferguson, the player was asked what made the Scotsman such a great manager. The reply came back: 'He is my Daddy in football.' Ronaldo's own Madeiran father Dinis Aveiro, who served as a conscript with the army in Angola when it was a Portuguese colony, died as a tragic alcoholic while the player was in his first period at United.

The Ronaldo who arrived in Manchester in the summer of 2003 was a star in the making, a prodigy as far as technique and skill were concerned, but immature, exuberant and selfish. Ferguson helped him grow in character, and as a player, working on him like a master jeweller might polish a precious diamond. The young Cristiano, from his early days in Manchester, had a personality that grated with some team-mates and broad sections of the media, because of his narcissism, which was out of step with the club's team ethos, and which challenged the macho culture that had long prevailed in English football. Ronaldo's showboating on and off the pitch was in no small measure a response to his burning desire to be noticed, the need some naturally gifted players had to show off their talent; but he was determined to get to a point when what he showed off was of such brilliance that anyone who watched him was in awe of his talent.

On 1 November 2003, ten games into his first season in the Premier League, Ronaldo finally opened his account in a match against Portsmouth, when he took what would come to be seen as one of his trademark free kicks – curling the ball in at an angle from the left, over the wall and into the net.

In his first six years at Manchester United, Ronaldo scored 118 goals in 292 games, winning three Premier League titles, the Champions League, the FA Cup and two League Cups. He is worthy of being remembered for having completed one of the most remarkable periods of high performance the English game has ever seen. Bravado and showmanship backed up by huge creativity and awe-inspiring goals. Defenders seemed to bounce off him; he had an extra yard of pace and vastly more mental acuity. The ball always seemed to be breaking into his path or popping up at the far post as he arrived. Across the country, fans debated what the secret to his free kicks was and whether they were possible to stop. He succeeded nationally and internationally.

In December 2008, he won his first *Ballon D'Or*. Ronaldo's triumph made him the first Manchester United player to claim the award since George Best in 1968, joining Denis Law (1964) and Bobby Charlton (1966) in United's Golden Ball pantheon. The two other players from the English league who had won the *Ballon D'Or* were Stanley Matthews (1956) and Michael Owen (2001). No other Premier League player has won the award since (at the time of writing), but Ronaldo went on to win it four more times when he was at Real Madrid.

For ten years of pre-Covid club history (2008-2018), Ronaldo shared with Messi the accolade of best elite footballer in the world, each winning five prestigious *Ballon D'Or* titles and extending the potential of modern football with the unprecedented scope of their achievement. They broke goal-scoring records as well as showing extraordinary physical resilience and sublime skills that had firmly established them both in a leading position among the pantheon of sporting gods.

As the *La Liga* 2017/18 season reached its end on 17 May, Ronaldo scored two goals in Real Madrid's match against Celta Vigo, breaking Jimmy Greaves's record as the all-time top scorer in the top five European leagues and securing a championship title that had evaded '*los blancos*' since 2012. He also contributed to Real Madrid's successful European campaign, scoring a spectacular bicycle kick in the quarter-final against Juventus, before going on to win his own fifth Champions League title in the final against Liverpool on 26 May. He finished his campaign that season with a total of 15 goals and was the top scorer of the tournament for the sixth season running.

Real Madrid fans were not unanimously happy with Ronaldo's departure to Juventus that summer. Many of them felt it was worth paying him more to keep him at the club. They respected what he had achieved and believed in what he still had in him, given his unflagging athleticism. In his sensational nine seasons at Real Madrid, he had defined a golden era, scoring 450 goals and helping to win European championships, easily overtaking Raul as the club's all-time top scorer.

In his first season at Juventus, given that he and Messi now played in different national leagues, it was inevitable that it was at the highest competitive level of the Champions League that their rivalry came under greater scrutiny. Ronaldo was instrumental in taking Juventus to the top of *Serie A* but also helping his team heroically overcome a 0-2 deficit against Simeone's Atlético Madrid in the second leg of their last 16 clash in the Champions League . In the quarter-finals, Ronaldo scored an away goal against Ajax with a spectacular header, precise and powerful, his fifth Champions League goal of the season. It confirmed Ronaldo as the top goal scorer in the history of the Champions League, with 125 goals to Messi's 108. But Ajax fought back in Turin, Juventus lost on aggregate and Ronaldo's hopes of winning another European crown were dashed.

Ronaldo's return to Manchester United at the start of the 2021/22 season was a public relations dream, lifting fans from their Covid gloom and raising expectations that the good times were back. The club was under the management of Ole Gunnar Solskjaer, who was most famously remembered as a player for his part in the 1999 Champions League Final heroics. That night, United turned what seemed certain defeat into victory by scoring two goals in stoppage time. Solskjaer came off the bench and within ten minutes prodded home the winning goal against Bayern Munich in the Nou Camp. Within 20 seconds, the final whistle had sounded and the most stunning comeback imaginable had been completed.

His return to the Premier League had Ronaldo's Instagram account, among the most-followed globally, going into overdrive. His post read, 'Everyone who knows me, knows about my never-ending love for Manchester United. The years I spent in this club were absolutely amazing and the path we've made together is written in gold letters in the history of this great and amazing institution. I can't even start to explain my feelings right now, as I see my return to Old Trafford announced worldwide. It's like a dream come true, after all the times that I went back to play against Man United, and even as an opponent, to have always felt such love and respect from the supporters in the stands. This is absolutely 100 per cent the stuff that dreams are made of!

'My first domestic league, my first cup, my first call to the Portuguese national team, my first Champions League, my first Golden Boot and my first *Ballon d'Or*, they were all born from this special connection between me and the Red Devils. History has been written in the past and history will be written once again! You have my word. I'm right here! I'm back where I belong! Let's make it happen once again! PS – Sir Alex, this one is for you.'

But it was tilting at windmills. United had come second in the Premier League in the previous season, thus qualifying for the Champions League , and they added two star signings to their squad – Jadon Sancho and Raphaël Varane. In their first game against a very bad Newcastle, Ronaldo scored twice in a 4-1 win and fans celebrated him as a redeemer. As *The Guardian*'s Jonathan Wilson wrote, 'Grown men wept: the prodigal son had returned.' But then, 'The Solskjaer nostalgia project was derailed … frolic in past glories obscured the chaos of the present. Solskjaer's football was about sitting deep and striking on the break, but Ronaldo meant there was no pace in the forward line. The game plan disintegrated.'

In November 2021, Solskjaer was sacked after a humiliating defeat by Watford in a dismal run that had left the manager facing mounting criticism and played havoc with the club's morale. Former midfielder Michael Carrick took charge for the next three games, before the appointment of the German Ralf Rangnick as interim manager until the end of the season. On 21 April 2022, Erik ten Hag was announced as the manager from the end of the season, signing a contract until June 2025 with the option of extending for a further year.

During the 2021/22 season Ronaldo scored 18 goals, eight more than anybody else in the squad, but accommodating him meant United managed 16 fewer goals than in the 2020/21 season and ended in 13th place, their worst finish in Premier League history.

As the new 2022/23 Premier campaign got under way, Ronaldo remained, wrote Jonathan Wilson, 'a totem of a club that, having lost faith in its capacity for the future, knows only how to look back.'

On Super Sunday, 7 August, one of the most totemic stadiums in world football, Old Trafford, was the scene for United's first game of the season, against Brighton & Hove Albion FC – better known as Brighton, one of southern England's most popular seaside resorts, hence the club's crest and nickname 'the Seagulls'. Compared to United's glory days, Brighton had little in their history to boast about. Their financial power was far less than that of the Red

Devils who had built a global brand, made-to-measure for the Premier League.

In the late 1990s, Brighton were in the lower tiers of English football and were having financial difficulties. After narrowly avoiding further relegation in 1997, a boardroom takeover saved the club from liquidation. Successive promotions in 2001 and 2002 brought Brighton back to the second tier. The club was a late-comer to the big spectacle, promoted to the Premier League in the 2017/18 season, ending a 34-year absence from the top flight.

Brighton were a low-budget club that punched above their weight. They cut good deals, bought players from very obscure clubs, but some of those players had real potential, like the Belgian Leandro Trossard. Their manager Graham Potter was credited with having done a reasonable job of building a team with humility – not a defining trait among the more internationally famous managers. His reward, halfway through the season, was to be snapped up by Chelsea – only to be ditched.

By contrast, United's reputation had floundered, according to their most acerbic critics, thanks to being undermined by their ownership under the Glazers and the unwieldy superstructure they had set up, with multiple advisers and consultants and brains trusts, all of them feeding into a board that seemed to regularly get its big decisions wrong.

Among the fans, the jury was out as to whether one of the club's biggest errors of recent times was bringing back Ronaldo on £26.8m a year, when he was 38 years old, an age that for most players represented a declining phase of their career, and when other clubs who could afford him did not seem to want him. Supporters who wanted him to stay pointed to his 24 goals in 38 games in the last season. He remained an iconic figure, an enduring memory of his stardom during the best of the Ferguson era, and there was no doubting his impressive form in *La Liga* at Real Madrid, and at international level as Portugal's talisman. Such was Ronaldo's celebrity mass-following that even a club with such a great history as United ended up being drawn into its gravitational field.

Ronaldo, on his return from summer holidays in 2022, signalled he would like a transfer in pursuit of another Champions League triumph that would put him statistically beyond the reach of Messi, who with PSG had a guaranteed place in the biggest European club tournament. United had failed to qualify.

After a disastrous previous season under his predecessor, United's new manager Ten Hag had stepped into the hottest of football hotseats, with a mission to rebuild a champion team that while not excluding him, was not dependent on Ronaldo. The first game of the season began with the superstar's ego dented, on the bench.

United played badly from the outset. Ronaldo and Ten Hag were a study in contrasts. The player raised his arms in the air to rally the fans, while Ten Hag showed no sign of emotion, surveying the players dispassionately like a stoic Dutch general who felt his one priority was to keep faith in his troops without raising his voice.

Brighton easily tore through a ragged United defence and Pascal Gross scored one goal in the 30th minute and a second nine minutes later. The England manager Gareth Southgate was among those watching from the VIP section. Three England internationals – Marcus Rashford, Luke Shaw and Harry Maguire – underperformed. United were mocked by the chanting of the Brighton fans and booed at half-time by their own followers. It all looked too easy for Brighton, the minnows, and United seemed a team without shape or purpose, staring down a black hole.

From the commentator's box, the ex-Manchester United player Roy Keane – part of the club's legacy of past glories – told an audience of millions that Ronaldo must be brought into the game, and he was, seven minutes into the second half.

Ten Hag was left with no option but to bring on Ronaldo in the hope that he could galvanise the troops, writing his own script in a way that has made him one of the best players in the world. There was a palpable uplift in the atmosphere in Old Trafford, with the belief that United's ragged performance at least now has a focal point of genius in the attack.

But the expected touch or two of magic was missing and when United's first and only goal of the match was scored it was the result of a poor clearance that backfired into the net as an own goal by Brighton's Alexis Mac Allister.

Brighton, with no superstars to speak of, cheekily showed off their skills in an extended period of possession to the sound of '*Ole*'s' from their fans, and hung on to their lead to increasingly loud cheers from their faithful.

To a growing number of United fans, the team, with or without Ronaldo, was in urgent need of a major overhaul. As for the club culture under the Glazers, focusing on making money as much as making footballing memories, it needed to change.

Premier League history is not short of games in which David slays Goliath, but the presence of Ronaldo in a United shirt unable to crush a club that barely registered as a known entity outside English shores had a memorable feel about it, savoured by Brighton fans, not least the older ones.

After the match, I received a text from an old friend who had watched the game in South Africa. 'For years and years my late uncle, a wounded veteran of the Great War suffered as he watched Brighton & Hove Albion remain at the bottom of the [then] Third Division. He would have enjoyed seeing Brighton beating Manchester United.'

* * *

On 22 August 2022, Manchester United restored a sense of hope among their fans, securing their first win of their season at Old Trafford, beating Liverpool with goals by Rashford and Sancho and leapfrogging their old northern enemy in the Premier League table. Manager Ten Hag declared: 'We can talk about technique but it's all about attitude. Now you see we bring the attitude. There was communication, there was a fighting spirit and especially there was a team, and you can see what they can achieve. Because they can play good football.'

Ronaldo stayed on the bench throughout the game and the team seemed to work better without him. His future continued to be the subject of debate. The journalist and long-term Manchester United fan Andy Mitten was near prophetic in his *The Athletic* podcast: 'Ten Hag played it well. He saw the impact on this happy squad when he brought them home from the tour and Ronaldo joined it – the mood didn't improve, it got worse. If that negative can be turned into a positive, I think Ronaldo can still offer United something great, but there's got to be some compromise from his side. Ten Hag has got to think of the collective, not just about one player.'

\* \* \*

### 7 August 2022: West-Ham vs Manchester City

Of all the encounters on the first weekend of the new Premier season, this Super Sunday match was one that guaranteed spectacle, entertainment, tough play and huge skill.

Clubs up and down the country had rebuilt their squads ahead of one of the most anticipated seasons of all time. Teams had spent big money over the summer, ready to confirm the Premier as the best and most competitive league in the world.

One club that had carefully gone about their business, and by all accounts with largely underrated transfer activity, was West Ham United. Four departing players included club legend Mark Noble who ended his long association with the Hammers, as he retired at the end of the season. Born just a stone's throw away from the club in Canning Town, Noble had made 472 appearances in an 18-year club career.

Despite wanting to go one better in the new season, West Ham had remained patient and spent wisely. Their star signing was the Italian international Gianluca Scamacca who had left *Serie A* club Sassuolo for a Premier League stint, joining for an initial £32 million. Scamacca was the striker West Ham needed. For a while in the match against Manchester City, he led the line very well.

Another element in West Ham's favour was that the club had managed to retain, despite attempts by United and Chelsea to sign him, the talented English international, 23-year-old Declan Rice. A defensive-minded midfielder, who was known for his tenacity and clean tackling, Rice had recently told a small audience of English journalists. 'Do you know what? Until this day, I have never had a beer and I am 22,' the West Ham and England midfielder told *The Guardian*'s David Hytner, 'That is the truth, never had a pint. Don't drink it.'

Rice had sacrificed plenty on his journey to the top, which had ramped up in earnest over the past few seasons. 'When I moved from home [in Kingston-upon-Thames] to West Ham at 14 [after his release from Chelsea], that was a sacrifice,' he said. 'Obviously, loads of parties with best friends. Going out on weekends, the drinking side of it – seeing all of my mates partying, sending me videos while I'm stuck in hotels.'

West Ham were unfazed by the prospect of facing bigger richer clubs. They relished it, and fans could not ask for a better challenge to kick off the new season in August 2022 than facing Guardiola's thoroughbreds on a celebrity stage made to measure. There was a record crowd of 62,000 at West Ham's impressive new London Stadium, one of the most dynamic flagship venues in the UK. Built to host the London 2012 Olympics, the stadium had become home to West Ham United and UK Athletics along with other crowd-pulling events such as rock concerts, the Rugby World Cup, and the first Major League Baseball games to be played in

Europe. With a commitment to serve as the heart of the local community, the stadium's stand-out features included the longest cantilevered roof in the world and re-configurable lower-tier seating that brought West Ham's passionate football fans closer to the action while providing the flexibility to reveal additional floor space for concerts and athletics. The stadium has a hothouse atmosphere on the big occasions and West Ham fans like to remind visitors why they take pride in their reputation as among the most hostile and loudest in the Premier League.

The match on that early August day nonetheless underlined the quality and skills that Guardiola's Manchester City could draw on to demolish a motivated team not lacking in talent – after all, Guardiola had so far managed to come out on top in one of the most extraordinary rivalries of modern club history, head-to-head with Klopp's Liverpool.

Guardiola was a proven master of the modern game. Over the previous year, Manchester City's playing style had continued to evolve. Guardiola's teams always kept the ball for long periods but now they were doing it more slowly, before suddenly speeding up, looking for that killer goal, the one that does most damage – and now the team had a proven goal scorer in the newly signed Norwegian Erling Haaland.

His first goal for Manchester City came after half an hour, after West Ham's first-choice goalkeeper Łukasz Fabiański was forced out with an injury and was replaced by Alphonse Areola. Less than five minutes later, Haaland picked up a pass from İlkay Gündoğan between the two centre-halves, and with an extraordinary display of strength and pace, powered his way behind a deep-lying defence, forcing Areola to rush and commit himself, and trip the Norwegian, who had reached the ball first. Haaland coolly took a penalty shot that easily beat Areola.

Ignoring the boos of the West Ham fans, Haaland headed off and sat in a Zen-like pose of a man at peace, if not with the world, certainly with Pep Guardiola and the Premier League, replicating the faith the Catalan had in the Norwegian not just as a talented player but a born winner who was young and with a great future.

City's second goal came in the 65th minute, in a sequence of pure tactical genius and execution. With West Ham pressing them right back into their own half, City kept calm in possession and played the ball, with Kevin De Bruyne delivering the perfect pass to Haaland, who scored.

After the match, Guardiola reflected: 'The way he [Haaland] took the ball to take the penalty, I said "Oh, I like it". I think if someone were to take the ball, he would have punched his team-mates in the face. That is a good sign. You've got to be self-confident, ambitious and have a ruthless mentality.

'And of course, he scored it. I was fortunate as a manager to be with Messi and if he scored three, he wanted four and if he got four, he wanted five. The top goal scorers, the strikers, they are never satisfied. They are always hungry, starving, they always want more and more.'

Haaland had struggled to impose himself in his first City appearance, against Liverpool in the Community Shield match prior to the start of the Premier season. But he had few doubters after becoming the second City player to score two goals on his Premier League debut, after Agüero in August 2011. Some people had thought Haaland might be a player who would not adapt to the Premier League. Now they were saying he was going to be an Alan Shearer. Haaland was the stand-out player on the first weekend of a new Premier season and his combination play with De Bruyne drew comparison with some of the legendary partnerships in the modern history of English club football: Toshack and Keegan, Dalglish and Rush, Cole and Yorke, Shearer and Sutton. Now Guardiola's latest star mix had the potential to prove the most devastating partnership in European football.

In that Super Sunday clash, after a brief flurry of West Ham attacks in the first few minutes, the visiting team dominated play in the first half, with 373 successful passes compared to 74 by Moyes' players. Manchester City remained a team of champions, West Ham a team with a beating heart and a loud mouth.

* * *

*Conte's Tottenham Summer 2022*

YouTube images of Tottenham players vomiting during gruelling sprint sessions in Korea in July 2022 went viral. It was a reminder, in case anyone had forgotten, that Tottenham's manager Antonio Conte was among the toughest task-masters in the Premier League, almost to an obsessive degree, and it brought results. 'Eat Grass' was Conte's legendary message to players when he was manager of Juventus, by which he meant, work harder, run further than anybody else.

Conte was appointed Tottenham's manager in November 2021, replacing Nuno Espírito Santo, who was fired by the club's owner after 17 games in charge.

Juventus was only one of the names on Conte's impressive curriculum vitae as a player and manager. During nearly two decades as a coach, he had been in charge of Chelsea, Inter Milan and Italy's national team. Conte was no stranger to the pressure of high-level European football – but on his return to the increasingly competitive and high-quality Premier, he was facing perhaps the biggest challenge of his career. His mission at Tottenham was to lift the club above and beyond the level achieved under Pochettino when Spurs finished second in the 2016/17 season, their highest league placing since the 1962/63 season, and when they advanced to the UEFA Champions League Final in May 2019, where they lost to Liverpool.

As the Tottenham fans roared across the impressive new Tottenham Hotspur Stadium in the first match of the Premier League against Southampton, Conte's players came out quite literally as giants – pumped up and fit, the average height of his team was more than 6ft. The squad had also noticeably increased in quality of depth thanks to an intelligent, structured recruitment which covered various areas of the team. While none of the six summer signings, Ivan Perišić, Fraser Forster, Yves Bissouma, Richarlison, Clément Lenglet and Djed Spence, were named in the starting team, it was soon evident that fresh competition in key places in defence and attack had raised the levels of existing players at Spurs.

Under Conte, the squad had been greatly improved to the point that it was considered among the strongest in the Premier League. Tottenham functioned as a coherent team with players combining well. They could be more pragmatic than Liverpool and Manchester City, winning the ball back quickly and letting their more versatile players excel.

Richarlison came in from Everton for £60 million, making him, by some distance, Tottenham's most expensive signing over the summer. The Brazilian star was suspended by the Football Association for the game against Southampton after being charged for throwing a flare into the stands during Everton's win against Chelsea the previous season.

For the price paid for him, Richarlison had his sights set on becoming a regular first-team starter. Working in Richarlison's favour was the fact there would be no shortage of opportunities, as Conte rotated his players to keep them fresh and made strategic in-game changes across four competitions.

Harry Kane remained a key part of Conte's armoury but Tottenham's impressive 4-1 victory over Southampton, with three different scorers – Sessegnon, Eric Dier, and Kulusevski (Southampton's Mohammed Salusi scored an own goal) suggested the club was evolving into a collective project that was not dependent on any one player.

* * *

Of all the matches getting under way at the start of a new season, that between two of the smaller clubs of the Premier, Leicester City and Brentford, was the one that promised to enthuse loyal fans, even if it was not at the top of the watch-list of a wider international audience.

The recent history of each showed that the Premier raised the prospects of smaller clubs promoted from the lower divisions, only to have their optimism dampened when faced with the commanding presence of some of the leading clubs in European club football, who had much bigger treasure chests and could afford to sign up top managers and impressive squads of players that are among the best in the world.

But English football is about more than money. It is about the heart and soul of its fans. Over 30,000 supporters packed into the King Power Stadium to see the home team, Leicester City, one-time Premier champions, and Brentford, one of the less famous London clubs.

Leicester City, founded in 1884 when the city was developing as a major manufacturing and engineering hub of the Victorian era, had had mixed fortunes in the Premier League. They were promoted into the top flight, only to be relegated after finishing second from bottom in the 1994/95 season. They returned to the Premier League before the decade was out and established themselves with four successive top-ten finishes, but then were relegated again at the end of the 2001/02 season.

A period of decline followed, until the club's fortunes revived in spectacular fashion. Leicester started 2014/15, their first season in the Premier League since 2004, with a good run of results in their first five league matches. On 21 September 2014, Leicester went on to produce one of the greatest comebacks in Premier League history when they beat Manchester United at the King Power Stadium after coming back from 3-1 down with 30 minutes left, to score four goals.

Leicester appointed former Chelsea manager Claudio Ranieri as their new manager for the 2015/16 season and despite being widely considered the clear underdogs by the bookies, won the Premier League on 2 May 2016. Leicester, the football club and the city, attracted global attention and several commentators viewed them as an inspiration to other clubs, fundamentally transforming the expectations faced in English football.

The success story was to prove ephemeral. On 23 February 2017, Ranieri was dismissed due to the club's poor form, which had resulted in them being only one point above the relegation zone. By Christmas 2017, Leicester were in eighth position in the Premier League and went on to finish one place lower in ninth at the end of the season. They finished the 2018/19 season again in ninth place. The 2019/20 season, under the new manager Brendan Rodgers, took them to fifth in the table – their second-highest Premier League finish in their history – only to fall back into eighth the following season.

Leicester's 2-2 draw against Brentford at the start of the 2022/23 season, which drew boos from the home support, underlined the structural weakness of their squad and raised the expectation that Rodgers' future might be on the line as, with the arrival of autumn, the club sunk to the bottom of the table.

Leicester had gone into the match against Brentford as the only club in the Premier League not to have invested in new players, while also facing strong interest from the richest clubs in the Premier League for three of their key players, James Maddison, Wesley Fofana, and Youri Tielemans. Fofana would soon be sold for £70m to Chelsea.

The club had kept Jamie Vardy, still a standout figure in the Premier League both as a player and a controversial personality. In the 2021/22 season he broke a record as the most prolific 'old timer' in the Premier. In March 2022, the former England striker struck late in a match against relegation-bound Burnley to make it 94 league goals since he turned 30. But starting a new season in the summer of 2022, Vardy, at 35, looked less sharp than he was when he helped lead his club to championship history. He was destined to find himself on the bench when autumn came, but he was a recognised legend at Leicester. He had come a long way as the son of a crane driver, from working in a carbon fibre factory in Sheffield and having to leave due to the stress on his back.

Vardy had been an obscure name when he joined Fleetwood Town from Halifax of the Northern Premier League, level eight of the English Football League pyramid. Despite his declining form, Vardy's own personal rags-to-riches journey remained a source of inspiration for footballers from lower levels, including the players who had gone into the professional game via Vardy's V9 Academy, which was set up in 2016 with a view to providing non-league talent with a chance to impress.

But the fact remained that Leicester were struggling to remain in the Premier, with their troubled manager Rodgers facing questions over how he could strengthen the squad, and equally crucially whether he could hang on to star players.

The club had invested £100m in a new training ground as way of attracting major signings and also developed home-grown talent which had served Leicester so well in the past. They had also unveiled plans for a new 220-room hotel, an events and entertainment venue and the expansion of the King Power Stadium by 8,000 seats to a total of 40,000 – still only half the size of Old Trafford. When the plans were announced in August 2021, the club stated: 'To continue competing in the Premier League … requires a disciplined, sustainable and innovative business model.' But to compete with the best in the Premier League, you had to get closer to competing with them on the pitch, as well as off it. Leicester's glory days seemed a distant memory.

*Leicester City's open-top bus parade celebrating the club's Premier League title win, 16 May 2016. Chairman Vichai Srivaddhanaprabha and manager Claudio Ranieri are either side of the trophy.*

*Stanley Matthews and Alfredo Di Stefano shake hands before Stoke City host Real Madrid in a friendly match to celebrate the Potters' centenary at the Victoria Ground on 24 April 1963. The game ended 2-2.*

*Euro 96 – Group A – England v Scotland. England's Paul Gascoigne (top) celebrates with team-mate Gary Neville after scoring the second goal.*

*Tottenham Hotspur manager Bill Nicholson looks on as his players enjoy a bath after winning the FA Cup Final 2-0 against Leicester City on 6 May 1961. The victory secured Spurs the first Double of the 20th century.*

*German international striker Jürgen Klinsmann playing for Tottenham Hotspur against Everton on 6 December 1995.*

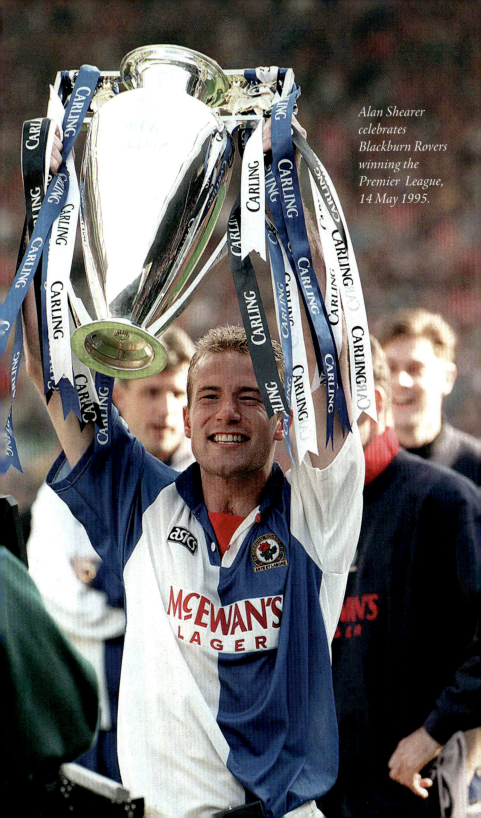

*Alan Shearer celebrates Blackburn Rovers winning the Premier League, 14 May 1995.*

*Newcastle United fans in good voice during the Premier League match at West Ham United's London Stadium on 5 April 2023.*

*England captain David Beckham looks forward to the World Cup finals in Germany, June 2006.*

*David and Victoria Beckham in 2007 at an American awards ceremony.*

*Wayne Rooney on the ball during Manchester United's Premier League fixture against Portsmouth at Old Trafford on 22 April 2009.*

*19 January 2022. Harry Kane of Tottenham during the Premier League match at the King Power Stadium, Leicester.*

*21 December 2022. Presenters Gary Lineker, Gabby Logan, Clare Balding and Alex Scott arrive on the red carpet at the BBC Sports Personality of the Year awards 2022.*

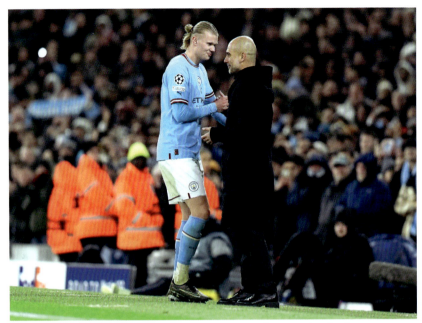

*Manchester City manager Pep Guardiola greets Erling Haaland as he is substituted off during a Premier League match at the Etihad Stadium. Picture date: Saturday, 13 August 2022.*

*Manchester United's Cristiano Ronaldo (right) shoots past Tottenham Hotspur's Cristian Romero during the Premier League match at Old Trafford on Saturday, 12 March 2022.*

*Heung-Min Son of Spurs during the Premier League match between Tottenham Hotspur and AFC Bournemouth at the Tottenham Hotspur Stadium on 30 November 2019.*

*Cole Palmer of Chelsea celebrates after he scores from the penalty spot for 1-1 – Tottenham Hotspur v Chelsea, Premier League, Tottenham Hotspur Stadium, 6 November 2023.*

*21 April 2021. Phil Foden of Manchester City is challenged by Aston Villa's Ollie Watkins during the Premier League match at Villa Park.*

*Jude Bellingham of Real Madrid during the La Liga EA Sports match between FC Barcelona and Real Madrid at the Estadi Olimpic Lluis Companys on 28 October 2023 in Barcelona, Spain.*

By contrast Brentford's Danish manager Thomas Frank deserved credit for creating, with a modest budget, a well-motivated team that fans enjoyed watching. The team was tactically adaptable, playing short or long passes and switching from game to game. The rising English star Ivan Toney personified the team's versatility, playing up front but also dropping to the midfield for a change of play. The Dane, Christian Nørgaard was an impressive playmaker in midfield.

Brentford, in that summer's transfer window, brought in the young Scottish full-back Aaron Hickey, one of the below-radar summer transfers with a great deal of promise. Like other British youngsters before him, Hickey had bet on himself by making the move abroad – to Bologna – and after just one season in Italy, Brentford had brought him to the Premier League, prior to the 2022/23 season that saw the west London club improve their position over the previous season from 13th to ninth.

Hickey suffered a set-back in October 2023, when a hamstring injury he suffered during training put him out of action for an extended period of the 2023/24 season.

# Chapter Twenty-two

# Anglo-Spanish Exchange

THE FLOW of humanity between countries over the decades has sometimes had a productive outcome when it comes to English and Spanish football players and managers moving between their respective countries with a claim to having the best leagues in the world.

Precisely when the first football game was played by the English on Spanish soil remains a subject of dispute. Old photographs and other historical research suggest that it was on the local feast day of San Roque on 16 August 1887, in the Andalucian town of Minas de Rio Tinto. The playing field was where the then-British-owned Rio Tinto mining company's English Club had its office, near the mayor's building, along a street of Andalucian white-washed houses and very English, red-tiled houses. There, a group of English mining staff gathered for their inaugural kick-off between two teams picked exclusively from non-Spaniards.

The founding kick-around of English expatriates on Spanish soil was played with the restless rules-free abandon of amateurs. It mirrored the primitive folk years of football in England, the land where it all began. As Hunter Davies records in his social history of the British game, *Postcards from the Edge of Football*, football in its early days in England was usually held on festive days, with two teams of unlimited numbers trying to get a ball from one village or neighbourhood to another and reaching a designated goal: 'Kicking each other, fighting, settling old scores, using weapons or any sort of physical violence was allowed, and people did get badly injured and, sometimes, killed.'

The first football match recorded in Spanish history near the mines of Rio Tinto was almost as loosely played, although non-violent. *Los Ingleses* aspired to bring a culture of civilisation to one of the least developed areas of southern Europe, with its backward feudal economy and endemic political turmoil.

Not so far away, on an estuary leading out to the Atlantic coast, Huelva Recreativo Club (later renamed Recreativo Club de Huelva), was officially founded in December 1889 by Andrew Mackay, a Scottish doctor employed by the British-owned Rio Tinto mining company. To this day the club disputes with Minas de Rio Tinto its claim to be the *'cuna del futbol Espanol'*, the birthplace of Spanish football. It was registered as the first Spanish club although its first team was built by Englishmen and Scots.

In the Basque country, the game also had strong Anglo-Saxon roots. As in Rio Tinto, the English in Bilbao were linked to the local mines, with one of Athletic Bilbao's ritual chants, *'Aliron, Aliron, Athletic Campon'* deriving from the phrase 'All Iron', which an English mining technician would write in chalk if a mined rock was found to have more than 70 per cent iron content.

The Spaniards would soon learn from their football teachers and would in time develop their own style and autonomy, producing great clubs with a following that crossed borders – but for much of the 20th century, it was English players and coaches who made their mark in Spanish domestic football, rather than vice-versa. That would change with the Premier League.

FC Barcelona (founded in 1899) had several Englishmen among the foreigners in their first team. The goalkeeper was called Brown, the club's first secretary Wild, and two key players were the brothers Arthur and Ernest Witty. In 1998, six years after the foundation of the Premier League, I interviewed the veteran Frederick Witty, the then-longest-surviving descendant of the early Barca players, who later died in an old people's home near Castelldefels. Frederick was frail but received me with his dignity intact, dressed in a tweed jacket and silk cravat, the epitome of an English gentleman. We drank tea on the well-watered lawn of the nursing home, as the Mediterranean sun went down, and his breathing became laboured. He told me of his father's playing days with Barca. 'He never did any specialised training – none of the stuff you see these days, with players having orders shouted at them by coaches acting like camp commandants. But he knew how to keep fit, and did so by going for long runs. He played with a combination of acceleration, toughness, ball control and goal-scoring potential.'

Real Madrid (founded as Madrid FC in 1902) had as one of their first players a veteran of the game called Arthur Johnson. He was a free-thinking English businessman who shared his footballing skills and philosophy of life with a group of young Spanish disciples of Francisco Giner de Los Ríos, founder of the *Institucion Libre de Ensenanza* an enlightened free-thinking secular educational movement which flourished in pre-Franco Spain. Johnson, as the captain of the team, distinguished himself with his precise tackling, agility, and elegance of body. He played in several positions, centre-half, centre-forward and goalkeeper.

A few English legends in Spain stand out in the interwar years. Among the early English coaches was Fred Pentland. A former player with several English clubs and an English international, Pentland crossed the Pyrenees into Spain, after famously organising football games in a German detention camp during World War One. He became a coach of the Cantabrian club Racing, where he showed himself an advocate of the short-passing game, focused on technique and ball skills, courage and determination he had learned as a player with Blackburn Rovers.

When he moved as 'boss' to Bilbao, Pentland smoked cigars and wore a bowler hat – on and off the field – for which he earned the nickname *El Bombin*, which is Spanish for bowler hat. He told his players they could celebrate a famous victory by collectively stamping on his hat as he had a good stock he could replenish them from. The fact that he got through several hats was an enduring testimony to his success at the club. Pentland became the most successful manager ever to sit on the bench at San Mames, in two spells at the club taking Athletic Bilbao to five cup wins and two league championships, becoming the first manager in the history of Spanish football to win a *La Liga* and cup double. In 1929, Pentland helped coach the Spanish national squad to its first significant international achievement since winning a medal in the 1920 Olympics: Spain beat England 4-3, the first time the English team had lost a match outside a Home Championship against Scotland.

Years later in this Anglo-Spanish history, the Englishman Laurie Cunningham, the son of Jamaican parents and one of the most gifted players of his generation, signed for Real Madrid from West Bromwich Albion in 1979. Vicente del Bosque who played with Cunningham years before managing the most successful Spanish national squad in history, told me: 'He was a great kid. His problem was that despite being a strong player with considerable skills, he lacked consistency. He played some brilliant games but then there would be matches in which one would hardly notice him. He fitted in really well with the team, settled down well even though ours was a different culture … He felt happy and adapted himself perfectly to the Spanish way of life and Real Madrid.'

Cunningham scored twice on his debut and helped the Spanish giants win the league and cup double in his first season. Known as the 'Black Pearl' in Madrid, Cunningham impressed the fans with his flamboyance, but injuries and an enjoyment of Madrid's nightlife limited his overall impact.

The approach of a new millennium had national teams being eclipsed by the inexorable rise and global commercial clout of Real Madrid, FC Barcelona and Manchester United. For talented players, their agents and their clubs, globalisation and ever-increasing TV money meant that selling or being sold to the highest bidder competed against traditional ties and national identity. Two watershed moments which reinforced each other were the foundation of the Premier League in 1992 and the European Court ruling in 1995 in favour of the Belgium player Jean-Marc Bosman who challenged the restrictions placed on footballers from European countries playing within the national leagues of Europe. The Bosman ruling allowed professional footballers in the EU to move freely to another club at the end of their contract, in accordance with the new competition rules established by the EU's single market in 1992. This meant players could demand even higher salaries, whether they were renewing a contract or moving on, as clubs fought to avoid losing their assets for nothing. This in turn inflated transfer fees, creating an elite group of clubs able to out-muscle under-resourced clubs in both countries.

In 2003, Real Madrid's 'Galactico's Galactico', David Beckham was signed for £25 million from Manchester United. During the following two decades other star English players went to Spain but their numbers were dwarfed by the number of Spaniards who went to the Premier. While the debate over which was truly the best league in the world rumbled on, the one area where the Premier League excelled over its Spanish rival related to the money involved – specifically when it came to TV deals. Until the pandemic crisis, this wasn't an issue if you joined Real Madrid or Barcelona but it would be if a player decided to sign for one of the other Spanish teams, whose budgets were considerably smaller.

According to a report published by the Premier League in April 2020, 144 Spaniards had by then played in the English club competition, making Spain the fifth most-represented country. Cesc Fàbregas led the Spanish list for both appearances and assists, having set up 111 goals in 350 matches for Arsenal and Chelsea and been a champion twice with the Blues. Fàbregas was one of five Spanish players to have set up four goals in a match, a Premier League record, alongside fellow Spaniards Santi Cazorla and José Antonio Reyes. While at Chelsea and Manchester United, Juan Mata amassed a total of 103 goals and assists. César Azpilicueta, who joined Chelsea in 2012, helped win two league titles. In his better days, goalkeeper David de Gea kept 108 clean sheets and won the Manchester United player of the year award four times.

Of the best Spanish players among the more than 140 who have played in the Premier, I would include: Diego Costa – in his time at Chelsea, the club won the Premier League twice, (2014/15 and 2016/17); Xabi Alonso – one of Rafa Benítez's most trustworthy performers in defensive midfield while at Liverpool; and Fernando Torres, who joined Benítez's Liverpool in 2007.

As Simon Kuper wrote in *The Football Men*, 'Torres was given the choice between betraying his club and betraying his talent and chose to leave Atlético de Madrid. He returned from the ends of the earth [a Polynesian holiday] to talk to Liverpool.'

At his new English club, Torres won over the fans. The player recounted how years ago some of his Madrid friends had tattoos with Liverpool's slogan, 'You'll Never Walk Alone'. Torres couldn't get the tattoo at the time, but his friends bought him an armband bearing the slogan. Not all of Spain's best players found it easy to emigrate. But manager Rafa Benítez reassured Spanish players that his Liverpool was a small corner of Spain.

After joining the club in 2007, Torres showed himself to be a thrilling attacker and scored a total of 81 goals in all competitions with the Reds. However, some Liverpool fans will never forgive him for departing four years later for Chelsea, when he was quoted as saying he had finally joined one of the world's 'top clubs' upon his arrival at Stamford Bridge.

Torres's time at Chelsea, between January 2011 and December 2014, had the club winning the FA Cup, UEFA Champions League and UEFA Europa League, although his goalscoring rate and performances, not helped by injuries, declined.

David Silva is also on my list of the Premier League's best Spanish players. During his time at Manchester City (2010-2020), he helped the club build towards its success, scoring 60 goals in 309 appearances in the Premier League.

Silva's charismatic performances helped Manchester City to win the league title in 2012. He was one of the key players in Premier League history for any team. Nicknamed 'the magician' by City fans, the unassuming Spanish World Cup winner was the main man for much of his ten-year stay at the Etihad. Signed from Valencia in 2010, he played 436 times for City, winning four Premier League titles, two FA Cups and five League Cups. A statue of him – constructed by welding thousands of pieces of galvanised steel, the creation of the award-winning Scottish figurative sculptor, Andy Scott – was unveiled at the Etihad in 2021. Silva loves the statue, in which he is in possession of the ball in midfield, looking for who to pass to.

'Being at City changed my life. I'm proud of what we did together and I feel emotional that it has been recognised like this,' Silva told Manchester City fans on the club website after he left the club. 'When I first saw the statue, I felt good, I thought it was like me. This statue really represents the way I like to play, I love the pose the sculptor has chosen. It really reminds me of those times I was on the pitch playing and that moment when I had to find the striker. It's an exciting thing to be a part of, creating something that becomes part of that landscape that means so much to so many people.'

As the popular Spanish sports daily *Marca* noted in August 2021, the Premier League gained a reputation as the best league in the world due to the big names that played there and the hefty sums that were moved around during every transfer window, which led to an increasing amount of young talent from Spain heading to England to ply their trade. Spanish clubs were finding it increasingly difficult to compete with the amount of money on offer in England, which led to even the smaller Premier League clubs prying away talent from *La Liga*.

A rising Spanish star Marc Cucurella began his *La Liga* career at FC Barcelona but spent most of the time there in the reserve team. After playing over 100 *La Liga* games for Eibar and Getafe, in 2021 he joined Brighton & Hove Albion, who had finished 16th in the Premier League the previous season. In the summer of 2022, he joined Chelsea for an initial £56m with a possible £7m in add-ons.

'You earn a lot of money, yet somehow it counts for nothing because the one thing that can make life bearable when you are a long way from home, both physically and emotionally, is playing the game you love,' wrote *La Liga* TV pundit Guillem Balagué in an article for the *Bleacher Report* in 2014. Balagué recalled how Santi Cazorla openly admitted that when he first came to Arsenal, had it not been for Mikel Arteta taking him under his wing and showing him around, he might well not have settled in England.

For years now Spain has produced some of the best players on the planet. But the main competitor of *La Liga* in terms of club football became the Premier League, as it attracted a growing share of the world's elite footballers as well as many of the potential young stars, who matured and flourished in its competitive environment, supported by the most passionate fans anywhere on the globe.

There was a time, long ago, when the caricature narrative was that Spanish players, however gifted, were not suited mentally or physically to playing the faster, less technical, more aggressive English club football. Pep Guardiola broke down stereotypes, adapting his artistry and conquering the Premier working his alchemy at Manchester City with a mix of English and foreign talent.

Not every Spanish speaker had a happy experience of the Premier League. The Argentine Ángel Di María joined Manchester United from a successful time at Real Madrid in 2014, for £60m – the highest fee paid by a British club at the time – but he lasted just one season and fans and commentators regarded him as a failure. He made 27 appearances, scoring only three goals, and left for Paris Saint Germain with United accepting a cut-down fee of about £15m less than they had paid for him.

Di María's experience of English life was not helped by having to suffer an attempted burglary at his country residence outside Manchester, in the idyllic and usually peaceful landscape of the 'Golden Triangle' of Cheshire, near the picturesque commuter village of Alderley Edge. The attempted burglary shocked Di María, who carried memories of his birth town Rosario, an Argentine city with a reputation for violent drug-related criminality as well as producing star players. Messi was also born there.

According to Di María's wife Jorgelina Cardoso, the player's move to Manchester was a terrible mistake. 'I didn't like it all … I can tell you. People are weird. You walk around and you don't know if they are going to kill you. The food is disgusting. The women look like porcelain,' she told an Argentinian TV programme *LAM* in August 2022. 'Ángel and I were in Madrid, with the best team in the world, perfect food, perfect weather, everything was perfect. And then came

United's proposal. I told him no way, no way, but he kept saying we will be a little more financially secure.'

Many Spaniards and Englishmen who know the city of Manchester will find it difficult to recognise her description. From 1996, when an IRA bomb destroyed a major shopping centre, the city finally rose from its post-war decline. Old industrial warehouses were converted into cultural centres including a magnificent Spanish one, the Instituto Cervantes. Manchester had become as cosmopolitan in its cuisine as in its football. In 2016, two years after his son signed for the Red Devils from Chelsea, Juan Manuel Mata, a businessman and football agent, opened Spanish restaurant Tapeo and Wine in Manchester's Deansgate, near the Cervantes Institute and another Spanish icon, the main city branch of Santander Bank. José Mourinho was a regular customer during his two-and-a-half years as manager of Manchester United. Guardiola, who arrived in Manchester at the same time to take over at crosstown rivals City, also frequented the eatery.

In 2018, Guardiola together with Manchester City's chief executive officer Ferran Soriano and director of football Txiki Begiristain, invested in Tast Cuina Catalana, a restaurant that had Paco Pérez, a top chef, bringing a taste of his native Catalonia to the city.

It is perhaps Guardiola who best personifies a Spanish success story in the Premier League, adapting to and getting to love the local environment with the same sense of engagement as he did in Munich, having improved his English during a year-long sabbatical in New York, after leaving Barca.

'Here, after four or five years I feel so good ... I have always had the feeling, the dream to come here, to train in the Shakespeare country, in the Beatles' country, in Oasis country, the theatres, the movies. This country is special for many, many, many reasons and I wanted to live this. I hate November, December, January and February in England because I would like better weather, but I have everything

[I need] to do my job, that is the reason why I extended my contract,' Guardiola told the former Manchester United player Rio Ferdinand in March 2021 during BT Sport's *Rio Meets* series.

At the time of the interview, Guardiola was on his way to winning a fourth Premier League title in five years in 2021/22 as well as reaching the Champions League semi-final. The Catalan made a stunning start to life at City, winning his first 11 games in charge and was twice nominated for the Premier League manager of the month award, in August and September 2016. In his second season he guided the Blues to the Premier League title and the Carabao Cup, smashing records along the way in a stunning season.

He picked up four successive manager of the month awards and was voted the Premier League manager of the season and the LMA manager of the year. He was again voted Premier League manager of the year after guiding City to four more trophies in 2018/19, to become the club's most successful boss ever with six trophies in three seasons.

Guardiola has flourished under an Arab ownership with money to spend, and in the broader context of a powerful and acquisitive English domestic league. The ten transfers from *La Liga* to the 2022/23 Premier League even before the summer transfer window was over in August totalled almost £300m, with the spend on foreigners, totalling over £1.6bn, higher than pre-Covid levels.

From 1 January 2021 the UK government implemented new rules which threatened to make international player recruitment more complicated, after Brexit ended the freedom of movement between the UK and the EU. The policy change added bureaucratic steps to international football transfers. For instance, like other overseas workers, Spanish footballers and managers would have to pass a points-based system before moving to the UK. As noted in a previous chapter, the continuing arrival of European players and coaches to the

Premier League suggests that in terms of the well-paid, highly-qualified top flight of football, the dissuasive impact of Brexit has not been as great as some had feared. Talented European coaches following in Guardiola and Klopp's footsteps have had little difficulty in meeting the rules agreed as part of Britain leaving the European Union, whereby they would need to satisfy the English authorities that they were of the highest calibre and able to contribute significantly to the development of the game at the top level in England. To qualify, potential managers have to meet specific criteria, which includes a total of 36 months first-team management in a major league within the previous five years, or 24 months consecutively in post, and the club they are planning to join must be without a manager.

In 2007, less than 20 per cent of top-flight managers in the Premier League were from overseas. In contrast, at the end of the 2020/21 season, nine of the managers in post were from overseas and that increased by two by the following season, to more than 50 per cent of managers in the Premier League, with the top clubs all managed by Europeans, among them Spaniards Guardiola and Arteta at Manchester City and Arsenal respectively, the Germans Klopp (Liverpool) and Tuchel (Chelsea), the Italian Conte (Tottenham) and Ten Hag (Dutch) at Manchester United.

As for the players, Tom Allnutt, a former Agence France Press journalist with expertise in both *La Liga* and the Premier suggested in an article for *The Times* that English recruitment departments no longer dismissed players from Spain, as they once did, as technically excellent, but too slight to handle the rough and tumble of the English Premier. There was a belief in fact that small but elite players – as shown by the likes of Santi Cazorla, Silva, Juan Mata and Fàbregas – could thrive in England, in part because they offered some of the subtlety the Premier League lacked, wrote Allnutt.

However there remained a 'base level of physicality required – a willingness to fight, not only to match the intensity of English games, but also as a means of being accepted.'

In considering the challenges facing imports into the Premier League from *La Liga*, Allnutt wrote that Basque and Catalan players were better at learning English, Andalucians too easily get home-sick, while Galicians and Basques were less likely to worry about the weather. In the end there were uncontrollable factors like the demographics of a dressing room, the faith of the manager, and the mood of the club. Even luck will play its part.

# Chapter Twenty-three

# The Premier, *Quo Vadis?*

KICK-AROUNDS OF a ball on the British Isles are thought to date back to the early Celts of the sixth century, and the time when, according to myth and legend, the noble King Arthur and his equally chivalrous knights of the round table protected the downtrodden and persecuted from their fantastic city of Camelot.

In those early times the physical demands of everyday life were so great as to leave little time for leisure. Ball games were played sporadically and without rules. It was only in the 19th century that football became professionalised, with organised teams and rules. It began to be played in a way that not only helped distract the industrialised working classes, but also as a sport worth exporting as imperial Britain extended its cultural as well as socio-economic influence beyond its shores.

Along with the game, the British developed the sporting ethos of 'fair play'. In its essence there were two aims: the first to establish a complementary balance between a person's physical and mental development from a young age, instilling in the individual and in the team the acceptance of alternating experiences of winning and losing with nobility and grace, respecting the opponent. The second was at the level of community and international relations, sublimating rivalries and resentments and transferring them from military conflict to the sports fields.

As Norman Davies writes in his history of the English, *The Isles*: 'It is not surprising that these aims emerged in Britain, the world's first urban and modernised country. It was worked out in the evolutions of games that have assumed global importance ... above all football.'

In time, football attracted support from all classes in England – the nearest there ever was to a national game – even if in its formative years it was almost exclusively reserved for male participants. The first all-male English Football League was formed in 1888 with 12 member clubs.

Later, in the 20th century, the country that had founded the game fell behind its inheritors in one respect. The English national team's fall from grace in the rankings of world football, proceeding largely unchecked for decades, seemed a mirror of England's post-imperial decline. England's World Cup win in 1966 was a rare achievement for the national squad. In 1999, the country that laid claim to having invented football beyond its primitive beginnings, was in 11th place in FIFA world rankings.

And yet the underachievement of the English national squad was deceptive. The European Cup was dominated by English clubs in the late 1970s and early 1980s, when from 1977 until 1982, English teams – Liverpool, Aston Villa and Nottingham Forest – won the European Cup every single year.

Other than Real Madrid's five consecutive wins in the early days of the competition, between 1956 and 1960, and the Dutch domination of the European Cup when Feyenoord and Ajax lifted the huge trophy four times between them at the start of the 1970s, never had one country held such a monopoly over Europe's elite competition.

English domestic club football was destined to undergo a transformation with the approach of a new millennium, with the Premier transforming the business of the English game into a global commercial powerhouse. This exciting new era in modern football began on 15 August 1992, as remembered in snapshots on the Premier League's website on its 30th anniversary:

> The first Premier League goal arrived after only five minutes of action, when Sheffield United's Brian Deane scored against Manchester United. He added a second from the penalty spot just after half-time, as Sir Alex Ferguson's team suffered an opening-day loss.
>
> Leeds United had won the First Division title the previous season and they got their Premier League campaign off to a winning start, with Lee Chapman scoring both goals in a 2-1 victory over Wimbledon.
>
> At Selhurst Park, Alan Shearer gave a hint as to the record-breaking goalscoring exploits that were to follow when he scored two superb goals on his Blackburn debut.
>
> Norwich City stunned Arsenal at Highbury, coming from two goals down to record a 4-2 win, with Mark Robins sealing the victory with a sublime chip over David Seaman.
>
> David Smith struck from close range to help Coventry City start off with a 2-1 home success over Middlesbrough, and a fine Barry Horne strike gave Everton a 1-1 draw with Sheffield Wednesday.
>
> Aston Villa and Oldham Athletic also came from behind to draw their first Premier League matches, at Ipswich Town and Chelsea respectively, while Southampton and Tottenham Hotspur played out a stalemate at The Dell.
>
> Nottingham Forest and Liverpool would have to wait until Sunday afternoon before starting their campaigns, in the first live televised Premier League fixture.

The first live televised goal was scored by Teddy Sheringham, which was enough for Forest to claim a 1-0 win.

'What a goal to start off that era,' said Sheringham. 'David James was in goal and he looked huge. I remember thinking, "How am I going to score this?" so I hit it as hard as I could into the top corner.

'I don't think we all realised quite what the Premier League was going to become 30 years ago. It was a new thing and exciting times. There were dancing girls on a Monday night and it was all fan-dabby-dozy.'

Three decades after its launch, the Premier announced a six-year American TV deal that would push the league's annual turnover above £6bn, marking the moment when income from foreign media rights exceeded domestic income. As noted by the author David Goldblatt, it was a fitting marker for the Premier's 30th season and its three decades of hyper-globalisation. It had become the most-watched football league in the world, with the biggest spread of high-quality foreign coaches and star foreign players as well as the best of the English.

If the satellite and the internet had reached out to a massive audience beyond the relatively small market of the British Isles, the attraction of the Premier was in part down to the deep-rooted local identities of English clubs and the passion and loyalty of their fans that animated the matches and fuelled the competitive spirit of managers and players.

Only people who bought satellite dishes could initially watch the new league live on their TV screens. But the government allowed it, because post-Thatcher Britain trusted the free market – an essential condition for the Premier League's success. Meanwhile, with the modernisation of stadiums, there came more customers, including women, but an enduring unreconstructed, if reduced, hooligan element retained the capacity to intimidate rather than welcome visitors. Football encounters could propagate acts of violence rather than fair play, not least in times of festering social and political tension.

In its publicity, the Premier League authorities marked the 30th anniversary by the progress made in promoting diversity and anti-racism, and funding being channelled to football academies and the sports education of the disadvantaged. But lucrative broadcasting rights and sponsorship deals have gone hand in hand with massive transfer deals. Elite players, agents, managers, celebrity TV pundits and their legal advisers, have earned astronomical sums that contrast with the economic misfortunes and hardships of large swathes of society, battered by Covid, energy prices and the negative trade repercussions of Brexit.

The Premier League, in the summer transfer window of 2022, spent almost £2bn on players, bouncing back after two seasons of Covid. The figure compared with the previous record of £1.4bn in 2017 and dwarfed its European rivals. Premier League clubs spent more than Spain's *La Liga*, Italy's *Serie A* and the German *Bundesliga* combined, according to research by financial services firm Deloitte. Of the top 20 signings in Europe, 15 joined the Premier League, giving top-tier English clubs a competitive edge in competitions at home and abroad, and ensuring not only packed stadiums but an ever-growing global market of TV and digital viewers.

Tim Bridge, lead partner in Deloitte's Sports Business Group, said in September 2022: 'The record level of spending during this transfer window is a clear indication of Premier League clubs' confidence, as fans return to stadia and a new broadcast cycle begins.'

However, as Bridge also noted, English top-flight clubs would have to face up to the uncertainty surrounding the UK economy. He predicted that it was going to be incredibly expensive for clubs and organisations to put matches on and to really work hard to keep attracting fans and keep ensuring that they had the opportunity to engage. 'What we have to do is think about the responsibility that the industry has, in general, around financial sustainability. Ensuring that the clubs are there for the long term and recognising their real community asset status. We must step forward through this cost-of-living crisis and ensure that the football clubs continue to play what is a fantastic role above and beyond these headline numbers.'

The Premier has produced stories of solidarity, with some individual players speaking out on racism and poverty, and fans protesting against the ESL, while English women have aspired to a bigger role in football than at any time in their history thanks to the success of the Lionesses. However, the Premier as a business model is a ruthless profit-seeking machine that has some way to go in terms of redistributing more fairly and justly its extraordinary wealth.

It may well be, as Simon Kuper commented in the *Financial Times* in 2022, that fans were as much part of the machine as they were exploited victims. 'Like the groundlings of Shakespeare's day, English fans consider themselves participants in the show, co-creating it with their cheers and songs. They aren't fixated on winning. Defeats become fodder for self-mocking humour, as in the comedian Jasper Carrott explaining life as a Birmingham City fan: "You lose some, you draw some".'

Football is more of an escape than a long-term remedy – a periodical short-term fix that allows fans to forget what is wrong in their lives rather than exacerbate their fears and frustrations. It produces moments of huge joy, as well as despair, in tribal communion with others who wear the same colours, share the same stories, songs, and chants. The behaviour of a tribe is affected by individual circumstances as well as submersion in the group. English fans also have lives beyond football, where suffering and inequality and bad governance have their limits of tolerance.

The foundation of the Premier League was driven by technology and by the urge to exploit new ways of consuming. Thirty years on, in August 2022, *The Guardian*'s Barney Ronay wrote that, 'Football is basically just moving shapes on a screen now, a digital product, a dopamine hit across the internet, there to be consumed as part of a wider fandom.'

As long ago as 1995, the English Labour politician Tony Blair, two years before he became prime minister, spoke at a dinner of the English Football Writers' Association in honour of Sir Stanley Matthews's 80th birthday, and warned about the direction the Premier League might be taking. He expressed his unease with the 'get rich quick, something for nothing philosophy and the erosion of values like service to the community and wider responsibility that people in the public eye have for those we follow and idolise.

'A nation that neglects sport at grass roots because it is obsessed with the commercial gains from the sport at the top is a nation set for sporting and social decline,' Blair told his audience.

Three decades on, the Premier League could boast that it was a huge commercial success that was not tied to place, or tradition or to rules that stifle profit. Just three weekends into the new season in late August 2022, a thrilling edge-of-the seat match between Newcastle and Manchester City was already a contender for game of the season. It ended in a 3-3 draw after a match characterised by great goals, passion and pressing, and a moment of dramatic human and technological controversy when the Newcastle player Kieran Trippier received a red card for a reckless lunge only to have the decision reversed at the prompting of the VAR (Video Assistant Referee).

The closer the season got to its end – and clubs fought for those top places needed to qualify for the rich pickings to be had in international club competitions, and less successful clubs fought to avoid relegation – the bigger the games. In one weekend alone in March, there were two edge-of-the-seat games which would endure in collective memories: Arsenal coming back from two goals down to beat Bournemouth 3-2 at the Emirates and Liverpool's trouncing of Manchester United, 7-0 at Anfield.

Earlier in the season, against Newcastle, Guardiola's team had been faced with a team managed by Eddie Howe who – according to the Zimbabwean tabloid *H-Metro* – played with, 'daring, dashing, destructive football good enough to scare the daylights of arguably Europe's best football team'. The very existence of that comment underlines the popular global reach of the Premier in former British colonies. Newcastle led 3-1 in front of their euphoric fans at St James' Park before City fought back with goals by two of their international stars, Erling Haaland and Bernardo Silva.

Just a year before, Newcastle had been second-bottom of the league, in seemingly terminal decline under the failing ownership of English businessman Mike Ashley. Now they were reviving after the politically questionable Saudi takeover of the club. They were an emerging force, while City showed why they were still champions. The encounter had all the elements that gave the Premier identity and brand as the most-watched sporting competition in the world.

The Premier was still, in the words of *The Guardian*'s Barney Ronay, 'robustly and unapologetically a profit machine, and like every model predicated on greed and growth, it must take ever larger mouthfuls to survive happily.'

Amidst the celebration of the glory years of the Premier, the great games it has made more accessible, the sheer spectacle on offer and the quality and competitiveness of those playing still gave one a sense, to echo Ronay's words, 'of something gorging itself towards a state of unravelling.'

On the other hand, the glory days of the Premier had already defined an era of modern football. The English, throughout their history, had had a sense of entitlement, of being different, but had shown themselves capable of exemplary resilience, solidarity with a greater good and capacity to renew. For the Premier League to find a way of continuing to be not only more open to the world, but also a true emblem of fair play, more redistributionist perhaps, would be a positive English story taking us into a better future, to be admired as well as enjoyed by football fans around the world.

## Chapter Twenty-four

# Post-scripts From the Edge

### An English fan

My friend Andy Mitten is an Englishman, journalist and author and enduring football fan. Born and bred in Manchester, he divides his time between his city of birth and Spain, travelling to more than 80 games each season, most of them in the Premier League. He founded the best-selling *United We Stand* fanzine as a 15-year-old before studying journalism at university and has gone on to interview many famous footballers and cover memorable games. Writing about football has taken him from Israel to Iran, Brazil to Barbados.

Andy's great-uncle, Charlie Mitten, was one of the first English players to move abroad after World War Two. He left Manchester United for Bogotá, Colombia in 1950. While in South America, Charlie's wages rose from £10 to £100. While he was in Bogotá, he was visited by Santiago Bernabeu who was building up a legendary Real Madrid into European champions and was interested in three players who were living there: Alfredo di Stéfano, Héctor Rial and Charlie Mitten. Di Stéfano and Rial moved to Madrid, but Charlie was homesick and wanted his children to be educated in an English school, back in Manchester, so he returned there. Not joining Real Madrid was Charlie's greatest regret but he still pursued a rewarding career back in England. He was a record signing for Fulham and went on to manage Newcastle United.

Andy has lived between Spain and Manchester since 2001. His father, also called Charlie, loved his travels to the Spanish mainland, its coasts and mountains and its islands. In 2018, Andy was on the fast AVE train from Barcelona to Madrid to cover Atlético de Madrid vs Arsenal when Charlie called him to share the news that the cancer he was suffering from had got worse. Following further treatment at Manchester's Christie hospital, and spending his final days being cared for at St Ann's hospice, Andy's dad died before the year was out. As Andy later recalled: 'A man who never stopped complaining about Manchester United, seldom complained about his pain. I wanted to do something.'

So, Andy decided to raise £40,000 to support hospices around Manchester by riding a bicycle from Barcelona to Manchester across the Pyrenees, through France, and then across England. Each day the sponsorship money rose. In a pub near Birmingham, a lady in the kitchen donated her day's wages. In a pub near Stoke, regular drinkers contributed nearly £200. Those who had least gave the most until those who had more also helped. Liverpool FC gave Andy a shirt signed by a player who had worn it in the 2019 Champions League Final in Madrid. It raised £5,000. Just 40 miles before Andy reached Manchester, he had hit his target of £40,000.

When Andy arrived at Old Trafford, former United players Ryan Giggs, Gary Neville and Andy Cole came out to greet him. 'You look like a skeleton,' said Giggs. Andy had lost weight on a long, challenging journey. The money raised went towards buying one ambulance and paid two-thirds of the cost of a second one. The first ambulance was delivered the week before the pandemic locked Andy down for the first time.

In the autumn of 2022, Andy, kindly shared some of his thoughts as I came towards the end of writing the bulk of this book and asked him about his love of English football.

JB – *Why did you become a Manchester United fan?*
AM – I'm from a big football family in Manchester. My great uncle Charlie was a star in Sir Matt Busby's first great United side, the 1948 FA Cup winners, and my grandad played football professionally, as did his other brother. My dad, his brothers, his cousins, my brothers – they all received money to play football. One cousin, John, played first-class cricket for Leicestershire and football for Leicester City in the same year. I'm the odd one out, I pay to play.

Everyone in the family is United. I grew up on the Urmston/Stretford border, two miles from Old Trafford. I could hear the roar of the stadium when I delivered newspapers as a young teenager in Manchester and I started the *United We Stand* magazine in 1989.

I was 15 and felt the British government – Thatcher was still prime minister – were taking the piss out of football fans. They thought we were all hooligans with no brains and wanted to bring in ID cards on our behalf after Hillsborough. I felt strongly about that, as I did about rip-off ticket prices and poor facilities at stadiums. We put some words down, I borrowed £20 off my mum to photocopy a fanzine – which was terrible content-wise, looking back – but within a year we were selling thousands and it started to take off.

Since 2000 I've divided my time between Manchester and Barcelona, where I'm married with two girls. Barcelona is probably my favourite city in the world. It has everything. I also cover Barça and go to around 20 games per season at Camp Nou.

JB – *How do you explain your enduring loyalty?*
AM – I love football, love stadiums, travelling to new places and meeting people. Football clubs are really important in their communities and that should be cherished and not tampered with. They're community assets. I love watching games live, hearing the roar of a crowd, seeing floodlights at

night. And I still think Manchester United are going to win every game, even though the team has been mediocre to poor since Sir Alex Ferguson stepped down.

As a football journalist, I've been fortunate enough to interview Maradona in Sinaloa, Sócrates in Sao Paulo, Juan Sebastián Verón in La Plata, Lucas Radebe in Soweto, Carlos Queiroz in Tehran, Lionel Messi in Barcelona, Roy Keane in Philadelphia, [as well as] travelling around Asia with Gary Neville, Ryan Giggs, Paul Scholes, Nicky Butt and Phil Neville. I work very hard, but I've been fortunate too.

JB – *What about Manchester United's controversial ownership?*
AM – The highly leveraged buyout in 2005 should never have been allowed, neither by the UK government, nor the football authorities, who were limp to stop debt being piled on to the club. United has been asked to swim with a tonne of bricks on its back ever since.

JB – *What makes Old Trafford and the club still so special?*
AM – Seeing that pitch for the first time as a ten-year-old was one of the greatest moments of my life. It was so green amid the billowing factories of the Trafford Park industrial estate where my father worked. That was 1984. Old Trafford, opened in 1910, is one of the great football stadiums. It survived Second World War bombs and the Taylor Report into the Hillsborough stadium disaster which recommended that all major stadiums convert to an all-seater model, restrictions on the sale of alcohol, etc.

It was the first club in England with executive boxes, in 1965. When the cantilever stand opened for the 1966 World Cup it was the best in England.

The success of the team in the 1990s came at just the right time as money from that success (merchandising, commercial and TV) helped pay for United's extensive development between 1992 (when the Stretford End terrace was pulled down) to 2006. That shouldn't be taken for granted since former chairman Martin Edwards was so worried about financing the Stretford End that he was prepared to sell the club to someone who could afford it.

During those 1993-2006 developments, Old Trafford became an all-seater stadium, the Stretford End was rebuilt to make a full 44,000-seater bowl in 1993 and the giant North Stand, which, with 25,300 seats is still the biggest in Britain, boosted the capacity to 55,000. Another 6,000 seats were added on to either end to push the capacity to 68,000, before the quadrants linking them added another 8,000 seats. All were delivered on time and on budget. That's how we see the stadium today, a giant cavity of Redness (and red always invokes more passion than blue!) with the Sir Bobby Charlton Stand the only single tier one left. That stand needs developing, expanding and modernising. There's little reason why Old Trafford can't hold 90,000 – the demand is there.

JB – *How do Manchester United compare with Guardiola's Manchester City and Klopp's Liverpool?*
AM – It's a bigger club than both, but a distant second right now on the pitch. They're two of the best teams in football. It's frustrating for United fans, but those same fans saw the team crowned champions of England 13 times in 20 years up to 2013.

JB – *What was your most memorable match or moment?*
AM – Juventus 2 Manchester United 3. The semi-final of the 1999 Champions League. The Italians were perceived to be the best team in the world and raced into a 2-0 lead inside 11 minutes. Then a magnificent Manchester United got in their groove, came back, won the tie, reached the final and won that with two dramatic late goals against Bayern Munich to win the treble. That was in the Camp Nou where I've long been a regular attender.

## The Catalan who loves the Beatles and El Premier

Multiculturalism came to form part of the Premier League's attraction, and along with the quality came the diversity of nationalities that enriched English football. It was in Spain, and specifically in the Catalan coastal town of Sitges which I frequently visit, that I came to understand the extent to which the popularity of English football reflected the best of that other great English export, the 'Fab Four', John, Paul, George and Ringo.

This a small tribute to my good friend Carlos Batalla, owner of the Quiosco El Alba, a newsagent, bookseller, musician and Premier League fanatic. He is a West Ham United – 'Up the Hammers', he will always greet me with – as well as a Liverpool fan.

Carlos spent his favourite family holiday in Liverpool, on a pilgrimage that took in iconic places like the Cavern Club, Strawberry Fields and Anfield. Carlos never felt he was walking alone. Along with my football books and those of other local authors, Carlos had the grace to add a wonderful new box collection of works by the Beatles to his universal shop.

For years Carlos, accompanied by his wife Marta, has been an inspiration and a popular figure in Sitges with local Catalans, expats, and tourists. He is not just an excellent rock musician (a great bass player who has shown his talent in numerous local bands) and an English football fan, but a hugely engaging and *simpatico* citizen of the world who makes every customer who comes to his small but generously and diversely stocked Quiosco near the beach, feel welcome, and part of a community that extends beyond municipalities and nationalistic prejudice.

'It was more than fifty years ago today' that the Beatles broke up, a seminal moment in post-war history. It left millions of their followers bereft and dislocated, wondering what life would become without them. Both in their songs and as a group, John, Paul, George and Ringo had combined into being global ambassadors for their country England and the English language, but also a discipleship for humanity in modern times. Their songs and personalities made millions of pounds and also combined into a unique collective phenomenon that spoke to us of love, brotherhood and the fragility of our lives, and why music, not least theirs, still mattered in a fractious world.

As Lennon famously said in 1966, when the group's popularity had spread across the world, the Beatles at the time seemed to have become 'more popular than Jesus', a phrase that some fundamentalists found offensive, and forced Lennon, always the most rebellious of the four, to clarify.

'I'm sorry I opened my mouth. I'm not anti-God, anti-Christ, or anti-religion. I was not knocking it. I was not saying we are greater or better.' Lennon stressed that he had been commenting on how people popularised the Beatles. He described his own view of God by quoting the English Bishop of Woolwich, 'not as an old man in the sky. I believe that what people call God is something in all of us.'

Thankfully there was life after the Beatles, with John, Paul and George each pursuing their careers in a way that, in their own ways, proved inspirational, while Ringo, the most self-effacing as well as least creative, was also the happiest to take a lower profile. The music they had created together continued to inspire across generations and countries after Lennon and Harrison's deaths.

But to go back to Carlos, it seemed perfectly in character that he should choose to give the Beatles' collection and McCartney's autobiography pride of place in his shop in Sitges, as English music has inspired him in parallel with the Premiership, and his favourite English phrase 'Up the Hammers', and occasional visits to Liverpool.

## The boys in Battersea Park

There was nothing like watching football played in the times of Covid to help one reflect on the world's most popular sport and what if anything we might learn from it. It was November 2020, between lockdowns, nine months into the pandemic, and in my London neighbourhood my local beloved Battersea Park was alive with the sound and sight of young boys enjoying an outing in the glow of a gentle autumn sun, their teacher half-heartedly trying to impose some rhythm and order on his young charges' play. Hard as the tracksuited sports master tried to channel the ball and encourage a decent combination of a pass or two among the short-trousered minnows, he miserably failed to impose any kind of system.

Instead, the boys joyously kicked the ball in whatever direction they fancied, or simply ignored it, jumping or running around each other in a collective carefree dance of sheer frivolity across an open field.

These boys I should add, judging by their pampered physical demeanour and accents, not to mention the colour of their skin, were not exactly under-privileged, let alone streetwise. But exempt from their lockdown for an afternoon in the park, they were damned if they were going to get, well, locked down.

It was quite a different scene from another occasion when, in the early hours of a dry night, I stood and watched another group of kids play on a nearby all-weather pitch under floodlight. Here was a mix of mini-Messis, Ronaldinhos, and Jordi Albas, with a couple of unshaven Harry Kanes and Raheem Sterling lookalikes hard on their heels, all running on and off the ball, in a series of quick, perfectly timed and choreographed moves. I was struck by the effortless display of poetry in motion, but also by their evident hunger for the ball, which had these boys rising above their social condition and feeling good about themselves.

Trusted by their Brazilian coach, these boys were left to play with minimum interference. They belonged to a local community football club. They were there, these young amateurs, because they really wanted to learn and play to their best of their ability, rather than as an excuse to get away from the classroom and indulge themselves because they could afford to or were paid to do so.

Which takes me to the sight during lockdown of elite, hugely overpaid adult footballers playing their league and championship matches, their televised and livestreamed encounters sound-tracked with invisible audiences roaring their support, a pre-recorded passion, no longer a spectacle but simply a game, stripped of its razzamatazz, 11 adult men kicking a ball around in an empty shell and trying to make a show of celebration whenever it found the opposing net. We were expected to believe that the players really were inspired and motivated to play their best without the atmosphere of live fans and with the knowledge that their real value now stood exposed against the suffering and dislocation that Covid had inflicted on so many people.

The stadium during the pandemic lost its heartbeat, it became soulless without fans, the players visibly diminished, struggling with their egos amidst the emptiness, keeping up the pretence that they deserved to be watched virtually but also still being paid massively for it.

But then I caught a glimpse of football as they must have played it before they made a lot of money from it – some really skilled, naturally talented players, the boys I saw on the all-weather pitch. The girls, young aspiring Lionesses, would soon arrive.

## The Premier and the Qatar World Cup

The Qatar World Cup in late 2022 was played in temporary stadiums erected in the desert and maintained artificially refrigerated. It interrupted the European club season including the Premier, with an unprecedented interlude of a month.

Not every fan could afford the price of a return airline ticket to Doha, the Qatari capital, or an unpredictable stay there, and those who did manage to secure a place to watch their team live in a stadium had to put up with a ban on alcohol.

Such restrictions seemed to have had a minimal impact on Argentine, Moroccan and a mixture of other Arab fans whose presence loomed large. English fans by comparison were smaller in numbers and not so vociferous as those who usually accompany English teams and clubs. They were still loyal but less fanatically tribal, perhaps because, apart from the cost, they sensed the artificial and controlled nature of the location, lacking the intensity and passion at most matches of the Premier.

The World Cup in Doha was played out in the context of an unresolved political debate over the host nation's human rights record of exploitation of cheap immigrant labour and intolerance towards the LGBT community. And yet, after the Qatari team's early exit, politics receded as the tournament progressed, and the game took centre stage, full of unexpected results.

In the end the World Cup was won by one of the best teams, Argentina. There was no need to relegate the memory of Maradona to make way for Messi. After Qatar the two joined each other on the pantheon of Argentine football Gods.

And yet, the feeling persisted that this World Cup marked the end or at least the beginning of the end of a golden era in football, which had been dominated for a decade by the extraordinary achievement at club level of Messi and Cristiano Ronaldo, both of whom broke statistical records and won numerous competitions and *Ballon D'Ors*.

Of the two, it was Ronaldo who seemed to be on the descent, his decline marked by the fact that he was no longer considered indispensable by his national team and by Manchester United, and he departed from European football. After playing part of the first half of the 2022/23 season from the bench, Ronaldo's contract with United was rescinded after he gave a widely publicised interview with the TV journalist, Piers Morgan during which he said that he felt betrayed by the club and felt no respect towards the Dutch coach Erik ten Hag. Signalling a significant exit from the elite football of the Premier, Ronaldo signed a transfer deal worth an estimated £177 million a year with the Saudi Arabian club Al Nassr.

As for Messi, in the euphoric aftermath of his World Cup conquest in Qatar, he gave no indication of retiring from international football, nor were the universal fans in a hurry to see him disappear. They wanted to enjoy the latest deification while it lasted. Messi continued to be a key point of reference, almost insurmountable for any emerging claimant to the throne, even after he moved away from European football. In the summer of 2023, the greatest player transferred from Paris Saint Germain to Inter Miami FC, co-owned by David Beckham, reportedly earning between $50m (£39.6m) and $60m (£47.55m) annually, excluding additional revenue-sharing deals from sponsors.

Elite players were now increasingly cogs in a commercial machine, playing for clubs that invested fortunes in collective talent of the highest quality and teams that were resilient enough to chase trophies in an environment of high physical and commercial pressure.

In Qatar, England dreamed of emerging as one of the great World Cup winners, promising much in early victories only to lose to France in the quarter-final. It was a team that perhaps deserved better.

Football is not rational and much less moral.

For all the efforts by some Western media to expose the abuse of immigrant labour and intolerance of LGBT rights, David Beckham told the British media that the World Cup in Qatar would be a platform for 'progress, inclusion and tolerance'. And yet the fact that the England team took the knee before every match during the tournament endured as a visible and necessary reminder that human rights were worth a statement amidst all the football hype that this was the greatest of World Cup tournaments.

Even journalists with a conscience couldn't help but get caught up in the hyperbole of the game, and almost wished the tournament would go Argentina's way, in order to ensure the best possible result for soccer fans, broadcasters, sponsors all over the world – that Messi could finally wear the crown that glorified football as he played it, at his best and most convincing at the age of 35, but also in the countless games in which he showcased his unique talent, first at FC Barcelona and then at Paris Saint Germain.

Messi has never played for an English club, but the global reach of the Premier League was still very much present in Qatar. The Premier contributed more players than any other league to the 32 teams competing for the biggest prize in world sport, almost a quarter of all the players involved. With 136 players from the top tier of English club football called up to their respective international teams (followed by 83 from *La Liga*, 76 from the *Bundesliga*, 68 from *Serie A* and 54 from France's *Ligue 1*), perhaps it underlined why many describe the Premier League as the best league in the world.

However, no league could boast of having dominated the tournament. Messi and Mbappé, the two top scorers who played in the final with Argentina and France respectively, both played for French champions Paris Saint Germain. World champions Argentina and runners-up France nonetheless each included five Premier players in their squads.

Among the most controversial stars at the tournament was Argentinian goalkeeper Emiliano Martínez of Aston Villa, whose saves, after provocative and distracting gestures directed at the opposing kicker, were instrumental in his team's penalty shoot-out wins against both France in the final and the Netherlands in the quarter-finals.

Another standout star in the Argentina national team was Manchester City striker Julián Álvarez, who started the tournament as a substitute in Argentina's disastrous opening game against Saudi Arabia and finished it as a national hero after scoring four goals en route to the ultimate victory. His best performance came in Argentina's 3-0 semi-final victory over Croatia, playing a role in all three goals, including the first, a Messi penalty after Álvarez was brought down by Croatian goalkeeper Livaković. The second goal came from Álvarez scoring at the end of a long and very fast solo run from midfield, stumbling through two defenders. The third, after the half-time break, had Messi, after a dazzling dribble, setting up Álvarez for a shot.

Among the new-found heroes of the Argentine team was Alexis Mac Allister of Premier club Brighton & Hove Albion – subsequently transferred to Liverpool – who showed his quality and resilience in midfield during the tournament. In the final in Doha, he was a key element in creating a magically contrived second goal. His assist was finding Messi with a clever short pass, then running forward and carrying the ball back to the right of goal before playing the ball left into the path of Di María to guide it into the net.

The ability of respect for talent and good play to break old political and cultural prejudices – as is the case of an Anglo-Argentine antagonism – was demonstrated by the warm reception that Brighton fans gave to their world star, the Argentine Mac Allister upon his return to the United Kingdom after the victory in Doha and the great Buenos Aires party. With a replica of the World Cup held high in the air, he was carried on the shoulders of the supporters, to chants of support from his team-mates, the English among them as enthusiastic as the foreign standouts in the squad.

For Mac Allister, at the age of 24, playing with Messi in Qatar was a learning experience. In each match he played with the superstar he found himself more attuned. Thanks to the World Cup, the midfielder returned to England as one of the Premier's most valued players and although he declared how good he felt in Brighton, the possibility had opened up that the market would lead him to a richer and more competitive club in the Champions League.

Perhaps with the exception of Messi, no player defined the tournament on his own. Both in their competitiveness and in their quality of play, the best games fell short of the best games seen regularly in the Premier League, which can boast the most intense and deep-rooted participation of the fans, but lack the presence of Messi.

In addition to Julián Álvarez, other Premier League players among the goal scorers in Qatar were England's Marcus Rashford, Bukayo Saka, Harry Kane, Raheem Sterling and Richarlison, whose beautiful *jogo bonito*, executing a scissor kick in the 73rd minute of the opening match for Brazil against Serbia, was voted the best goal of the tournament by the fans.

Manchester City were the English club that contributed the most players to the tournament, followed by Manchester United, Chelsea, Tottenham Hotspur and Arsenal.

### AFC Bournemouth
**2 players:** Chris Mepham, Kieffer Moore (Wales).

### Arsenal
**10 players:** Gabriel Jesus, Gabriel Martinelli (Brazil), Takehiro Tomiyasu (Japan), Granit Xhaka (Switzerland), William Saliba (France), Matt Turner (USA), Aaron Ramsdale, Ben White, Bukayo Saka (England), Thomas Partey (Ghana).

## Aston Villa
**4 players:** Leander Dendoncker (Belgium), Jan Bednarek, Matty Cash (both Poland), Emiliano Martínez (Argentina).

## Brentford
**6 players**: Mikkel Damsgaard, Mathias Jensen, Christian Norgaard (Denmark), Bryan Mbeumo (Cameroon), David Raya (Spain), Saman Ghoddos (Iran).

## Brighton
**8 players:** Kaoru Mitoma (Japan), Leandro Trossard (Belgium), Robert Sánchez (Spain), Alexis Mac Allister (Argentina), Tariq Lamptey (Ghana), Pervis Estupiñán, Moisés Caicedo, Jeremy Sarmiento ( Ecuador).

## Chelsea
**12 players**: Mateo Kovačić (Croatia), Thiago Silva (Brazil), Denis Zakaria (Switzerland), Christian Pulisic (USA), Hakim Ziyech (Morocco), Kai Havertz (Germany), Mason Mount, Conor Gallagher, Raheem Sterling (England), Édouard Mendy, Kalidou Koulibaly (Senegal), César Azpilicueta (Spain).

## Crystal Palace
**2 players:** Joachim Andersen (Denmark), Jordan Ayew (Ghana).

## Everton
**4 players:** Jordan Pickford, Conor Coady (England), Amadou Onana (Belgium), Idrissa Gana Gueye (Senegal).

## Fulham
**6 players:** Harry Wilson, Daniel James (Wales), Tim
Ream, Antonee Robinson (USA), João
Palhinha (Portugal), Aleksandar Mitrović (Serbia).

## Leeds United
**3 players:** Rasmus Kristensen (Denmark), Brenden
Aaronson, Tyler Adams (USA).

## Leicester City
**7 players:** Danny Ward (Wales), Wout Faes, Timothy
Castagne, Youri Tielemans (Belgium), James
Maddison (England), Nampalys Mendy (Senegal), Daniel
Amartey (Ghana).

## Liverpool
**7 players:** Alisson, Fabinho (Brazil), Ibrahima
Konaté (France), Trent Alexander-Arnold, Jordan
Henderson (England), Darwin Núñez (Uruguay), Virgil van
Dijk (Holland).

## Man City
**16 players:** Manuel
Akanji (Switzerland), Ederson (Brazil), Kevin De
Bruyne (Belgium), İlkay Gündoğan (Germany), John
Stones, Kyle Walker, Kalvin Phillips, Phil Foden, Jack
Grealish (England), João Cancelo, Rúben Dias, Bernardo
Silva (Portugal), Nathan Aké (Holland), Aymeric
Laporte, Rodri (Spain), Julián Álvarez (Argentina).

## Man Utd
**13 players:** Antony, Casemiro, Fred (Brazil), Christian
Eriksen (Denmark), Raphael Varane (France), Harry
Maguire, Luke Shaw, Marcus Rashford (England), Diogo

Dalot, Bruno Fernandes (Portugal), Facundo
Pellistri (Uruguay), Tyrell Malacia (Holland), Lisandro
Martínez (Argentina).

## Newcastle United
**5 players:** Bruno Guimarães (Brazil), Fabian
Schär (Switzerland), Nick Pope, Kieran Trippier, Callum
Wilson (England).

## Nottingham Forest
**5 players:** Remo Freuler (Switzerland), Wayne
Hennessey, Neco Williams, Brennan
Johnson (Wales), Cheikhou Kouyaté (Senegal).

## Southampton
**2 players:** Armel Bella-Kotchap (Germany), Mohammed
Salisu (Ghana).

## Tottenham Hotspur
**11 players:** Pierre-Emile Højbjerg (Denmark), Ivan Perišić
(Croatia), Richarlison (Brazil), Ben Davies (Wales), Hugo
Lloris (France), Eric Dier, Harry Kane (England), Rodrigo
Bentancur (Uruguay), Pape Matar Sarr (Senegal), Cristian
Romero (Argentina), Son Heung-min (South Korea).

## West Ham United
**5 players:** Lucas Paquetá (Brazil), Alphonse
Areola (France), Nayef Aguerd (Morocco), Thilo
Kehrer (Germany), Declan Rice (England).

## Wolverhampton Wanderers
**5 players :** Matheus Nunes, Rúben Neves, José
Sa (Portugal), Hwang Hee-chan (South Korea), Raúl
Jiménez (Mexico).

Source *Premier League, November 2022.*

# Chapter Twenty-five

# Dreams, Big Business

ENGLAND'S DEFEAT by Spain in the final of the European Championships in Berlin on 14 July 2024 was a story foretold, with English fans and players seeing another shattering of the dream of having their national men's squad win its first international tournament since the World Cup of 1966.

I approached the final with mixed feelings. I was born in Madrid (the son of a Spanish mother and English father), educated in England, but brought up bilingually and in a constant interchange between the two countries I inherited. I am an Anglo-Spaniard in heart and soul, my loyalties when it comes to football never defined by national prejudice but by my love for a game played at its best, with passion, beauty and decency. Certainly, as an Anglo-Spanish football fan, I couldn't have hoped for a better major international final.

During the days leading up to the final, I visited a bar in Madrid which was largely filled with Real Madrid fans, setting aside their club prejudices and celebrating the rites of passage to international stardom of the Barca teenager Lamine Yamal as he made history by scoring a magnificent goal. Subsequently a photograph of him as a baby alongside a smiling adult Messi taken in 2007 went viral on social media, as if Yamal's joining the pantheon of football gods was by anointment.

The following evening, I watched England beat the Netherlands. This time I took refuge in the safety and comfort of my Madrid hotel room, before opening my balcony to the sound of a group of English fans chanting that hymn to the shattered hopes and dreams which span the past 58 years: 'It's coming home, it's coming home, football's coming home.'

England had been close to what they were capable of, after underperforming through the early matches of the Euro 2024 tournament. Close to full time against the Dutch team that Wednesday, a winning goal by Aston Villa's Ollie Watkins booked a place in English football folklore, underlining England's resilience and ability to recover from impending disaster.

Before that, there was Jude Bellingham, who after failing to replicate the best form he had shown during the season with Real Madrid, produced a stunning 95th minute bicycle kick goal, equalising in the last 16 when England were just seconds away from defeat. (They went on to beat Slovakia in extra time.) That Bellingham was with the England team and yet owed his international stardom to his success playing for the Spanish and European club champions Real Madrid, epitomised the cultural fluidity and quality that prevailed in Euro 2024 despite any instincts of nationalist bigotry.

Among Bellingham's English team colleagues were Arsenal's Declan Rice and Bukayo Saka, and Manchester City's John Stones, Kyle Walker and Phil Foden, who at club level between them played for arguably two of the best managers in the Premier League, Arsenal's Mikel Arteta and Manchester City's Pep Guardiola – both Spaniards. Spain meanwhile had three Premier players among their number: substitute goalkeeper, Arsenal's David Raya, Manchester City's Rodri and Chelsea's Marc Cucurella.

Both Spain and England drew on the player quality that existed in their respective national leagues, the best in Europe, and a long and proud football history, with England the founder of the game and Spaniards laying their own claim to supremacy and developing in their own creative way.

Three Premier League players, Walker, Rodri and Cucurella, made it into the UEFA Euro 2024 team of the tournament. Among the other English players who distinguished themselves was midfielder Kobbie Mainoo, who only made his first Premier League start with Manchester United in the 3-0 win at Everton in November 2023 and has emerged as one of the best young players in Europe. Chelsea fans meanwhile took some pride in the fact that the underused Cole Palmer seemed to energise the English team in attack when brought on as a sub, while Cucurella redeemed himself as a key player in the Spanish team, not least in the eyes of club legend Frank Leboeuf who admitted he may have been too harsh when criticising him earlier in the season.

The best team won Euro 2024, with Spain playing the beautiful game on and off the ball, committed, creative, pure poetry in motion. A cultural symbiosis was evident, showing that national identity in football is not necessarily one of bigotry fuelled by history, mythology and politics. Both England and Spain have had to face up to the toxic nature of racism and sexism in their football, as a result of attitudes in politics and society at large. Human empathy – expressed as a respect of racial and sexual diversity and a belief in the capacity of football to restore a nation's belief in itself as a decent society with a sense of the common good – had been at the heart of the English team moulded by Gareth Southgate. All but three of his first-choice players were from immigrant family backgrounds, who have maintained their sense of integrity despite being victims of racial abuse.

Two of Spain's star players, Lamine Yamal and Nico Williams, owed their identity to being born in Spain to immigrant parents in regions – the Basque country and Catalonia – with strong cultural sentiments of their own. Their elevation to hero status among Spanish fans of varying club and political prejudices during the tournament, and in the moment of victory, after Williams scored the opening goal of the final, was a further reminder that football has the capacity to build human bridges.

Ahead of the Anglo-Spanish Euro 2024 Final, I asked my good friend and spiritual adviser Fr Shaun Middleton – a Welshman – how I should discern my own feelings as an Anglo-Spaniard football fan. Back came his answer: 'Rejoice with the winners, empathise with the losers and give thanks to the sportsmanship of the game.'

I rejoiced in Spain's wonderful football and empathised with England as they accepted defeat gracefully, while sharing in some of the disillusionment that English fans felt. After the game, Alan Shearer, commentator for the BBC, paid tribute to the soon-to-depart English manager Southgate as someone who had dragged the English national team from the bottom and taken it to near-success. But, as he pointed out, getting to the final when you have the quality of players like England was never going to be good enough.

And yet there was hope, with the candidates initially touted as possible successors to Southgate a reminder of the management talent that has flourished in the Premier League.

In terms of an evolving story of women's football that has formed part of this book, Spain and England reached the World Cup Final in August 2023, in Sydney, Australia, showing, in the words of FIFA boss Gianni Infantino, 'what women's football can do, what women can do on the biggest stage. How they can light up each nation, how they can inspire generations.'

The Lionesses' 1-0 defeat did not take away from the achievement of becoming European champions under manager Sarina Wiegman in 2022. As King Charles's message to the team after the final whistle eloquently put it: 'To have reached the final at all is an immense tribute to your skill, determination and team spirit in the finest sporting tradition.

More than that, though, it will serve as an inspiration for generations to come – and, for that, your place in the history books is assured.'

The Spanish players proved the better team, the women's *La Roja* shining throughout the tournament with their brand of attractive, attacking football. They also secured a hard-fought victory for women's rights after *La Roja's* Jenni Hermoso claimed she had been forcibly kissed on the lips and harassed afterwards by Luis Rubiales, the president of the Spanish Football Federation. Rubiales resigned but denied any wrongdoing amid mounting condemnation, with Spanish players insisting they would not play again for their country unless he was removed.

The Lionesses meanwhile issued a joint statement of solidarity, underlining an important cultural shift toward ensuring greater diversity and equality in football across national boundaries. The Lionesses' statement read: 'Unacceptable actions allowed to happen by a sexist and patriarchal organisation. Abuse is abuse and we have all seen the truth. The behaviour of those who think they are invincible must not be tolerated and people shouldn't need convincing to take action against any form of harassment. We all stand with you, Jenni Hermoso and all players of the Spanish team.'

In January 2024 FIFA's appeal committee confirmed a three-year ban on Rubiales after dismissing his appeal. The following May it was announced by a Spanish high court judge that Rubiales would stand trial for sexual assault. Rubiales strenuously denied wrongdoing, alleging the kiss was consensual while claiming he had been the victim of 'social assassination'.

But back to the male players. The kind of beautiful game Spain played in Euro 2024 was the kind some English Premier clubs are capable of producing domestically and internationally. If some of the best English players in Euro

2024 looked tired and below form in the tournament, including Harry Kane, Bellingham, and Foden, it was because they had come to it after a very demanding season. It was a reminder of the physical and psychological pressures put on highly paid elite players by the modern business of football, in extremely competitive national leagues like the Premier, plus the growth of 'supersize' tournaments.

Foden had been named the Premier League's Player of the Season and the English Football Writers' Association Footballer of the Year, after a career-best 17 goals and eight assists, before he scored two more goals for Manchester City in their final game, a 3-1 victory over West Ham. At Euro 2024, he showed touches of his brilliance in the game against the Dutch, but otherwise failed to come alight, unable to get on the ball and score, as he had been doing under Guardiola's management.

Spain beat England despite having to play the second half without Rodri, among the best midfielders in the world, who was substituted at half-time, deemed not fit enough to feature in the second period. Yet data on workload published in the *Financial Times* ahead of the final suggested Spain had a slight but crucial fitness edge on England.

Euros aside, the final games of the 2023/24 season showed the Premier at its best among the world's club leagues. The prize-fighters took it to the final round, preceded by no clear knockout, with Manchester City and Arsenal keeping the outcome tantalisingly unpredictable until the final day, giving their global following reasons to be hopeful.

Similarly other clubs slugged it out for a place in the following season's European competitions, while the excitement of those struggling in the relegation zone was surpassed by those securing top places in the Championship and either an early return to the Premier – Leicester City – or, in the case of Ipswich Town, a first chance in 22 years to bite at the most lucrative of cherries. Ed Sheeran, one of Ipswich's sponsors, called to congratulate team and fans after their 2-0 victory over Huddersfield Town at their Portman Road home, showing yet again the extent to which football has become a celebrity sport.

By early May 2024, after several English teams had crashed out of European competitions, the Premier League had consequently lost a coefficient ranking place so only four teams would qualify for the 2024/25 Champions League. Manchester City, Arsenal and Liverpool already had their spots in the bag and Aston Villa were set to easily beat Tottenham for the remaining spot.

The season ended with Manchester City winning the Premier and Manchester United, after a poor season, clinching a place in the Europa League after beating City in the FA Cup Final. That ensured manager Erik ten Hag's survival, at least in the short term, despite ending eighth in the Premier, following Sir Jim Ratcliffe's purchase of a 27.7 per cent stake in United, which enabled his INEOS company to take control of football operations at the club.

Chelsea ended in a respectable sixth position in the Premier and qualified for the Europa Conference after another topsy-turvy season, with the Italian Enzo Maresca replacing the Argentine Mauricio Pochettino as new head coach. Newcastle ended up in seventh position in the Premier, failing to secure their return to Europe, a disappointing contrast with the previous season's promising campaign which, thanks to manager Eddie Howe's attacking approach, had led the club to Champions League qualification.

West Ham were pipped to the post in their quest for a fourth consecutive European campaign, with the Scots manager David Moyes unable to galvanise the troops after announcing his impending departure from the club at the end of 2023/24.

In terms of an enduring success story, it was Guardiola's Manchester City that secured their place in Premier history, becoming the first men's team in English football to win four top-flight titles in a row. With team, individual players and manager setting new records with consistent on-pitch success, driving commercial and matchday revenues, City consolidated their position as the Premier League's most valuable football club brand, with their value increasing to £1.4 billion according to Brand Finance, the independent brand valuation and strategy consultancy.

On Sunday, 19 May 2024, the final day of the season, Manchester City, with a team moulded and finessed by Guardiola's tactical and creative genius, sealed their latest success, finishing just two points ahead of Arteta's Arsenal, who enjoyed their best season under their Spanish coach. It was Manchester City's tenth top-flight league title – and the sixth time in seven seasons they had won the Premier League, continuing Guardiola's remarkable record since taking charge of City back in 2016. The season ended with the club still facing judgement of their financial affairs, 15 months on from being hit with 115 Premier League charges for alleged irregularity – charges the club strongly denied. Whatever the outcome of the case, its unresolved nature as the 2023/24 season came to a close, cast a shadow over the club's future and the Premier League's reputation for being the most competitive league in the world.

For the business of football to be truly transparent and accountable, the onus is on legislators and governing bodies to ensure against distortions and imbalances. The new Labour government, elected in July 2024, pledged to push ahead with plans for a football regulator, independent of government and football authorities, to be included in a Football Governance Bill. The aim was to ensure the long-term financial stability of the men's professional game and the safeguarding of English football's heritage.

A statement from the Premier League warned that 'mindful that its future growth was not guaranteed', it remained concerned about 'any unintended consequences' that could weaken the competitiveness and appeal of English football.

But as *The Guardian*'s Jonathan Liew wrote after City won the Premier in May 2024, the tendency of the Premier League over the years has been 'to turn a blind eye to immeasurable autocrat wealth, bathed in the reflected glory, gripped above all by a faith in the intrinsic virtue of its product, a belief that competitive balance would just happen, was simply its essential nature'.

And yet there was still no denying the quality of managers and players in the Premier, exemplified by City's collective achievement under Guardiola, with all of the squad contributing to their success, and some notable individual milestones, too.

Two other Spaniards continued to excel as Premier League managers. Arsenal under Mikel Arteta enjoyed some of the best football played by the club since the Wenger glory days, and were worthy challengers to the Premier crown. At Aston Villa, Unai Emery consolidated his presence, agreeing to a new five-year contract after guiding the club to a fourth-place finish in the Premier League in the 2023/24 season, securing a place in the Champions League for the first time in Villa's history [they had won the European Cup in 1982].

Since his arrival in 2022, Emery transformed the club's fortunes. He steered them from 17th to seventh in the table in his first season, with the side benefitting from the brilliance of Ollie Watkins, who at 28 years of age was called up for his first major tournament with England at Euro 2024 after his best season yet in the Premier, scoring 19 goals and a competition-high 13 assists.

Over at Chelsea, Pochettino quit his managerial role by mutual consent after only 11 months, the latest manager to fall out with the club's American owners, following the sacking of Thomas Tuchel and Graham Potter, the latter's demise leading to Frank Lampard taking charge on a temporary basis.

Manchester City's striker Erling Haaland finished the league season on 27 goals, winning the Premier League Golden Boot for the second season in a row, while their midfielder, Spaniard Rodri, was described by Gary Neville as 'City's most important player by a mile'.

The Premier League might lay claim to being the best league in the world, but its top clubs are not necessarily the best in Europe, with both Manchester City and Arsenal knocked out of the Champions League at the quarter-final stage in the spring of 2024, losing to Real Madrid and Bayern Munich respectively. The results meant there was no English club in the semi-finals for the first time since 2020, and only the second time since 2017.

Real Madrid, whose DNA includes a sense of historic entitlement to the 'European Cup', and with Bellingham one of its big stars, sealed a record-setting 15th Champions League, beating Borussia Dortmund. The final at Wembley included loud pre-match cheers in support of German national Jürgen Klopp and an emotional rendering of 'You'll Never Walk Alone' after he had ended his time as one of the best-loved and most iconic managers at Liverpool FC. Liverpool fans had paid their own fond farewell to their charismatic manager with songs, murals and other tributes as Klopp led his beloved Reds for the 491st and final time against Wolverhampton Wanderers in front of a sell-out crowd at Anfield. Having won seven trophies, including Europe's Champions League in 2019 and a first English league title in three decades in 2020, Klopp was leaving of his own volition to recharge his batteries.

It was not just success that endeared Klopp to fans, and he never claimed to be 'invincible'. It was his personality, understanding and identification early on with the club's heart and soul, and not only being part of it but also nourishing it.

He recognised the power as well as loyalty through good and bad times of Liverpool fans, referring to them as the 12th man, responsible for supplying energy to the squad.

Klopp's persona as a man of the people put him up in the pantheon of club managerial legends, leaving a legacy similar to that of Liverpool's iconic manager, Bill Shankly. However, while Shankly belonged to a past era of English football between 1959 and 1974, Klopp was a German with an international outlook beyond borders, who restored Liverpool's pride and belief in itself after decades of mediocrity and underachievement. His irresistible passion and tactical zeal – fist-pumps at the end of games, bear hugs for players, time for charitable causes, indignant protests at dubious decisions, and insistence on a high-energy aggressive counter-pressing style of football – helped usher in a golden age of the Premier League through his rivalry with Guardiola, the one Premier League manager he was never able to eclipse.

Despite the antagonism rival fans developed for each other over the years, Klopp and Guardiola never came to a serious fall-out, preferring to learn from each other's tactics and playing up their role as showmen on a big stage – cool, casual dressers, dynamic personalities, the action men on the touchline, barking orders at their men, gesticulating and expressing in ways that connected not just with loyal fans but a global audience.

If their football styles were once considered divergent – in simplified terms, Guardiola's short-passing game full of artifice perfected since his early years at Barca, contrasts with the raw attacking aggression of Klopp's players – the two managers increasingly developed around each other, constantly anticipating and reacting to stratagems and movement on and off the ball. For Guardiola, it was a question of countering Liverpool's counter, drawing on ideas pioneered by Johan Cruyff when he was manager at Barca, pushing his full-backs into midfield when his team was in possession. For Klopp it became a question of a better-organised, less anarchic team, with stricter training regimes focused on more reliable ways of recycling the ball without losing possession, and more structured attacking patterns.

In the words of *The Guardian*'s Jonathan Liew, as Klopp's era at Liverpool came to an end, 'there was a kind of symbiosis at work, a shadow war, most evident in the games they played against each other, but it helped the Premier flourish'.

The Premier League provided the perfect setting for coaches of such a calibre, with super-rich owners, passionate and loyal fan bases and a footballing culture steeped in history but increasingly refined and global in its outreach.

The enduring loyalty of English fans remained one of the more endearing features of the Premier League which is not say that there were no rumblings of discontent, not least among the smaller clubs who felt themselves at a financial disadvantage when it came to retaining successful teams and buying star players.

Setting aside the tendency to romanticise a past when fans were cramped into poorly built stadiums and aggression on and off the pitch and long balls were necessarily seen as virtuous, fans understandably moaned and groaned not just about the money that others had and they didn't or that owners of small clubs had wasted, but the rising cost of following your team beyond the goggle-box and armchair.

While the subject of money – its use and misuse and the shadowy transactions that might lie behind it – remained very much part of the Premier League story as it entered the new 2024/25 season, there was also the ongoing debate about the technological intrusion and interruptions of VAR, a cold pedestrian brake on the emotional free-flow of the game. Yet it seemed that fans would have to put up with it, as part of the reality of a world increasingly dominated by technology.

By contrast English fans' opposition to the formation of a breakaway European Super League managed to persuade the big

Premier Clubs to withdraw from the project – but the growing tendency for a few successful clubs to become global businesses seemed unstoppable.

In June 2024, Juventus became the latest big club of the 12 who originally signed up to the ESL to drop its support, favouring re-joining the European Club Association (ECA) instead. The 12, including six from the Premier League – Manchester United, Manchester City, Liverpool, Chelsea, Arsenal and Tottenham – had faced a backlash across Europe in 2021 and the ESL seemed to collapse. Juventus's departure left Real Madrid and FC Barcelona still clinging to the European Super League dream.

Just days earlier, a Spanish commercial court had ruled that UEFA and FIFA were wrong to ban clubs from joining the ESL, because it amounted to anti-competitive behaviour and abuse of their dominant position as the two big governing bodies of international football. A similar decision had been made by the European Court of Justice in December 2023. The company behind the ESL A22, celebrated the court's ruling and re-declared its ambition to shake up the structure of European soccer, with pan-European competitions governed by the participating clubs themselves.

'We have won the right to compete,' A22 CEO Bernd Reichart said in a statement after the ruling. 'European club football is free. The near-70-year UEFA monopoly is finally over, and the court's decision has far-ranging and positive consequences for football. We will continue working with clubs, leagues and other stakeholders without fear of sanctions to create the best and most fan-centric football competitions in Europe. For the first time since 1955, pan-European competitions can now be governed by the participating clubs themselves as is the case in virtually all European domestic leagues.'

Real Madrid, still the key actor in the ESL plan, given their unrivalled history of success in European club competitions and global reach, declared through their president Florentino Pérez, 'We are at the beginning of a new era where we can work freely, in constructive dialogue, without threats, without acting against anything or anyone and with the aim to innovate and modernise club football to bring passion back to the fans.'

He added: 'From today, the present and future of European football is finally in the hands of clubs, the players and their fans. Our destiny belongs to us and we have a great responsibility before us. This day will mark a before and after. It is a great day for the history of football and for the history of sport.'

The other consistent ESL backer, FC Barcelona, also welcomed the court's ruling, restating their support for a 'new elite level football competition that would address such issues as fixture overload and the excessive number of games between national teams, that will work towards regulation of financial fair play among participating teams, and that will put local and international players and supporters at the centre. This system must respect the functions and sustainability of domestic competitions and should be a meritocracy that is primarily based on results on the pitch.'

The Premier maintained its opposition to the ESL. 'The ruling does not endorse the so-called "European Super League" and the Premier League continues to reject any such concept,' it said. 'Supporters are of vital importance to the game and they have time and again made clear their opposition to a "breakaway" competition that severs the link between domestic and European football.'

The future shape of European club football and how it might impact on the Premier League was an ongoing saga as the season ended in the summer of 2024, with continuing competing statements, the tectonic plates of power politics and big business susceptible to unpredictable shifts, not always in the interests of ordinary fans, not least those fearing a growing financial divide between a limited number of big clubs and the rest.

The Premier League ended the 2023/24 season with Leicester City returning to it after a season's absence, as winners of the Championship. Relegation from the top flight has the potential to inflict stagnation or worse, a spiralling downturn into limbo if a club doesn't get back after a season or two – see the examples of Stoke City, Blackburn Rovers and Middlesbrough. By contrast the Foxes went up, went down and went up again, with a revamped stadium and training ground, but with the challenge of strengthening the team with new players in a highly competitive market and stabilising the club during the first season back among the giants with their big pockets.

Leicester City's remarkable comeback party rekindles the fairy tale which saw the club win the Premier in 2015/16. But as Jon Holmes, a long-term fan put it to me, the Premier League had become a battleground in the struggle between the US and the oil-producing nations of the Middle East. It was a war being carried on elsewhere in football and other sports.

The 2023/24 season underlined the dynamic nature of top-flight football, with managers' contracts subject to demanding outcomes in terms not just of building competitive teams but also winning trophies. Managers were sacked for underperforming or rewarded for their success after being brought into richer clubs. The transfer market saw players come and go earnings salaries way above most of the working population, with a labour mobility denied to lesser mortals by Brexit, and with the cost of travel to and attendance at live games testing the loyalty of most football fans.

But the season's minnow achievement award went to Kieran McKenna's Ipswich Town, whose solution-focused psychology in the final games of the Championship included turning off televisions around the club whenever Leicester and the two other parachuted clubs, Leeds and Southampton also battling for promotion, were playing.

Something else worked for Ipswich as they booked their place for their first Premier League season in 22 years, and that was the brilliance of 38-year-old Northern Irishman McKenna. In a season notable for managerial falls from grace, he resurrected memories of the golden days at the club of Sir Alf Ramsey and Sir Bobby Robson.

Ipswich chief executive Mark Ashton, who inherited a club stranded in mid-table of League One when he joined three years earlier, predicted in May 2024 that Ipswich would be 'brave and bold' in the summer transfer market, backed by the club's owner, US group Gamechanger 20, and the private equity firm Bright Path Sports, which bought a 40 per cent stake in March.

The club was looking forward to its fourth season of sponsorship by the Suffolk superstar Ed Sheeran, a fan from childhood who had helped boost shirt sales. They needed to be realistic, though, about the limits imposed by current profitability and sustainability regulations and financial fair play (FFP), which aim to check what football writer Jonathan Wilson described in a column for *The Observer* as 'the endless cycle of the rich winning and so getting richer and so winning more'.

Perhaps the horse of big business and foreign investments had well and truly bolted, but a more stringent version of FFP, under an independent regulator and a Labour government, was required, with the Premier striking the right balance between clubs representing their communities and the elite becoming global brands and seducing a worldwide fan base.

# Thanks/*Gracias*

AS I mentioned in my opening chapter, I owe the inspiration for this book to my late parents, my English father Tom, and my Spanish mother Mabel – *Que en Paz Descansen* – thanks to whom my life as a writer has straddled two cultures with a love of life, not least good football: the English and Spanish.

Earlier books of mine have included a history of Spanish football, where the English roots and coming and goings between players and managers between the two countries have played a formative role. After also writing about *La Liga* and its great clubs and icons, I have turned my focus in this book to the history of English club football and a narrative that shares a personal perspective on the emerging force of the Premier League in global sport, written in the year of the 30th anniversary of its foundation for a Spanish publisher, and now updated with a new chapter for the English edition.

It draws on my own experience of the most emblematic clubs involved, the league's stadiums, players, managers, owners and chroniclers, and I acknowledge the additional insights and writings of friends, colleagues and fans below.

Those I owe a special debt include: Simon Kuper, Jonathan Wilson, Krishan Puvvada, Vinay Patel, Henry Winter, Rob Smith, John Cross, Barney Ronay, Dan Einav, David Hendrick, Andy Mitten, Dan Coombs, Jim White, Paul MacInnes, Barry Glendenning, David Conn, David Goldblatt, Simon Burnton, Andrew Antony, Glyn Wilmshurst, Mark Wright, Eric S. Hoffman, Peter Sharland,

Chris Lawrence, Tom Allnutt, Jon Holmes, Gary Lineker, Patrick Harverson, Peter Sharland, Carlos Oppe, Anthony Oppe, Ignacio Peyro, Walter Oppenheimer, José Luis Martinez Hens, Vicente del Bosque, Rory Compton, Deidre Fitzgerald, Susan Wrack, Roger Blitz, George Parker, Carlos Batalla, and Dominic Begg.

In Spain, *gracias* to Gloria Gutierrez, Maria Borras and Manuel Pimentel, and in the UK to Annabel Merullo and Daisy Chandley at Peters, Fraser, & Dunlop, and Paul Camillin at Pitch Publishing, for their encouragement with this project.

And a very special thank you to Kidge, Julia, Miriam and Nadia for their constant support and patience, not least during a hot, hard-working summer of writing.

# Select Bibliography

**Books:**

Belton, Catherine, *Putin's People* (William Collins, 2021)

Burford, Bill, *Among the Thugs* (Arrow, 1992)

Burns, Jimmy, *When Beckham went to Spain* (Penguin, 2005)

Burns, Jimmy, *Barca, A People's Passion* (Bloomsbury, 2016)

Burns, Jimmy, *La Roja, A Journey Through Spanish Football* (Simon & Schuster, 2012)

Burns, Jimmy, *Cristiano & Leo* (Macmillan, 2018)

Cashmore, Ellis, *Beckham* (Polity, 2003)

Crick, Michael, *The Boss* (Simon & Schuster, 2003)

Davies, Hunter, *The Glory Game* (Mainstream, 1992)

Davies, Norman, *The Isles* (Papermac, 2000)

Davies, Peter, *All Played Out* (Yellow Press, 1998)

Ferguson, Alex, *My Autobiography* (Hodder, 2014)

Ferguson, Alex, *Leading* (Hodder, 2016)

Gascoigne, Paul, *Gazza* (Headine, 2005)

Goldblatt, David, *The Ball is Round* (Penguin, 2007)

Goldblatt, David, *The Game of our Lives* (Penguin, 2014)

Groom, Brian, *Northerners* (HarperNorth, 2022)

Hamilton, Ian, *The Faber Book of Soccer* (Faber & Faber, 1993)

Hamman, Dietmar, *The Didi Man* (Headline, 2012)

Kelly, Stephen F., *Not Just a Game* (Headline, 1995)

Kelly, Stephen F., *The Pick of the Season* (Mainstream, 1997)

Keane, Roy, *Keane* (Penguin, 2003)

Kuper, Simon, *The Football Men* (Simon & Schuster, 2011)

Kuper, Simon, *Barca* (Short Books, 2021)

Neville, Gary, *Red* (Transworld, 2012)
Neville, Gary, *The People's Game* (Hodder & Stoughton, 2022)
Obama, Michelle, *The Light We Carry* (Viking, 2022)
Robson, Bobby, *My Autobiography* (Macmillan, 1998)
Savage, John, *1966* (Faber & Faber, 2021)
Scovell, Brian, *Bill Nicholson* (Blake Publishing, 2010)
Wrack, Suzanne, *A Woman's Game* (Faber, 2022)

**Films:**

*Gazza* (BBC, 2022)
*All or Nothing – Arsenal* (Amazon, 2022)
*United* (BBC, 2011)
*Arsène Wenger: Invincible* (Amazon, 2021)

**TV:**

Sky Sport, BBC *Match of the Day*, Eurosport.

**Newspapers, Magazines, Websites, Podcasts:**

The Athletic, Bleacher Report, El Pais, The Guardian, The Financial Times, Forbes Magazine, BBC, FourFourTwo Magazine, The Times, The Sun, The Mirror, the Daily Mail, Mail on Sunday, Marca, New Statesman, The Week, The Observer, The Oldie, The Telegraph, The Game, United in Focus, www.heroesandhumans.com.